CW00823294

# TUNING FOR SPEED

How to increase the performance of a standard
motorcycle engine for racing and
competition work

BY

## P. E. IRVING
M.I.Mech.E., M.S.A.E.

Published by
**FLOYD CLYMER PUBLICATIONS**
*World's Largest Publisher of Books Relating to
Automobile, Motorcycles, Motor Racing, and Americana*
**222 NO. VIRGIL AVENUE, LOS ANGELES , CALIF. 90004**

# INTRODUCTION

Welcome to the world of digital publishing ~ the book you now hold in your hand, while unchanged from the original edition, was printed using the latest state of the art digital technology. The advent of print-on-demand has forever changed the publishing process, never has information been so accessible and it is our hope that this book serves your informational needs for years to come. If this is your first exposure to digital publishing, we hope that you are pleased with the results. Many more titles of interest to the classic automobile and motorcycle enthusiast, collector and restorer are available via our website at www.VelocePress.com. We hope that you find this title as interesting as we do.

## NOTE FROM THE PUBLISHER

The information presented is true and complete to the best of our knowledge. All recommendations are made without any guarantees on the part of the author or the publisher, who also disclaim all liability incurred with the use of this information.

## TRADEMARKS

We recognize that some words, model names and designations, for example, mentioned herein are the property of the trademark holder. We use them for identification purposes only. This is not an official publication.

## INFORMATION ON THE USE OF THIS PUBLICATION

In today's information age we are constantly subject to changes in common practice, new technology, availability of improved materials and increased awareness of chemical toxicity. As such, it is advised that the user consult with an experienced professional prior to undertaking any procedure described herein. While every care has been taken to ensure correctness of information, it is obviously not possible to guarantee complete freedom from errors or omissions or to accept liability arising from such errors or omissions. Therefore, any individual that uses the information contained within, or elects to perform or participate in 'do-it-yourself' modifications acknowledges that there is a risk factor involved and that the publisher or its associates cannot be held responsible for personal injury or property damage resulting from the use of the information or the outcome of such procedures.

## WARNING!

One final word of advice, this publication is intended to be used as a reference guide, and when in doubt the reader should consult with a qualified technician.

# ANNOUNCEMENT

This is a practical how-to-do-it book for riders, mechanics, sportsmen and enthusiasts who are interested in speed tuning either single or twin-cylinder engines of two or four-stroke design.

The author, P. E. Irving, is not only a famous author of motorcycle and automobile books, but a graduate engineer. He knows the subjects he writes about from A to Z.

Probably no other book published anywhere in the world offers as many authentic hints and tips on how to get the job done properly, and it deals with every phase of high performance engine tuning.

This title was published for the first time by Temple Press Books of London in 1948. Eight editions, revised and brought up to date, have since been published for worldwide distribution. We purchased the United States publishing rights from Temple Press Books, and we trust you will enjoy and find useful this unique book which it is our pleasure to publish.

*Floyd Clymer*

# INTRODUCTION

SINCE time immemorial man has sought to travel faster than his fellow man. This inborn human urge gained tremendous impetus some 60 years ago with the introduction of the petrol engine as a practical proposition for vehicle propulsion. Inevitably, users of the new form of transport felt their competitive instincts aroused. Their demands for more power and more miles per hour were met initially by the simple expedient of fitting larger and still larger engines. In this "brute force" era, in which sheer volume counted for more than volumetric efficiency, the results of hit-or-miss experiments were all too obvious, the scientific reasons for those results all too seldom understood.

Clearly a halt had to be called to this "Frankenstein's Monster" method of progression. With a growing understanding of basic principles in internal-combustion power production, allied with practical experiments on the road, designers turned their attention to obtaining increased performance from engines of more moderate cubic capacity. So far as motorcycles were concerned, this more scientific form of development was encouraged by the introduction of the Isle of Man Tourist Trophy Races with their strict limitation of engine sizes. This second era was one in which the observant mechanically-minded amateur rider sometimes discovered a "secret of tune" which enabled him for a time to score over his professional rivals.

With advances in metallurgy and a complete appreciation of basic principles, the point has now been reached in this, the third era, where there are no longer any "secrets". Science has replaced brute force and guesswork. Success in international events depends upon the combined efforts of the designer and development engineer, plus a host of specialist technicians responsible for ancillary equipment.

But if the day has passed when the lone amateur could hope to beat the factory representative in a major event, tuning skill, combined with riding ability, continues to bring success to the private owner in a wide variety of competitions. Nor need he possess elaborate workshop facilities to improve the performance of his standard sports model or production-type racer. What he must have, however, is the necessary "know how" and that is supplied in this Manual. Written by a well-known technician responsible for the design, development and racing preparation of highly successful "factory" models, it embodies a wealth of hard-earned knowledge yet reflects throughout the author's ready understanding of the private owner's problems.

Although intended primarily for the racing motorcyclist, much of the text will prove equally useful to those drivers of Formula III racing cars who may lack practical experience in the tuning of high-performance air-cooled single- and twin-cylinder power units. Moreover the ordinary everyday motorcyclist, perhaps not in the least degree interested in racing, can benefit from a study of the special assembly methods employed by racing mechanics; a touring engine rebuilt to racing standards of accuracy could well be more efficient in overall performance, smoother running, cleaner and quieter in operation than hitherto.

The author emphasizes that in this textbook it has not been possible to delve deeply into details of specific makes of machines and power units. Thus, should the reader find that his advice runs counter to that given in some manufacturers' instruction manual, the latter should always be heeded or the maker consulted before modifications are undertaken. Similarly, where reference is made to machine tools, heat treatments and so forth, the information is given so that the reader may explain what is required to the engineer deputed to carry out the work; specialist technicians are not always well versed in the idiosyncrasies of motorcycles and will appreciate expert advice.

GRAHAM WALKER

# AUTHOR'S FOREWORD

As in every other branch of engineering, motorcycle design does not stand still. Steady progress is made from year to year and a book which was first written in 1948 cannot hope to remain of much value unless revised from time to time.     Much dead wood in the form of references to obsolete models has been deleted, although some has been retained to assist owners of "vintage" machines or to trace the lines of development which have led up to modern designs. Much new material has been added, and several passages rearranged or altered to avoid repetition and for the sake of greater clarity, without increasing the size of the book.

In fact, I have attempted to emulate, in literary form, what the tuner has to accomplish with an engine—pack a lot more punch into the same volume!

# CONTENTS

# TUNING FOR SPEED

WRITTEN for the motorcycle owner who wishes to obtain the utmost efficiency from his engine, this practical handbook explains how to increase the performance of the standard motorcycle engine for racing and competitive work.

This Edition includes the latest information on racing fuels, conversion kits, timing, tuning, carburetter sizes and settings, with additional information on racing sparking plugs, and a fuel analysis table. First published in 1948, this work is based upon many years of actual racing experience and is an essential part of a racing motorcyclist's library.

CHAPTER I

A PRELIMINARY SURVEY

SUCCESS in tuning an engine for speed depends upon three main factors. They are: (1) getting the maximum combustible charge into the cylinder the maximum number of times per minute; (2) turning as much as possible of the heat liberated into useful work, instead of absorbing it into the combustion-chamber walls or losing it down the exhaust pipe; and (3) eliminating all unnecessary sources of internal friction.

With these three points fixed firmly in mind, some time can be spent very profitably in planning a course of action which will ultimately give the maximum benefit without wasting too much time, or money, on non-essentials.

It must be assumed that certain indispensable equipment is available, such as a good workshop bench, well lighted, and in surroundings of such a nature that scrupulous cleanliness can be observed, particularly during the final stages of assembly. It is also a good plan to prepare suitable washing and draining trays, large enough to accommodate a complete crankcase, *before* commencing work.

External and internal micrometers of assorted sizes are useful, but expensive. As one will be concerned primarily with clearances and not actual dimensions, they are not absolutely vital, but a good set of narrow-bladed feeler gauges most definitely will be. Another very useful gadget is a cast-iron surface plate at least 12 in. square. Really accurate scraped plates, too, are expensive, but a slab of cast iron or mild steel plate, surface ground on both sides, makes an excellent substitute, and there are plenty of machine shops which will carry out the grinding at quite reasonable rates. In conjunction with the surface plate will

1

be needed a scribing block and dial gauge reading to .001 in., for checking squareness and parallelism of various components and assemblies, and a burette, or graduated glass jar, for measuring compression ratios.

A lot can be done without any equipment additional to the usual workshop hand tools, but a little capital invested at the outset is almost certain to pay a dividend later on. When lack of cash is a deciding factor, it is a good plan for several aspirants to speed honours to pool their resources and thus obtain a well-equipped workshop without an excessive drain on the pocket of each individual.

Then one must decide for what sort of event the machine is to be used—or, rather, for what it is *suitable*—grass, scrambles, hill-climb or road events. However well prepared, very few engines other than modern types can compete with any hope of even moderate success in long-distance racing when limited to non-alcoholic fuel, but they may do quite well in short-distance work—dirt or grass-tracking, hill-climbs or sprint stuff—or even long-distance track or road-racing where alcohol is permitted. Some of the engines built several years before the 1939-45 war are excellent for such work; they are usually lighter than their modern brethren, and although sometimes rather deficient in fin area judged by modern standards, this is not to their detriment if the engine is to run exclusively on "dope" fuel; in fact, it may even be an asset in short-distance events when a rapid warm-up to operating temperature is necessary.

Right from the start it is best to keep a record, rather than to trust to memory, of work done and the results which have been obtained, and, in order to know where you have started, commence operations by noting carefully the ignition timing, valve timing and compression ratio.

The latter is determined by setting the piston at t.d.c. with the valves closed, then filling the cylinder head from the burette until the liquid just reaches the lowest threads of the plug hole, the engine being positioned so that the plug hole is vertical. Then rock the mainshaft very slightly until the liquid reaches its maximum height and top-up, if necessary, until it reaches half-way up the hole. Now read off on the burette the amount of liquid poured into the head. Assuming this to be 80 c.c. and the correct volume of the engine to be 498 c.c., the C.R. would be

$$\frac{498 + 80}{80} = \frac{578}{80} = 7.22 \text{ to } 1$$

and so on for any other capacity (*see Chapter IV*). The level of liquid in the hole should be watched closely for a while, to verify that no leakage is taking place past the rings or valves. If there is a leakage, then the real volume

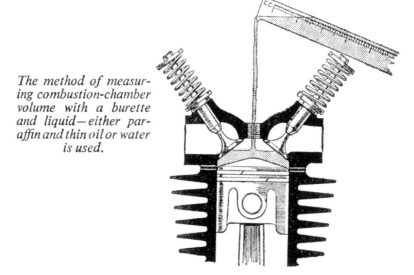

*The method of measuring combustion-chamber volume with a burette and liquid—either paraffin and thin oil or water is used.*

of the head will be somewhat less than the apparent volume but, unless the engine is in a very bad state indeed, the inaccuracy will rarely be bad enough to matter at this stage of the proceedings. If you really want to do the job accurately, then lift off the head and carefully apply grease around the valve heads and between the piston crown and barrel to form a temporary seal.

As to the liquid used, water is the best when there is any doubt about the condition of the valves or rings, because it is less likely to leak past these points than paraffin or light oil, particularly if a drop or two of engine oil is first squirted up the inlet and exhaust ports. For checking the ratio of a newly assembled engine, a mixture of paraffin and thin oil is preferable, as it does not leave a legacy of rust behind it.

Although burettes (which can be obtained from most wholesale chemists or scientific instrument suppliers) are mostly graduated in c.c.s, there is of course no absolute need to use either that instrument or that scale. The head volume could just as easily be measured in fluid ounces or cubic inches, provided that the same measure is used for the cylinder capacity. In working out the ratio remember that 35.2 fluid ounces equals one litre (1,000 c.c.) and, using this conversion factor, the volume of any cylinder can easily be determined.

If a timing disc is fitted to the mainshaft before measuring the clearance volume and a wire pointer is fixed at some convenient location, the pointer can be bent to fix accurately zero on the disc when the piston is absolutely at t.d.c., as indicated by the liquid in the plug hole having reached maximum height.

The ignition and valve timings can now be checked, and to avoid inconsistencies it is best to adopt a standard system of measurement, preferably that recommended by the makers. For measuring the ignition, first set the points to the correct gap (.012 in. in the case of most racing magnetos), insert a 1½-thou. feeler or a piece of tissue paper between the points, and, while applying slight resistance to the armature spindle (by holding the sprocket nut between the fingers or some such method), in order to take up any back-lash in the drive, turn the motor until the feeler is *just* released as the points commence to open, the control being, of course, set to full advance.

On machines fitted with automatic centrifugal advance mechanisms, it is best to lock the mechanism into full advance with a piece of metal or wood jammed between one pair of the fixed and moving stops; checking at full retard and adding the theoretical amount of advance given by the A.T.D. is not really accurate, although it is a good plan to determine for subsequent reference what the actual advance range is.

For the valves, methods vary: some cams are ground with " quietening curves " at the start and finish of lift, which give a very slow take-up, making the actual " lift " and " close " points difficult to determine. The recommendation in such cases is to measure the timing with the tappets set to a clearance much greater than the normal running clearance. This has the effect of making the opening and closing points more sharply defined, but, of course, it does not give the true figures, a point which must be borne in mind when comparing the timings for engines of different makes.

A table of representative valve timings and clearances is given in Chapter XII from which it will be seen that, on o.h.c. Nortons, the timing is quoted with *less* than the running clearance. As the clearance is adjusted by varying thicknesses of shims inside the valve caps on these models, the recommended checking clearance is obtained simply by using feeler gauges of the appropriate thickness between valve stem and cam follower.

On Vincent engines, it is not possible to measure the clearances with feelers; the method adopted is to set up a dial gauge in contact with the valve stem, and to adjust the tappets so that the valve is lifted one to two thous., making sure, of course, that the follower is on the base circle of the cam and not just at the start of lift. Then turn the engine until the valve lifts a further .005 in., and read off the timing at that point. This method is the one which should be used on any engine to get a really accurate reading of the valve timing.

The crank angle at which each valve reaches full lift, too, should be measured, and also the full height of lift of both valves and the amount each is open at both bottom and top dead centres *with correct running clearances.* You will then have a fairly complete picture of the valve-timing diagram, though to do the job properly, readings should be taken at, say, 2° intervals: the lift curve can then be plotted on squared paper and the effect of any subsequent cam modifications will be shown very clearly by plotting the new lift curves on the same sheet (*see Chapter XIII*).

All this measuring and note-taking may seem very upstage and time-wasting, but if you are to do any good at the game you must know what you are about, and you may as well start off correctly. You may, for instance, do something very silly later on, but will have all the information necessary to check back on earlier work and thus be able to put the motor back to a previously successful state, and then start again from there but along different lines.

The way is now clear to get down to business, the first step, obviously, being to strip the engine completely, keeping watch all the time for places where undue wear has occurred, for wear implies friction, which is one of the main things to be eliminated.

### Mechanical Condition

Regarding the general mechanical condition, any parts which show signs of bad wear should be replaced, the main thing being to decide what constitutes "severe" wear. Because a bit of mechanical noise does not matter, a certain amount of slackness here and there can be disregarded; but it is a mistake to think, as some do, that everything should be sloppy. Plain bearings in the cam gear and small-end should have a clearance of between .001 in. and .002 in. per inch of diameter, with a maximum of .003 in. Ball or roller bearings should have practically no slack in them at all, and the race tracks must be examined to see that no pitting has taken place.

When dismantling any engine containing more than one set of rollers, take particular care to avoid mixing up the sets. Take each bearing apart carefully, place each set of rollers in a matchbox, or tin, and make a note on the container stating the location of the contents. Injecting fresh oil into each bearing prior to dismantling will usually serve to retain the rollers in place long enough to stop them cascading all over the bench.

Sometimes a bearing will be slightly pitted in one small area but is otherwise in good condition. In this case, as a temporary expedient if no spare is available, the bearing can be refitted on its shaft or in its housing so that the damaged area comes into a position where it is not subjected to heavy load. The line of least load is at 9 o'clock on the drive-side main, at 3 o'clock on the timing-side main, and 9 o'clock on the crankpin—in each case looking at the crankcase from the drive side.

One point which needs to be watched closely is big-end lubrication, and another is whether the rod or cage shows any tendency to work over to one side and bear heavily against the flywheel. The latter state is a sign that roller-cage slots are not absolutely parallel with the axis. If all the slots have been incorrectly machined at the same small angle the rollers will clearly tend to screw their way to one side, though if they are out of parallel in random directions the errors may all cancel out. Feeding the oil into the bearing at one side has been known to cause trouble, but the scheme is used successfully on Velocettes from 1957 onwards.

If the compression is already fairly high, say, up to 7 to 1 or so, it is probable that enough metal can be turned off the cylinder to raise the C.R. sufficiently for petrol-benzole to be used while retaining the original piston, if this is in good condition and shows no signs of cracking in the gudgeon bosses. If "dope" is to be used, the old piston can be put quietly on the shelf, for a new high-domed pattern will be required in order to obtain the desirable 14 to 1, or so, ratio.

The condition of barrel and rings is especially important, for it is no use sucking in a lot of gas just to let it blow past the piston. If an area of wear exists at the top end of the barrel, the rings will lose contact with the walls at very high speeds, allowing pressure to escape.

Unfortunately, few cylinders will stand being rebored to

7

the full standard oversize without bringing the engine out-side the class cubic capacity limit, and you may have to look into the question of obtaining a new barrel or having the old one re-lined. The latter technique is quite a good idea for the arduous conditions of dirt-track or sand racing, because the liner can first be bored out .005 in. under-size, and, later, honed out to standard diameter: after that a new liner can be fitted and thus the expense of new barrels is avoided. If the wear is only to the extent of two or three thous. the barrel can be lapped out by hand.

The condition of the valves, guides and seats is important. Inlet valve stems should have between .002 in. and .004 in. clearance, but exhaust valves, if made of K.E. 965 or Jessop's G2 steel, need more, .002 per $\frac{1}{8}$ in. of stem diameter being a good figure to work to. If the clearance is less than this, the valve may bind at high temperatures; if more, it cannot get rid of heat properly, owing to insufficient contact with the guide.

This matter of heat dissipation is vital, and if the existing guide is of cast iron (which is a comparatively poor con-ductor of heat) it can, with advantage, be replaced by one of aluminium-bronze or phosphor-bronze, though the latter has been known to give trouble under extreme heat conditions through breaking away at the hot end near the port.

An alloy composed of copper with 1 per cent. chromium added, and known as chromium-copper, is even better for heat transference and its rate of wear is low; it is, however, difficult to machine and particularly hard to ream. It must be remembered that none of these non-ferrous materials will function satisfactorily without lubrication; cast-iron will work dry, but even it will benefit from the presence of a little oil. Cast iron is, however, quite satisfactory for the inlet valve guide, as heat conditions here are much less severe, and iron material can with advantage be used for exhaust guides in place of aluminium bronze in engines with aluminium heads using methanol, Shell A or 811, or similar fuels and a castor-base oil. This type of oil is soluble in methanol and, as the mixture in such engines is often excessively rich, the guide lubrication suffers and wear is rapid.

## Valve and Seat Modifications

If the exhaust valve has worn to a very thin edge or shows signs of being badly burnt under the head, it should be discarded in favour of a new one.

The silchrome or cobalt-chrome valves frequently fitted to sports engines are very satisfactory in ordinary road use for both inlet and exhaust, but where racing is concerned it is better to play safe and go in for an austenitic steel, i.e., K.E. 965 or Jessop's G2, for the exhaust valve, although the standard steel should be satisfactory for the inlet.

Apart from the faint chance that a crack may have occurred between the exhaust valve seat and plug hole (a defect which is sometimes difficult to detect), an old cylinder head which has seen much service usually shows a good deal of valve-seat wear—particularly on the inlet side— which causes the valves to be slightly masked and reduces their effective lift. If, as is frequently the case in sports engines, the valves are of equal size, the best way to cure this trouble will be to obtain a valve about $\frac{1}{8}$ in. larger in diameter, open out the inlet port to suit and recut the seat.

This procedure may not be possible in some engines where the valve is already of the maximum permissible diameter, as dictated by the position of the plug hole or the liability of fouling the edge of the exhaust valve when both valves are partially lifted. In such a case the masking must be removed by cutting it away with a tool similar to a valve seat cutter but with a much flatter angle; if the valve seat angle is 45°, it is often possible to utilize a cutter intended for a larger valve with a 30° seat. Some welding firms make a speciality of building-up worn seats by welding, and in some cases also will re-machine the head, though not of course to racing standards; both iron and aluminium-bronze heads can be reclaimed by this method, but there is a grave danger of melting the aluminium jacket or at least destroying the close adherence between the two metals in the case of bi-metal heads which have aluminium fins cast round a bronze "skull".

Boring out the seats and fitting inserts is an attractive method of head reclamation, since there is no risk of cracking or spoiling the head through excessive heat, and also the inserts can be made of material which is less prone to seat-sinkage than the original; cast aluminium-bronze is bad in this respect whereas wrought aluminium-bronze in the form of tube or extruded bar is good. Seat-rings made in plain cast-iron or austenitic cast-iron which is high-expansion, high-wear-resisting material, can be obtained from various firms—" Brico " and Wellworthy to mention only two—in standard sizes which may, however, need to be reduced in outsize diameter to be usable in some heads. Seat rings can also be purchased as spares from firms who supply aluminium heads with inserted seats as standard equipment. The nickel-iron alloy known as "Ni-resist" is of the austenitic type and is excellent raw material from which to make seat-rings.

When fitting seat-rings, the limiting factor is usually the thickness of metal which will be left between the recesses and the plug-hole and at the top of the sphere between the two recesses; if the thickness at the surface of the sphere is less than $\frac{1}{8}$ in. there is a risk that a crack will occur in service, particularly if there is much difference between the thermal coefficients of expansion of the metals of the seats and the head (p. 282). The most likely place for such a crack to start is between the plug-hole and exhaust seat, and it may be possible to improve the situation by using a seat-ring to suit an exhaust valve $\frac{1}{16}$ in. smaller; admittedly this will leave a small ridge in the port but this can be subsequently blended out and in any case the exact shape of the exhaust port is not of great importance.

Seat-rings of the same coefficient of expansion as the head do not need to be fitted very tightly : $1\frac{1}{2}$ to 2 thous. per inch of diameter will retain them indefinitely, provided that the mating surfaces are very accurate and smooth and the bottom of each recess and ring are square to the axis. For aluminium-bronze heads, use either Monel-metal or K-Monel (obtainable from Henry Wiggin and Company, Ltd., Birmingham) or wrought aluminium bronze, preferably in the form of tube.

Rings should always be shrunk in, never pressed in cold, as with the latter method there is always a risk of scoring the surfaces. With .002 in. per inch of diameter interference a ring should just drop into a cast-iron head at 200° C. temperature difference, but, to make sure, 250° C. is advisable. This can be obtained either by just heating the head to 250° C. or by heating it to 200° C. and freezing the ring in dry ice (frozen carbon dioxide) 200° C. (400° F.) head temperature without freezing is sufficient for a bronze head; this temperature can be obtained in a domestic gas or electric stove. To ensure quick and accurate fitting a mandrel (or mandrels) should first be made up from steel bar, with a pilot which fits the guide bore and a register on which the ring fits with a little more slack than the interference of the ring in the recess (otherwise the mandrel may be gripped by the ring). In use, a light coating of grease on the register will retain the ring whilst the mandrel is pushed quickly home and pressed down for some seconds until the ring is gripped by the head.

Aluminium-alloy heads with inserted seats have been used on racing engines for many years and are a feature of all post-war production racers. Various methods of fitting the rings have been tried, but the plain parallel form just described is much the simplest to make and to replace and never comes loose if properly fitted in the first place. Aluminium, besides having a high coefficient of expansion loses a large proportion of its strength at high temperatures, though some alloys such as Y-alloy and R.R. 53b are much better than others in this respect and are in consequence much used. Two conflicting factors accentuate the problem; if the initial fit is not tight enough the head will expand away from the ring and it will loosen; but if the fit is too tight, under certain circumstances the head metal may stretch or else the ring may be compressed so tightly that it collapses and in either event the ring will loosen. The most satisfactory seat materials seem to be austenitic cast iron for the inlet and wrought aluminium-bronze for the exhaust, and with these materials a cold interference of .002 to .003 in. per inch of diameter gives perfectly satisfactory operation in Y-alloy or R.R. 53b heads. Austenitic cast iron work-hardens very rapidly and any machining operations must be done with a perceptible depth of cut at a low speed; if the tool is allowed to skid on the work it will be very difficult to re-start the cut. For that reason, ordinary valve-seating cutters operated by hand are useless; the only satisfactory way to form the seats true to the valve axis in the first place is by means of a seat-grinder of the Black and Decker type.

Inserted seats which are worn but still tight cannot easily be removed by heating the head, as the temperature required to get the seat loose enough to drop out is so high that the heat-treatment of the head metal may be affected. The best method is to turn out the old seat very carefully to avoid damaging the recess, or else to run a flat-ended drill down through the ring at two or three places and break the ring into pieces. This operation must, however, be done very carefully to avoid making any cuts in the wall of the recess, or in the bottom face. Local damage of this sort is almost bound to lead to gas leakage and severe damage to the head.

Sometimes a seat ring will be found to be loose, or there will be some evidence that it has been loose when the head has been at running temperature. If the recess and ring are still otherwise in good condition, a satisfactory repair can be made by copper-plating the ring and finishing the deposited metal by turning or filing in a lathe to a size which will give the correct interference fit. All but the outside diameter of the ring should be "stopped off" with wax before plating to eliminate any possibility of plated metal flaking off under the action of heat inside the head.

Should the plug hole be tapped to take the old-fashioned 18 mm. size, which is now almost unobtainable in " hard " grades, it can be fitted with a 14 mm. adaptor sleeve, usually obtainable from one of the accessory houses. Perhaps a better plan is to screw in a solid steel plug, lying $\frac{3}{16}$ in. or so below the inner surface of the head, and to get this recess filled in by an acetylene welder with Sifbronze. This can be done at a dull-red heat, and will not harm the head if it is made of iron. A new plug hole can then be drilled slightly off-centre and at a different angle to the original, so as to get the plug points as near to the centre of the head as possible. The diagram gives the machining dimensions.

The remaining components still to be considered are the cams and rockers. Supposing that the valve-timing figures have worked out like this: Inlet opens 35° before t.d.c., closes 60° after b.d.c. Exhaust opens 65° before b.d.c., closes 30° after t.d.c.; the cams are of such a type as to be worth retaining—at least for the time being—unless they are badly worn or exhibit wavy grooves on the flanks. But if the timing is slower (i.e., of shorter duration) than that, and particularly if the overlap at t.d.c. is less, then a new set of cams should be obtained.

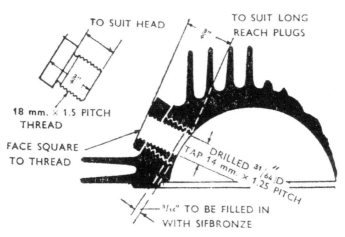

*An old-type cylinder head fitted with an 18 mm. sparking plug can be fitted with this special adaptor to carry a 14 mm. plug. The adaptor is drilled and tapped at an angle to bring the plug points into a more favourable position.*

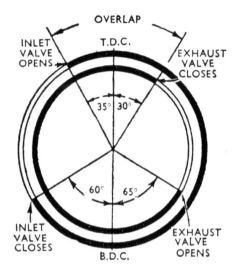

*If your cams give a timing approximate to this diagram and with not less than the overlap shown, they can be retained temporarily and the performance improved by other means.*

The lift must also be considered and should be slightly greater than one-quarter of the port diameter.*

Many makers will supply racing cams which can be fitted directly in place of touring or sports cams, and it is often possible to obtain higher lifts by utilizing cams made for an engine of similar make but of larger capacity.

The valve-timing diagram is determined not only by the cam contours but also by that of the cam-follower feet, and wear of their surfaces will affect the timing quite considerably. The grooves which eventually appear in cam followers with non-rotating solid feet have the effect of opening the valve earlier and closing it later; therefore, if considerable

*The quoted factor of one-quarter the diameter depends on the fact that the area of valve-opening measured round the circumference of the seat is equal to the area of the port at that lift, and hence, in theory, the gas-velocity is the same. However, as the valve is only at full lift momentarily, a ratio larger than one-quarter will give better total flow if the valve is on the small side, as it may be in engines of small bore-stroke ratio. On the other hand, if all other things are equal, the inertia loads and thus the spring-strength required varies in direct proportion to the lift and therefore for reasons of mechanical strength it may be necessary to keep the lift below one-quarter the diameter if the heads are very large.

wear of this nature is discovered, it is best to recheck the timing with new rockers, or with the old ones reground to the correct contour.

If the wear is more than 10 or 12 thous. in depth the rockers will, in any event, need to be reground and case-hardened anew unless new ones can be obtained, and this is obviously a job best done by the makers. In this connection it is sometimes found that an engine which has been going very well despite severely worn rockers, falls off in performance after new rockers have been installed. This is a clear indication that cams giving longer valve openings are required for maximum power at high revs.

The foregoing more or less covers the preliminary survey of the new parts which may be required and the work to be done. The methods of doing that work form the subject of subsequent chapters.

# CHAPTER II

# CARBURATION AND INDUCTION FACTORS

AT this juncture it is worth noting that a lot of fun can be obtained by "hotting-up" a side-valve engine; there have been quite a number of 90 m.p.h. s.v. "500 s" in existence at one time or another, and readers with long memories will recollect the astonishing little 250 c.c. J.A.P. engines which were reputed to be able to rev. at 8,000 r.p.m. The s.v. unit is usually much lighter than its o.h.v. counterpart, and can be screamed up to maximum revs. without danger of the valves hitting the piston or fouling each other.

Irrespective of the location of the valves or their method of operation, the prime necessity is to have the inlet passage as unobstructed as possible. An easy exit for the exhaust is also highly desirable, although this is as much for keeping this valve cool as for aiding power production.

There are three main factors to be considered in the inlet tract: (a) the size of the valve; (b) the shape and length of the port; and (c) the size of the carburetter. To some extent these are allied to each other. For example, it is no use using a very large-bore carburetter if the rest of the induction system is inadequate; such an instrument will give little or no extra power and will certainly spoil the acceleration. Improving the breathing capacity of the valve and port without increasing the choke size will, on the other hand, improve the power a little at high revs. without affecting the low speed end much; but, of course, the ideal arrangement is to make the whole induction system match, thus carrying out a principle once aptly described as " proportional tuning".

A 500 c.c. engine with a conventional cast-iron o.h.v. head will usually have a carburetter of $1\frac{1}{8}$-in. or $1\frac{1}{16}$-in. bore;

the latter is about the smallest size which will give anything like good results, and as progress is made, larger sizes can be tried. At the commencement it is unwise to use too big a choke, and the following ranges are recommended: 500 c.c. single o.h.v., $1\frac{1}{8}$ in.–$1\frac{3}{16}$ in.; 500 c.c. twin o.h.v., $\frac{15}{16}$ in.–1 in.; 350 c.c. o.h.v., 500 c.c. s.v., 1 in.–$1\frac{1}{16}$ in.; 250 c.c. o.h.v., 350 c.c. s.v., $\frac{13}{16}$ in.–$\frac{7}{8}$ in.; 250 c.c. s.v., $\frac{25}{32}$ in.

As to valve size, it is scarcely possible to lay down any hard and fast rule as so many factors are involved, but the following table gives an idea of the throat sizes which are advisable: 500 c.c., $1\frac{5}{8}$ in.; 350 c.c. $1\frac{1}{2}$ in.; 250 c.c., $1\frac{3}{16}$ in.

The capacities refer to the size of individual cylinders and *not* to the engine as a whole. At best, however, these figures can only be a rough guide, because other factors besides the cylinder capacity enter into the matter; the type of performance (i.e. the shape of the power curve) required, the valve timing, compression ratio, the design of carburetter and the nature of the exhaust system all exercise an effect. Generally speaking, the faster the engine is capable of revolving, judged from a purely mechanical sense, the larger the choke which can eventually be used, though a good deal of modification may be required before the ultimate size is attained; this line of development almost inevitably leads to a type of engine which, whilst it develops very high power at high r.p.m., is virtually useless below a certain minimum speed and in consequence has to be used in conjunction with very carefully chosen gear ratios and driven with great skill in order to keep it always pulling above its minimum speed. Such a power unit will show up at its best on a fast circuit, but may be equalled or even outclassed by an engine with less maximum power but with greater torque or pulling power at low or medium speeds, on a short course with many corners or in a vehicle such as a racing car where a very close set of gear ratios cannot be used. The Italians are notable exponents of large-bore induction systems; the

250 Guzzi has a choke of 32 mm. diameter, or just over
$1\frac{1}{4}$ in. and, therefore, $\frac{1}{16}$ in. larger than that normally fitted
to post-war 500 c.c. " Manx " Nortons, and this bore is con-
tinued right through the long induction pipe and inlet port
up to the throat of the valve. The 500 c.c. twin of the same
make, which is virtually two 250 singles, has even been
used with 35 mm. chokes and the same size is used on the
four-cylinder Gilera, in which one carburetter feeds a pair
of cylinders of which each is of course only 125 c.c. At
that time the fastest English "works" machines had not
gone to those extremes; the twin A.J.S. had one $1\frac{1}{8}$ in.
carburetter feeding each of its 250 c.c. cylinders, whilst
the "works" 500 c.c. Nortons and Velocettes used $1\frac{5}{16}$ in.
chokes. The foregoing data refer to engines built *circa*
1950–52. Since then engine speeds have gone higher
particularly in single-cylinder types, and chokes of $1\frac{1}{2}$ in.
diam. have been used on quite a number of 500 c.c. engines,
running in excess of 7,000 r.p.m.

Even these sizes, though smaller in relation to the
cylinder capacity than the Italian examples, furnish a gas
speed considerably lower than those stated by some authorities to be the theoretical optimum, this somewhat puzzling
paradox being probably caused by the aforesaid optimum
having been determined in manifold-type multi-cylinder
engines in which the fuel has to be vaporized and maintained
in that state before reaching the cylinders to obtain equal
distribution, whereas in motorcycle engines the bulk of
the fuel is not actually vaporized until after it enters the
hot cylinder; this process takes full advantage of the
latent heat of evaporation of the fuel to cool the charge
within the cylinder and so results in a greater weight of
charge being induced. (For later information see page 246.)

## Work on the Inlet Port

If your engine conforms reasonably well to the standards
so far described and is in good condition it may be well to
leave things as they are for the time being and experiment

with larger valves or carburetters later. In the meantime several jobs can be done to improve the breathing ability. As the valve is operating only partially open for much of the time, anything which will ease the passage of gas past the seat at low lifts is highly beneficial, and one step towards this is to reduce the seat width from the usual $\frac{3}{32}$ in. or so down to a mere $\frac{1}{32}$ in. by carefully radiusing the corners of the valve at the seat and the top edge, and performing a similar operation on the port.

*How to reduce the width of the seatings on valve face and inlet port.*

If the seat is very wide, as it frequently is when interchangeable valves are used, it is also possible to open out the port by perhaps $\frac{1}{16}$ in., which provides a useful increase in total area. The correct method is to use a cutter, similar to a valve-seat cutter, but with an included angle of 45°, but the job can be done by careful work with a file and scraper.

For rounding off the valve edges, hold the stem in the chuck of a lathe or drill, remove the bulk of the metal with a smooth file and finish off with emery cloth. Should the valve-seat in the head be very badly pocketed and you decide to fit a larger valve, it is often possible to utilize one from a larger engine of the same make, as it is a frequent practice to employ the same size of stem throughout the range; alternatively, racing editions of sports engines are often fitted with larger valves, and one of these could be employed.

The shape of the inlet valve under the head is of more importance than is often realized and depends upon the shape of port. It used to be the fashion to have a comparatively flat, straight port—a shape which directs the gas flow past the valve stem into the region nearest the exhaust valve—and in this case the valve head must be fairly flat underneath and joined to the stem with a small radius, so as to allow plenty of room for the gas to flow past into the operative region. This port shape—see sketch below—is by no means the best, partly because the area (B) is relatively ineffective owing to the acute change in direction which the gas is compelled to take, and partly because much of the charge coming in at (A) is liable to rush straight across and out through the still-open exhaust valve, particularly if a highly extractive exhaust system is in use.

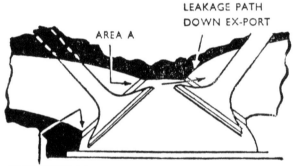

LEAKAGE PATH
DOWN EX-PORT

AREA A

INEFFECTIVE AREA B

*Limitations inherent in the old-type "flat" inlet port are depicted in this sketch. Note how the fresh charge tends to flow into the exhaust port.*

The shape shown in the second sketch—as used in modern engines—may not look so well to the casual eye, but is, in fact, better because almost the whole of the seat circumference is brought into effective use. This design of port works best in conjunction with a semi-tulip valve the shape of which has the effect of steering the gas towards the lower side of the seating. Some of the fresh charge is thus directed away from the exhaust valve, less will escape, and it will pick up less heat from that hot-headed component. Conversely, the latter is inclined to run hotter, a point which will have to be watched in petrol-benzole motors but is of less consequence with alcohol fuel.

By going up in valve size, it is possible to improve the shape of a flat port (as indicated in the third sketch by dotted

*The modern down-draught port used in conjunction with a tulip-shaped inlet valve overcomes the defects of the flat-port design.*

THIS AREA NOW
MORE EFFECTIVE

lines) in addition to increasing the valve area, but it may be better to leave this operation until a later stage, thus being able to pull something out of the bag which others may not suspect. In any case, the valve guide must be so treated as to offer the minimum obstruction, the usual method being to cut it off flush with the roof of the port. This sometimes reduces the guide length rather too drastically; equally good results can be obtained by fairing the guide off to a knife edge on the entering side and filing out the sharp corner between the guide and port, reducing the guide wall thickness down to $\frac{1}{32}$ in. or so at the sides. When a larger inlet valve is fitted, or sometimes even in standard heads, a certain amount of masking or interruption to smooth gas flow may exist in the area around the lower edge of the valve which may prevent this area being fully effective.

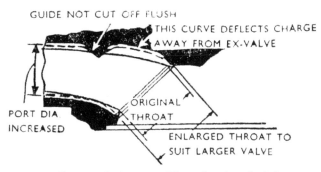

GUIDE NOT CUT OFF FLUSH

THIS CURVE DEFLECTS CHARGE
AWAY FROM EX-VALVE

PORT DIA.
INCREASED

ORIGINAL
THROAT

ENLARGED THROAT TO
SUIT LARGER VALVE

*How gas flow can be improved by enlarging the inlet tract to suit a bigger valve. The dotted lines indicate where metal should be removed.*

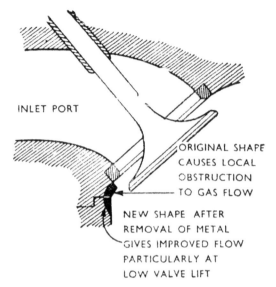

INLET PORT

ORIGINAL SHAPE
CAUSES LOCAL
OBSTRUCTION
TO GAS FLOW

NEW SHAPE AFTER
REMOVAL OF METAL
GIVES IMPROVED FLOW
PARTICULARLY AT
LOW VALVE LIFT

*Gas flow may be improved by reshaping the mating edges of the head and cylinder barrel adjacent to the inlet valve.*

It is often possible to cut away some metal from the head and in some instances the mating edge of the cylinder barrel also, and generally shape and smooth up the surfaces so that gas coming past the seat radially to the valve is gently guided into the cylinder instead of impinging against an irregular surface, or one which is too close to the valve to permit easy entry. For these port and head modifications, rotary files or emery wheels driven by a flexible shaft from an electric motor are invaluable, but the same effect can be produced with "rifflers" or bent files. Ordinary round files can be bent to shape after heating to redness, and re-hardened by plunging into water; after this treatment the steel is very hard and brittle, but if not knocked about, the teeth remain keen for a long time.

From the carburetter flange face or stub up to the valve guide boss there should be a gradual taper in the port, entirely free from ridges or hollows, and after the whole port has been brought to a satisfactory shape it must be polished with rough and fine emery cloth to a dead smooth finish. For rough port-polishing, one of the handiest tools is a piece of steel rod slotted across a diameter with a hacksaw for about $\frac{5}{8}$ in. in from the end. This rod is held in the flexible shaft chuck, and a strip of emery cloth or, better still, woven abrasive tape is slipped into the slot and wrapped round the rod up to about $\frac{3}{4}$ in. diameter. The wound-up tape must be inserted into the port before the power is turned on after which the flying end of the tape rough-polishes the port very rapidly. For final polishing, use felt bobs moistened with ordinary metal polish, or cotton material wound round the slotted bar. There is some controversy regarding the value of an absolutely mirror-like surface, but there is no doubt that a finish of this nature cannot do any harm, and is at least a source of envy to chance beholders; however, *shape* is of greater importance than mere polish.

### Side-valve Inlet Ports

The treatment described for o.h.v. inlet ports applies equally well to side-valve types. Except in those cases where the port has been purposely elevated in order to obtain clearance over a rear-mounted electrical installation, most s.v. ports have reasonably easy curves, and, so far as the approach of the gas to the underside of the valve is concerned, may be as good or better than the average o.h.v. type. As to valve shape, the same rules apply: a flattish

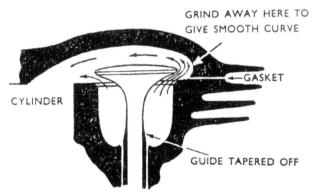

*In a side-valve unit the gas flow can usually be improved considerably by grinding away metal in the cylinder head at the point indicated. Great care is required in this oper-ation. Do not overdo it.*

port requires a flattish underhead profile, but a combination of a swept port with a semi-tulip shape of valve gives the best results.

The valve guide can be shortened a little or even cut off flush with the port without detriment, but the amount to which this is done depends largely on the port shape. It may be better to leave the guide fairly long and streamline it by tapering off to a very thin section at the upper end. Certain V-twin engines were built with the inlet ports lying horizontally in order to employ a plain T-shaped induction manifold, but an incidental advantage gained is the reduction in the angle of bend in the port itself. The front cylinder of such a motor mounted on a single-cylinder crankcase and equipped with a carburetter arranged to work at 25° upward inclination offers interesting possibilities.

It is obvious that after passing the valve the charge has to undergo another change in direction before it can reach the cylinder, and this, plus the fact that a third—possibly one-half—of the valve opening is partially masked by the valve chest wall is bound to impair the breathing. The change in direction cannot be avoided, but the effect of the masking can be reduced by clearing away the chest wall with a port-grinder and eliminating as far as possible all sharp angles.

### Further Aids to " Breathing "

In detachable-head engines, care must be taken to see that the inner edge of the gasket merges properly with the interior of the head. It may be advisable to cut a new gasket, from soft sheet aluminium or copper, which fits the head studs accurately, and to trim it up to the correct internal contour after bolting to the head.

As a further aid to " breathing", reduce the valve head diameter until the seat width is only $\frac{1}{16}$ in. and round off the edges of seat and valve as previously described. On account of the proximity of the chest wall, it is rarely of much use to attempt to use a larger valve, although it may be possible to do so if there is ample room available around

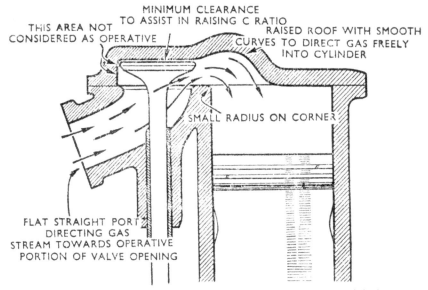

*A section of the inlet tract of a side-valve engine modified
for special high-performance valve timing.*

the head, or alternatively if there is sufficient metal in the
casting to allow for the necessary grinding-away.

Most side-valve engines have "slow" timings and low
valve lifts, with the intention of giving good low-speed
performance and, in keeping with this idea, are fitted with
small-bore carburetters. After due attention to the induction tract and timing (a point still to be dealt with), a larger
carburetter can be used, although it is not possible to go up
to quite the same size as an o.h.v. unit will take. As a
commencement. use the next size lower to that recommended
for an o.h.v. engine in the capacity choke scale on page 17.
Naturally, the inlet port must be increased in diameter to
match up with the larger-bore carburetter. One of the
difficulties associated with the obtaining of good breathing
in a side-valve engine on the lines just described is that, if
ample gas-flow areas are provided all round the valve head,
the compression ratio may become much too low. A possible
line of development worth pursuing only if valve-timing
modifications can also be carried out would be to regard

25

that portion of the valve opening furthest from the cylinder as being relatively useless anyway, and to re-design the combustion chamber with the space immediately above the inlet valve machined parallel to a radius only slightly greater than the largest inlet valve that can be worked in. The depth of this pocket should be about $\frac{1}{32}$ in. greater than the maximum valve lift, and the cam contour modified to slam the valve up to full lift as rapidly as possible and hold it at full lift for a considerable period.

The port likely to be most effective in this instance would be of the flattish type, as shown in the diagram on page 25, directing the gas stream mainly in the direction of the effective portion of the valve opening. To assist the gas in changing direction to enter the cylinder, the head may be hollowed out slightly and the top edge of the cylinder bore radiused off, though not so far down the bore that the top ring is deprived of the protection of the upper ring land.

## The Exhaust Port

The exhaust valve and port still remain to be dealt with, and it should be appreciated that the gas-flow conditions are quite different from those existing in the inlet. In the latter, the gas approaches from the back of the valve, and the pressure-difference between port and cylinder is (or should be) of the order of 5 or 6 lb. per sq. in. only as a *maximum* value, and must be much less than this at the finish of the induction stroke.

With the exhaust valve, however, the gas at the moment of opening is at high pressure—70 or 80 lb. per sq. in.—and is waiting all round the periphery of the head, ready to escape the moment the valve begins to lift. Thus, whatever the port shape, the whole of the circumference of the valve is operative, and 50% of the gas can escape straight down the port; only half of the gas is obstructed by the valve stem and guide, consequently these can be permitted to occupy quite a lot of space without detriment.

It is a mistake to carve away the guide and boss completely in order to get the maximum port area; by so doing more of the valve will be exposed to the outgoing gas and the stem will be robbed of much valuable contact area through which most of the heat picked up has to be conducted.

On the other hand, if the port is so shaped that a large proportion of the extremely hot gas is caused to impinge on the stem without a free path of escape, there is a grave risk of valve-failure, through overheating at the junction of the stem and head. Cutting away the side walls so that the port is considerably wider than the diameter at the throat reduces this effect very considerably, and is in fact the only course open in some engines where for the sake of compactness the port has purposely been kept flat.

Before doing much modification to port shape, the thickness of metal between the port and neighbouring pockets such as rocker-boxes, spring-boxes or the recess sometimes provided to accommodate coil valve springs, should be explored, preferably with indicating callipers, to ensure that there is ample metal present; nothing is more annoying (or expensive) than to find the port breaking through into a place where it should not do so, particularly just as the job is nearing completion. Also, on inserted-seat heads,

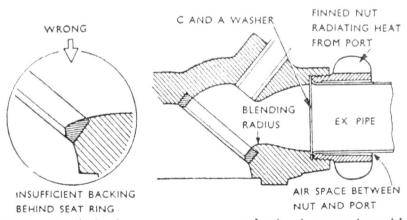

*(Right)* The ideal exhaust-port arrangement showing, in comparison with the inset sketch, the seat ring well supported and the valve guide protected from feed-back of heat from the exhaust pipe area.

never remove metal in any but the smallest amount from the seat ring itself, and also leave plenty of metal under the ring where it is closest to the port, as there is a possibility that explosion pressure may actually force the seat-ring back due to lack of support if there is insufficient port-metal backing up the ring at this point; the valve will then cease to be gas-tight and may shortly fail through over-heating.

It is not always appreciated that one of the most prolific causes of trouble in I.-C. engines is the large amount of waste heat absorbed by the exhaust-port walls and fed back into the head. Once the exhaust valve has opened, any heat left in the gas ceases to be of any value and becomes a waste product, and the less it is re-absorbed into the engine the better. Consequently, exhaust ports should be as short as possible, and there should be a path for heat conduction between the port and the exhaust pipe nut, but not between nut and pipe. These conditions are all assisted by using a male-threaded nut, with a perceptible clearance between the bore of the nut and the pipe; at one time long ports furnished with many fins to cool the port down were fashionable, but it is far better to prevent the heat being absorbed rather than to dissipate it afterwards: an examination of almost every engine which has been a successful performer on petrol or petrol-benzole will show that they all possess this feature of short, direct ports. The point is of less importance on engines designed specific-ally for alcohol fuel, but that does not impair the essential correctness of the principle.

Double-port heads which were popular some years ago are, in general, not nearly as efficient as those with single ports, and most engines so designed will perform better if one of the ports is blanked off completely and as close up to the valve as possible. The term "double port" is used here as applying to a single valve; if there are two exhaust valves, it is usual for each to have its own port, and in this event the criticism, of course, does not apply.

Once an exhaust port has been correctly shaped and

polished, it is best not to clean all carbon out of it, but to allow a thin skin to remain. Carbon is a poor heat conductor and acts as quite an effective insulator, which helps to limit the absorption of waste heat by the port walls.

Python engines (the name under which Rudge power units were supplied to other makers) were sometimes equipped with adaptors forced into the ports to suit $1\frac{3}{4}$-in. pipes (far too big, even for the 500 c.c. models), and these should be removed. This is done by removing the hexagon-headed setscrews which lock the adaptors in place; the latter can then be twisted out with the aid of a large Foot-print pipe-wrench, an operation best conducted before detaching the head from the cylinder. The right pipe size is that which just fits in the counterbore in the port from which the adaptors have been removed.

Much of the heat absorbed by the exhaust valve head gets away by conduction through the seat; the latter should, therefore, be reasonably wide—between .07 in. and .09 in., according to valve size. For sprint work, or on engines which will be regularly stripped down after every event, narrower seats can be used with safety, but more frequent valve-clearance adjustment may be necessary. It may pay on heads originally designed with both valves of equal size to reduce the diameter of the exhaust valve, and, therefore, the seat width, in order to fit a larger inlet valve and still maintain enough clearance between the two to prevent mutual interference in the overlap period when both are partially lifted. A slightly convex head is preferable to one which is dead flat or even concave, although it means a slight increase in weight. The edge must not be too thin, otherwise it will get very hot and may warp out of shape at running temperature; as with the inlet valve, the top edge should be slightly rounded off to improve gas-flow and to avoid a local hot area.

If there is any doubt as to the quality or age of the valve, play safe—discard it and get a new one of K.E. 965 or similar austenitic steel, conforming to the British speci-

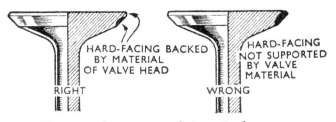

*Correct and incorrect techniques in the process
of hard-facing valve seat areas.*

fication D.T.D. 49b. Better still, if possible get hold of a
sodium-filled valve of the type commonly fitted to aero-
engines and used by our leading racing firms during the
last two or three years of racing before the war. These
valves are larger in the stem than the " solid " ones they
replace, and in consequence the guides will need to be
renewed or bored out. Valves which have worn thin near
the seats but are otherwise sound can be reclaimed by
building up the seat with " Stellite " No. 6 grade or
" Brightray ". Both these alloys are non-ferrous and have
the advantage that they are very resistant to attack by the
by-products of Ethyl fluid; in countries where heavily-
leaded fuel is obtainable and permissible for racing it is a
wise precaution to have the valves " Stellited " before they
become damaged by lead attack. There are other materials
such as " Cobalite " which can be used for hard-facing valves,
but it must be remembered that the deposited material
should always be backed up by the parent metal of the
valve, as shown in the diagram ; it is inadvisable to use hard-
facing to increase the diameter of the head or to build up a
very badly worn head to its original size. " Nimonic 80a ",
a non-ferrous nickel alloy, is another very good material
for exhaust valves.

### Side Exhaust Valves

Side exhaust valves are worse off than the o.h.v. type
as regards heat, because they get little cooling from the
incoming charge, and the part of the seat next the barrel is
bound to run very hot. Also they are usually rather small

in stem diameter, and have cast-iron guides; an improvement in heat dissipation can be effected by increasing the stem diameter by $\frac{1}{16}$ in. and using aluminium-bronze or Barronia-metal guides, but it will be necessary with these metals to ensure a small though positive supply of lubricant to prevent seizure. A flash-coating of hard chrome plate .0005 in–.001 in. thick on the valve stem will also assist in this direction.

Absorption of heat by the head is lessened by contouring the valve chest so that the outgoing gas is allowed to flow away as smoothly as possible; this is achieved by eliminating sharp corners in the valve chest and allowing plenty of room over the head of the valve when it is at full lift.

The scheme previously outlined for deliberately masking part of the inlet valve is definitely not applicable to the exhaust valve, for it is imperative that the whole circumference of this component is brought into action at the commencement of lift in order to liberate the high-pressure gas immediately.

## Valve Seat Angles

The majority of valve seats are formed at 45° to the axis, but some makers favour the flatter 30° seat, which is more effective at low lifts because the actual opening between valve and seat is greater by 22% or in the ratio of 86 to 70. This advantage ceases after the valve has lifted by an amount approximately equal to $1\frac{1}{2}$ times the seat width, and is, therefore, of less importance with narrow seats than with wide ones, but with the widths commonly employed the gain is worthwhile because much of the breathing must perforce be accomplished when either valve is only partially lifted. Conversely, the 45° seat has a greater self-centring effect on the valve, and may give better results mechanically in heads with short guides, or those in which distortion may occur at high temperatures. Some engines are made with 30° inlets and 45° exhausts for that reason.

CHAPTER III

## ATTENTION TO O.H.V. CYLINDER HEADS

So far we have progressed to the stage where the valve seats and ports have been attended to—at least, so far as the written word is concerned: carrying out the work in a really thorough manner takes a much longer time and far more patience than simply describing it.

Before proceeding further, the carburetter should be fitted temporarily to make sure that it lines up accurately with the port without a " step " anywhere around the circumference. If the mixing chamber pushes on to a stub, or has a spigoted flange, the two bores are almost bound to be concentric, but a " step " will exist if the diameters are unequal or if the port has been filed a trifle out of round during the cleaning-up process.

Once lined up, either of these types will always reassemble correctly, but the standard flange, which has no spigot, is sometimes a rather slack fit on its two studs. If the stud-holes are worn or have been filed out at some time, it pays to ream them out to ⅜ in. and fit bushes on to the studs;

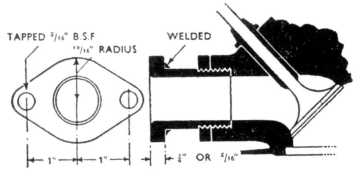

*Showing how an old-type induction stub can be modified to accept a modern flange-fitting carburetter. Note how the induction pipe is blended smoothly into the inlet port.*

the carburetter and port bores can then be blended into each other and you will be sure that, even if the carburetter has to be refitted hastily at some future date, it will go back correctly and cannot possibly work out of position at any time through vibration.

Sometimes these flanges become bent (usually through the use of a packing washer which is too soft and thick), and this fault must be rectified by truing up the face. For use in later experiments, it is worth while making up some extension blocks to go between the flange faces, in order to vary the length of the induction system ; the easiest way is to machine them from aluminium castings made from a wooden pattern the same shape as the flange and $\frac{1}{2}$-in. finished thickness. Four of these, plus the necessary longer studs, will enable the induction pipe length to be varied in $\frac{1}{2}$-in. steps up to 2 in.

The cylinder heads of early models were fitted with screwed-in stubs to take clip-fitting carburetters, and the engine makers concerned can often supply longer patterns; alternatively, in order to use a flange-fitting carburetter, a steel flange can be welded or brazed to the stub.

It may be advisable to make up a new stub altogether rather than to modify an old one; many induction systems are neither long enough nor large enough for maximum power at very high r.p.m. (*see Chapter XVIII*). New pipes can be made up quite easily from steel tube with flanges brazed or welded on. Another simple method is to use a piece of canvas-reinforced hose attached to the existing induction pipe and to an extension piece by Jubilee clips, though some care has to be taken to avoid a nasty step or change in diameter at each change from pipe to hose, particularly if an inch or so of hose is exposed; in that case, the best thing is to line the hose with a third piece of metallic tube to preserve a constant diameter. This scheme insulates the carburetter from the high-speed vibrations which sometimes cause a mysterious loss of r.p.m. through unsuspected flooding at a certain critical speed and so is referred to again in Chapter XVIII.

Amal carburetters are made in both flange- and clip-fitting forms. The largest bore which can safely be used with the standard 2-in. stud centre-distance is $1\frac{3}{16}$ in., and even then there is only just clearance for the nuts. Clip-fitting carburetters, i.e. those which fit on stubs, do not have this limitation, and when for reasons of space or to eliminate bends in the induction system, the mixing chamber has to be mounted out of the vertical, the clip-fitting type is easier to install because it can simply be swivelled round the stub into the correct position. The angle of the mixing chamber is immaterial, within limits, provided the float level is correct in relation to the jet, though if the inclination is greater than 15° flooding from the pilot jet into the engine will occur when standing if the fuel supply is not turned off.

Standard stub diameters are $1\frac{1}{8}$ in., $1\frac{1}{4}$ in., and $1\frac{3}{8}$ in., according to the bore of the carburetter. Adaptor stubs with any of these diameters can easily be made up to fit on standard flange studs, but it is best to use socket head screws of the Allen or "Unbrako" type with the largest size to avoid having to cut too far into the wall to obtain head clearance. By this method it is also possible to make up a stub of 1.422 in. diameter to utilize the 32 mm. carburetter.

Around 1950, a new standard Amal flange with 65 mm. bolt centres was introduced for very large carburetters and this point must be watched when contemplating a change-over. It is possible to make a double flanged adaptor with 2 in. hole centres in one flange and 65 mm. in the other, but the largest bore you can get without having two local flats adjacent to the Allen screw heads is $1\frac{7}{16}$ in.

## Coil and Hair-pin Springs

Hair-pin springs came into use many years ago for racing, because the coil springs in use at that period were not always reliable and became less so as engine speeds rose above 6,000 r.p.m. and valve lifts increased above $\frac{3}{8}$ in.; the combination of these two factors creates a difficult situation for any spring and even hair-pin springs have undergone considerable design modifications before reaching their present state of reliability. Most sports models and genuine " racers " of 1934–39 vintage were fitted with hair-pin springs with the notable exception of the speedway J.A.P. which has always retained coils, these being, in any case, sufficiently reliable for an engine intended primarily for short-distance events. Since 1945 there has been a considerable change back to coils, largely because of the difficulty of enclosing hair-pins without serious interruption to air-flow through the head fins, particularly on a parallel twin. Coil-spring fracture is mainly caused through " surging " or a state of rapid vibration of the centre coils, and the way to overcome this is by using only a limited number of coils; all modern coil springs are duplex or even triplex with not more than six free coils in the outer. The inner spring often has one or two more coils of lighter gauge wire and it is an advantage for it to be a push fit within the outer one as this provides a certain amount of friction damping and so helps to prevent surging.

Side-valve engines are usually equipped with single springs of fairly light poundage, sometimes of the " floppy " type, with a large number of coils. These should be replaced by others of similar proportions to those just described, which will probably entail replacing the top and bottom spring caps and the split collets. It is also probable that pieces will be required to make up for the reduced length of spring and these should be made with the smallest possible area in contact with the head to minimise transfer of heat to the uppermost coils.

With regard to spring pressure, it is a mistake to think that enormously strong springs are a *sine qua non*; any pressure in excess of that required to prevent valve chatter up to the usable maximum revs.—say, 7,000 for a 500 c.c. unit, up to 9,500 for a 250 c.c. plot—simply wastes a little more power and loads up the valve gear unnecessarily.

The actual strength required at full lift depends upon the cam contour and lift, as well as the revs. and weight of valve gear, so it just is not possible to give any hard-and-fast rule, but, apart from these considerations, it is usual in two-valve heads to provide 100–120 lb. pressure when the valve is seated, and, unless the cam design is very peculiar, 140–180 lb. should suffice at full lift (the greater figures obviously applying to the larger-size engines). Four-valve designs, with their much lighter individual components, require only about 80 lb. seat pressure per valve.

It is possible to make up a rig to test this pressure but makers' genuine replacements can be accepted as giving the correct amount provided that nothing has taken place to alter the installed length of the spring appreciably. Excessive seat wear, or possibly a stretched exhaust valve may account for this length being $\frac{1}{16}$ in. or so longer than it should be and this is sufficient to reduce the pressure by several pounds. For workshops which do a considerable amount of tuning work, it is a wise plan to acquire one of the special spring-testing machines that give an accurate measurement of the poundage given at any particular length. The actual installed poundage can then be determined by first measuring the distance between the top and bottom spring collars and then determining the pressure of the springs at that length on the machine.

Apart from being obviously broken, coil springs often shorten or settle and so lose their effective strength; attempting to restore the situation by packing up the lower seating is sometimes effective, but it is then essential to verify that the springs are not "coil-bound" at full lift; to do this see that the valve can be raised a further $\frac{1}{16}$ in. beyond the maximum point to which the rocker lifts it.

Another expedient is to place the weaker set of springs on the inlet valve, as insufficient strength on this component will at worst only reduce the top r.p.m. a little, but severe mechanical damage may result from lack of spring strength on the exhaust valve.

### Hair-pin Springs

Hair-pin springs were originally made with fairly small diameter coils and long legs, but the modern variety has much larger diameter coils and shorter legs. Further, the design is such that over the working range of the spring, the loop in contact with the valve moves almost in a straight line parallel to the valve stem and there is little or no tendency, as there was with earlier designs, for the stationary legs to move in and out on their abutments. When for reasons of space it has been necessary to reduce the overall width of the pair of springs, as, for instance, on parallel twins, like the twin-cylinder A.J.S. racing machine, the ends of each pair of springs are overlapped, and careful design is necessary to ensure that no interference occurs between the springs at any part of the valve movement. When fitting these overlapping springs, particularly to an engine for which they were not originally designed, care must be taken to see that the end loops do clear each other at all points from closed to full lift.

After a while, wear occurs on the straight piece of the loops of hair-pin springs, caused by rubbing against the spring retainer, and replacement is called for if this wear exceeds one quarter of the wire diameter. The force exerted by the springs in each pair should be equal to avoid tilting the valve, therefore it is essential to replace in pairs, not just one at a time. When they do break, hair-pins usually fail just where the top leg commences to bend round into the coil and every care must be taken to see that no cuts or deep scratches are made in the wire at this point when handling such springs.

It is often considered advisable to convert a coil-spring engine to hair-pins and this can be done with a little wangling in some o.h.v. designs. On MOV and MAC Velocettes of the original design with bolted-on rocker boxes, standard KTT springs, and spring collars can be used, but the rocker-box extensions which normally surround the spring cups have to be cut away, leaving the outer ends of the rockers exposed, and the rocker-box standards on the push-rod side must be thinned down to clear the springs which are installed at an angle.

Removal of the coil valve spring enclosure has the effect

of depriving the valve guides of lubrication which they normally receive by leakage from the rocker bearings and it is, therefore, desirable, particularly for long-distance work, to drill $\frac{3}{16}$ in. holes through the head into each valve guide to receive oil pipes which can be supplied with lubricant either from a small external tank or from the normal lubrication system with metering jets to limit the supply, which need only be small in quantity.

### Auxiliary Return Springs

Some designers prefer to utilize return springs on the rockers or push-rods, thereby either reducing the strength necessary in the valve springs or, alternatively, permitting higher revs for the same spring strength; examples are the hair-pin springs surrounding the rocker bosses on KTT Velocettes and the springs fitted on the lower ends of the push-rods of certain J.A.P. motors. The effect of such springs is to maintain the cam follower in contact with the cam continuously, and excessive pressure leads to local heating and wear of the cam-follower foot unless a roller is employed. A neat way of adding return springs to engines with hollow rockers is to house a coil spring loosely in the bore of the shank with one end fixed to the rocker arm and the other attached to the rocker enclosure in such a way that the spring can be wound up to any desired amount; this scheme has the merit that it is easy to experiment with varying

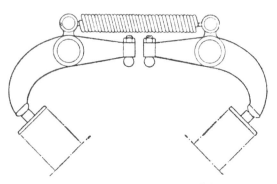

*A method of obtaining increased return-spring action without creating excessive cam-follower loading.*

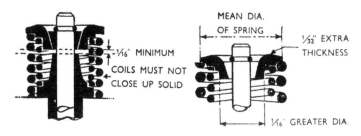

*(Left) (see page 42) At maximum valve lift there must be adequate clearance between valve guide and spring cap and between the spring coils. (Right) (see pages 40-1) Note how the outer diameter of the alloy cap is that of the mean diameter of the outer spring.*

amounts of pressure and thereby to discover whether stronger valve springs are required.

Another method is to attach a tension spring to a short vertical arm on each rocker; this idea is good because when the exhaust valve is closing, the inlet is lifting and, therefore, the tension in the spring is increased just when it is most wanted, and the required effect is gained without excessive cam-follower loading during other parts of the cycle.

In some designs the exhaust spring settles very quickly because the coils nearest the exhaust port become over-heated; a remedy can be effected by insulating the lower spring coils by mica washers, or packing the spring seat up on narrow washers so that there is the minimum of metallic contact and the maximum of air space between the spring seat and the hot port metal. Generally speaking, enclosed coil springs can be kept as cool or even cooler than open springs by the expedient of pouring enough oil over them through jets to carry away the heat.

Before leaving this subject of springs it may be well to dispel a popular misconception as to their function: some think that the cam pushes the valve open against the spring right up to full lift and after that the spring takes charge and performs the closing action. In fact, the cam operates against the spring plus the inertia of the valve for the first portion only of the lift; after a certain point and up to full lift, the spring is doing all the work of slowing the valve down until it is actually stopped by the time full lift is reached. After that, the spring accelerates the valve back again until a certain point is reached on the closing flank of the cam; from that point onwards the valve is being slowed down again by pressure between the cam-follower and cam so that it is eventually let down on to the seat at a very low velocity. In other words, the valve is under cam-control for the first and last portions of the motion but for the remainder of the action, i.e. over the nose of the cam, the valve is under spring control. The pressure between the cam and follower during periods of cam-control is equal to the spring pressure plus the inertia force or momentum of the valve gear, whilst during the periods of spring control, the pressure is the spring pressure minus the valve inertia, and if at any point the inertia becomes greater than the spring pressure the cam follower will leave the cam contour giving rise to the condition known as valve float. This may not be very noticeable, in fact if the cams are inadequate in lift or duration, may even be beneficial from the power production point of view, but if the speed rises still further, the separation will become greater and greater until the valve hits the piston or the other valve and suffers in the process, or else very heavy impact loads (as indicated by the onset of excessive noise) will be set up somewhere in the valve gear with the certainty of failure if the conditions are allowed to continue.

Touching on the matter of spring caps, many can be lightened judiciously by reducing their diameter to the

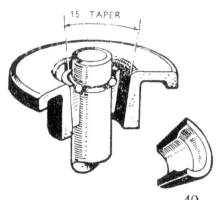

15 TAPER

*Construction of the split collet and circlip assembly used on J.A.P. and various valves.*

40

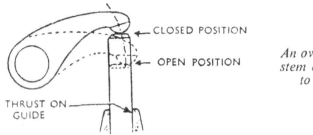

*An over-long valve stem causes thrust to the right.*

mean diameter of the outer spring and filing scallops in the edge, so that the spring bears only on six or eight projections. Alternatively, new caps can be turned from a *strong* light alloy (preferably R.R. 77, but, failing that, R.R. 56, or Duralumin B) to the same dimensions as the original steel ones, except for allowing a little extra thickness where the flange merges into the taper bore, and around the collet boss. Titanium is also suitable.

If you are rejuvenating an old engine and are using non-standard valves, the easiest way to retain the spring is by using a spring cap, collets and wire circlip of J.A.P. design, since all the machining called for is to turn in each stem a narrow semi-circular groove to accommodate the circlip, and to verify that the stems accurately fit the collets, which are obtainable with bore sizes of $\frac{5}{16}$ in., $\frac{11}{32}$ in., and $\frac{3}{8}$ in.

The position of the upper end of an o.h. valve-stem is important, but is difficult to check dimensionally without special measuring fixtures, so it will need to be done by eye. Assemble the rocker gear on the head and observe the behaviour of the rocker-tip relative to the valve stem as the mechanism is operated by hand from the closed to the full-lift position. If the stem is too long, the contact point will

*If the stem is too short the thrust will occur on the opposite side to that indicated by the above sketch.*

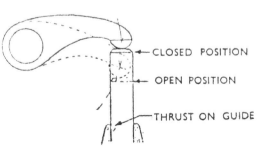

41

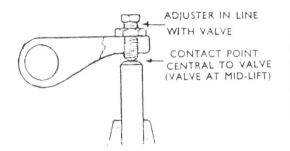

ADJUSTER IN LINE
WITH VALVE

CONTACT POINT
CENTRAL TO VALVE
(VALVE AT MID-LIFT)

*Just right! A valve
stem of the correct
length has the
rocker at right
angles to it, with
the adjuster dead
central, when in the
mid-lift position.*

move outwards, as shown in the diagram; if too short, the movement will be in the opposite direction. If the outer end of the rocker is fitted with a screwed adjuster, this should be exactly in line with the valve stem in the *half-lift* position with the contact point dead central to the stem at the same time.

There is little likelihood that a fairly new engine using standard components will not be correct, but numerous causes—excessive cutting-back of the valve seats, stretched or incorrect valves, or damaged rocker boxes—may all contribute their quota to incorrect alignment in old power units. Sometimes a cure can be effected by shortening the stem or fitting hardened end-caps of the appropriate thickness; in other cases packing up the rocker box will do the trick. The point may seem to be of little importance, but it must be remembered that, however strong the springs may be, as maximum revs. are approached they have less and less margin of strength over that required to return the valves to their seats; thus, an amount of friction anywhere in the whole of the valve gear, which is barely perceptible at hand-cranking speeds, becomes a serious item at top revs.

The clearance at full lift between the valve guide and spring collar must also be checked. This should be a full $\frac{1}{16}$ in., otherwise, if the motor is over-revved, the parts may hit, and no valve will stand up to impact of that nature for very long. Similarly, if coil springs are used, they must not be " coil-bound," i.e., compressed solid at full lift, which might occur if the bottom washers have been packed up to increase the spring pressure, or if incorrect springs are installed; this point is *most* important.

As a general rule, it is best to defer the assembly of the head until any necessary alterations to the barrel or piston have been effected; the subject is dealt with in Chapter X. Such modifications may be required to obtain the correct compression ratio, or to ensure that the valve-clearance "pockets" in the piston crown are deep enough and of the correct radius.

The correct compression ratio depends upon the cylinder capacity, type of fuel, material of the head and many other items, such as stroke-bore ratio, effectiveness of the induction system, and so forth, but the following table gives an approximate guide to the ratios which can be employed with safety in o.h.v. engines under racing conditions when using 50/50 petrol-benzole fuel, although they by no means represent the ultimate, or necessarily the most suitable, figures:

| Cylinder capacity | | | Iron | Cylinder-head Material Alum. Bronze | Alum. or Bi-metal |
|---|---|---|---|---|---|
| 250 c.c. | .. | .. | 8.5 | 9.5 | 10 |
| 350 c.c. | .. | .. | 8.2 | 9 | $9\frac{1}{2}$ |
| 500 c.c. | .. | .. | 7.8 | 8.5 | 9 |

Elderly engines with finning a bit on the scanty side may not be able to use ratios quite as high as those quoted, save

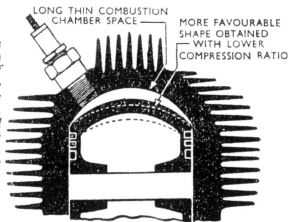

*The benefits of a higher compression piston can be lost if the resultant combustion space becomes unduly distorted. Better results will be attained with the lower piston dome, illustrated here by a dotted line.*

LONG THIN COMBUSTION CHAMBER SPACE

MORE FAVOURABLE SHAPE OBTAINED WITH LOWER COMPRESSION RATIO

for very short-distance events or when using alcohol fuel. Ratios as high as 16 to 1 can be used with fuels such as Shell " A ", J.A.P. fuel, or pure methanol, irrespective of the cylinder size, but in " square " engines—i.e., those in which the bore and stroke are equal, or nearly so—the piston may need to have such a pronounced dome on it that the shape of the combustion chamber becomes unfavourable to good combustion.

In such cases better results may be obtained by keeping the ratio down to, say, 12 to 1. Of course, " dope " fuels *can* be used with ratios suitable for petrol-benzole, but the engine will not give much more power—it will simply run cooler and be less liable to give trouble with valves or plugs. This subject is a wide one and has a section devoted to it in the next chapter.

Assuming that the compression ratio and valve clearances are correct, final-stage work on the head can be commenced by polishing the valve stems with dead-smooth emery cloth (rubbed *along* the surface, not round it) and then grinding-in in the normal manner, but using a fine abrasive, finishing off with powdered Turkey-stone or metal polish to obtain really smooth seatings entirely free from ridges or grooves. During this process the inlet-valve seat, which has been reduced to $\frac{1}{32}$ in. wide through rounding-off the edges of valve and port (*see page* 19), will increase slightly in width to 45 or 50 thous., at which it is wide enough to run for some time without undue hammering back. It is best to use some flexible device rather than a rigid tool for oscillating the valve so that it can seat itself freely ; a rubber suction-cup on a wooden handle fills the bill, though it may be necessary to apply a drop of Bostik to the polished valve head to obtain sufficient grip to turn it. Another method is to push a piece of tight-fitting canvas-lined hose on the end of the stem and oscillate it, either by twirling between the hands or with a hand drill. When grinding in Vincent valves the upper guide *must* be in place, for the lower one is too short to locate the valve accurately by itself and is not intended to do so.

After grinding in, wash away all traces of abrasive with petrol or paraffin, smear a drop of *clean* mineral oil on the seats, and assemble each valve in turn—first applying some graphited running-in compound to the stems to minimize the risk of scoring or "picking-up" when the engine is first started.

Make sure that the split collets are paired up correctly, and, after fitting the springs with the aid of the invaluable Terry spring compressor—an essential part of the shop equipment—verify that both collets are hard against the abutment on the stem and that the spring cap is fitting snugly on the taper; if not, one or two light blows with a hide mallet or the end of a hammer-handle on the spring cap (*not* the valve stem) will usually jar the assembly into position. If you are in any doubts as to the fit of the collets in the spring cap, it is advisable before assembling the valves to lap these components together in position on the stems, using ordinary valve-grinding paste as the abrasive.

Wire circlips sometimes become stretched when being removed and it is best to close them up before reassembly and then to make absolutely sure, even by using a magnifying glass, that each is actually seated in the groove and nestling snugly in the recess provided in the top of the split collets when the full pressure of the valve spring is on them. Occasional cases of valves dropping in with this form of fixing are usually attributable to failure to observe this point during assembly.

Split collets are often supplied in pairs, partially cut through. They should always be left in this condition until required, then separated and the small burr left in the cut cleaned up prior to fitting. Mixing up split collets indiscriminately is a fruitful source of valve failure, though it may take some time to develop.

Finally, don't leave the head on the back of the bench to get filled up with dust and swarf. Smear oil lightly inside the ports and block them with pieces of clean rag, or, better still, large corks, which are less likely to be left in place when they should have been removed.

# CHAPTER IV

# COMPRESSION RATIOS AND FUELS

THE previous note on compression ratios suitable for various engines needs amplification. In the first place, the ratios quoted are for racing only, being far too high for

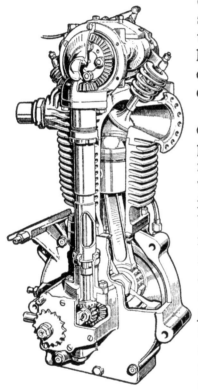

ordinary road work with silencer and "pump" fuel, one to one and a quarter ratios less being about as high as could be used in the latter circumstance.

Owing to the shape of the combustion chamber, it is impossible to obtain such high ratios in a side-valve cylinder without restricting the breathing ability—about 8 to 1 being as high as one can reach—and it must always be remembered that it is not the actual *measured* compression ratio which counts, but the *pressure of the gas* at the end of the compression stroke. This depends as much upon the perfection of cylinder filling as on the ratio; therefore a

*Scanty finning, characteristic of design of the 1920's, is still satisfactory where cool-running methanol and similar fuels are used.*

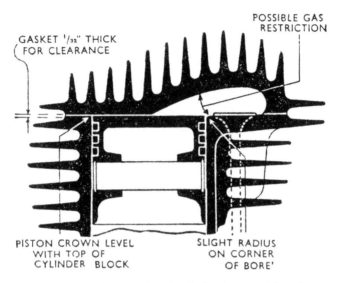

GASKET ⅟₃₂" THICK
( FOR CLEARANCE

POSSIBLE GAS
RESTRICTION

PISTON CROWN LEVEL
WITH TOP OF
CYLINDER BLOCK

SLIGHT RADIUS
ON CORNER
OF BORE'

*Points which must be checked when a side-valve cylinder head has been machined to raise the compression ratio.*

balance must be struck between the interior shape which gives the best gas-flow and that which gives the highest ratio.

Most s.v. engines are now of the detachable head pattern, with the combustion chamber concentrated over the valves, and in this type the throat between chamber and barrel sometimes constitutes a restriction, particularly if much metal has been machined off the head to raise the compression. A small radius on the top edge of the barrel next the valve chest will improve the flow lines, but must not be carried so far down that the top ring is in danger of being exposed. The thickness of the gasket is sufficient clearance between the flat portion of the head and the piston crown, which should, therefore, be just level with the top face of the barrel at t.d.c. An aluminium head is particularly desirable, except, perhaps, for alcohol fuel, when the cooling problem is not so acute.

Reverting to o.h.v. engines, the aim is to obtain the correct ratio with the least possible area of metal exposed to flame. However impressive it looks, an excessively domed piston crown is not desirable, partly because its exposed area is great, also because the "hump" hinders flame propagation, and anything in the nature of the converging pocket which is formed by the angle between dome and head produces a likely locality in which detonation can take place.

It is quite a good scheme to make a cast of the combustion chamber by pouring melted wax into the plug hole with the piston at t.d.c. This shows up any pockets or restrictions, and the wax can be softened and remoulded with the fingers after detaching the head, to give an improved shape with the same volume of wax and, therefore, the same compression. As quite a number of different makers have used the same bore diameters—74 mm., for instance, is a popular size for 350 c.c. power units—it is often possible to utilize a "foreign" piston of different proportions to replace a standard article and thereby obtain a better shape of combustion chamber.

Unless shims are already fitted under the barrel flange, the usual method of finally adjusting the ratio is by shortening the barrel. A great deal of laborious setting-up and remeasuring can be saved by making up a two-column table showing the C.R. and equivalent compression space and determining, as follows, the differences in barrel length which are equal to 1 c.c.

| Bore | | | 1 c.c.= |
|------|--|--|---------|
| 60 mm. | .. | .. | .014 in. |
| 70 mm. | .. | .. | .010 in. |
| 80 mm. | .. | .. | .008 in. |
| 90 mm. | .. | .. | .006 in. |

Knowing the existing ratio, a very simple piece of arithmetic will show how much length alteration is required for any other ratio. Skimming the barrel flange is an operation which has to be done very accurately to ensure that the new surface is dead square to the bore, and some prefer to turn the top joint face where squareness is not so vital. On the other hand, a little more than is necessary at the moment can be turned off the flange and thereafter adjustments to increase or decrease the ratio can readily be made by shims. These should be made up from good material of even thickness and free from wrinkles, and should be provided in assorted thicknesses, as a large number of thin shims do not provide a firm foundation for the cylinder.

Short-stroke Manx Norton engines are fitted with squish-type heads, and in these the gap between the flat lands on the piston crown and the steps machined in the combustion chamber *must* be maintained within the limits of 45 and 55 thou. This means that no significant alteration in compression ratio can be obtained by shimming the barrel, but only by changing the piston. On the other hand, shimming to obtain this optimum clearance may be necessary after any change of components or dimensional alteration has been made. The same remarks apply to late A.J.S. 7R and Matchless G50 engines.

## Determining Compression Ratios

For maximum power, the rule is to employ the highest ratio *at which the engine will run without distress*, on the fuel which is specified for the race in question. There are, of course, many factors, both internal and external to the engine, which have an effect on the ratio which can be used, but the prime factor is the quality of the fuel.

J.A.P. fuel, methanol and similar fuels composed mainly of alcohol can be run at anything up to 16 to 1, even in engines with iron heads and barrels and scanty finning, this being partly because alcohol is almost knock-free and partly because the large amount of heat required to vaporize these fuels exercises a great internal cooling effect.

Engines for use on official dirt tracks are, however, limited by the regulations to 14 to 1 ratio. Even in events where there is no such limitation, there is not much to be gained by going any higher as very often the obstruction in the combustion chamber caused by the high piston-crown required to obtain these ultra-high ratios more than offsets the slight increase in power which might otherwise be gained.

With petrol or petrol-benzole detonation will occur at much lower ratios than are usable with alcohol, the highest ratio that can be satisfactorily employed depending upon the "octane rating" of the fuel and the design of the engine. The octane rating varies from country to country, and may be as low as 70 in some and as high as 100 in others. If fast road work is the main objective, it is better to choose a ratio which will suit the octane value of the best fuel normally obtainable in the area where the machine will be used; as an instance of the effect of octane rating, engines which could be run at 10.5 to 1 in the 1939 T.T. races using 50/50 petrol-benzole mixture of around 87 octane rating, had to be dropped down to 7.5 to 1 when using plain petrol of 72 octane, which was the only fuel permitted in 1947 by the F.I.M. regulations.

Since then the regulations have been progressively relaxed and the requirement in 1959 is that the fuel must be only of the best quality commercially obtainable in the country where the race is being conducted, but in no case must it exceed 100 octane, Research method. This rules out the 100/130 aviation gasoline which is permitted for Formula 1 car racing, but even so allows ratios of 10.5 to be used if in fact 100 octane fuel is available. This may not be so, of course, in all countries and where "pump fuel" is specified in the local regulations, care should be taken to discover, well in advance, the octane rating which the available fuel possesses, and, if possible, obtain a sample.

The octane rating is improved either by the chemical analysis of the fuel or by the addition of tetra-ethyl-lead or "Ethyl fluid". This additive has the disadvantage that as a by-product of combustion it forms lead-bromide which attacks poor-quality exhaust valves with ferocity, but will have little effect on a well-cooled valve material corresponding to DTD49b or Nimonic 80. Consequently TEL additions of up to $3\frac{1}{2}$ c.c. per gallon can be tolerated by any good racing engine fitted with such valves.

Besides its inherent freedom from detonation, alcohol requires a great deal of heat to vapourize and if no external heat is applied, the result is a great reduction in charge-temperature, which can be seen by the rapidity with which ice forms on the induction-pipes. Methyl alcohol (methanol) has a greater cooling effect than the lesser-used ethyl alcohol (ethanol), but in either case the result is to allow a greater weight of air to be induced, since cold air is heavier than hot air. This improves the volumetric efficiency of the engine, and as the mixture will tolerate very high compression ratios and thus can be burnt at a higher efficiency, in theory a great increase in power should be obtained. In practice the increase is not as great as might be expected, partly because the engine must be run hot enough to give good burning and this offsets to some extent the cooling effect of the alcohol. Alcohol-engines are prone to be sluggish until fully warmed-up and usually perform best with limited cylinder cooling, so that this fuel is particularly suitable for getting a high performance from engines with ordinary cast-iron barrels and heads especially if the stroke is longer than the bore and a high compression ratio can be obtained without spoiling the combustion chamber shape.

Apart from this aspect, the amount of energy liberated in the cylinder per cubic inch of mixture of correct strength is very much the same whatever combustible substance is employed, the theoretical quantity being around 48 foot-pounds. No amount of juggling with any of the regular fuels will alter this fact, and the use of alcohol blends only increases the power for the reasons outlined above. On the other hand, the calorific value of alcohol is very much lower than that of petrol and for the same amount of power developed, the consumption is very much higher, up to two or even three times as great. This is naturally a serious matter in long-distance racing, as apart from the matter of expense, it entails either a vast tank capacity or too many pit stops, but a compromise may be affected by using alcohol blends such as 80 per cent methanol, 10 per cent benzole and 10 per cent petrol, or equal parts of methanol, benzole and petrol which will run very satisfactorily with a reasonable consumption at ratios of 10 or 11 to 1. The various oil companies used to supply such blends ready-mixed; a table of these with their approximate analyses and compression ratios appears on page 286, but this practice has now ceased in England. Instead, each company supplies a standard blend of methanol, and acetone, also quoted in the table of fuels, which can be blended with petrol and/or benzole to make any required mixture.

Blending methanol with petrol is not quite a straightforward matter; the methanol must be of the quality known as "anhydrous" or "dry blending", and even then it will only mix with some types of petrol if a proportion of benzole equal to that of the petrol is added as well. Acetone, besides being a fuel in itself, is a help in preventing the constituents from separating out after mixing and some of the present-day petrols, with this help, will mix with methanol without the addition of benzole. The point can always be checked by making a trial mixture in a bottle and observing whether the liquids settle into two layers or not after standing for a while.

For sprint work where a high consumption can be tolerated, it became fashionable to employ nitro-methane as an addition to alcohol fuel. This compound contains an excess of oxygen which is liberated during combustion and thus enables much larger amounts of alcohol to be burnt; in effect, it provides a sort of chemical supercharging, and as such its use is frowned upon by some race organizers. It is, however, permissible at the time of writing in sprint events, but it requires careful handling at all times, as unlike petrol or alcohol, it is chemically unstable.

For that reason, it is not supplied neat, but diluted with an equal proportion of methanol; even then, any containers must be de-pressurized occasionally by loosening the filler-caps. Drums, fuel tanks and so forth must be kept scrupulously free from any contaminants, and the entire fuel system should be drained completely after each event. Some riders are in the habit of flushing the system through with petrol but if this is done all petrol *must* be removed before starting-up on the nitro blend.

Fifty per cent nitro-methane can be used, with a theoretical power increase (according to W. B. Rowntree, M.Inst. Pet.) of 40 per cent, provided the engine is strong enough to stand it, but it is more usual to dilute the basic mixture with Shell A.M.1 (94 per cent methanol, 6 per cent acetone) to bring the nitro content down to 25 or 20 per cent which should give a theoretical power increase of 15 per cent. To utilize the liberated oxygen, much more fuel is required; if, say, an 1800 main jet is necessary for straight A.M.1 fuel, it may have to be increased to 2500 for 25 per cent nitro. In any case, it is wisest to err on the large side, partly because alcohol fuels give their best power at rich mixture strengths, and partly because the free oxygen present when there is a deficiency of fuel attacks and burns a hole in the piston crown with astonishing rapidity. Great care must be taken to see that the fuel can flow through to the carburetter absolutely freely; it may not do so under severe acceleration because the fuel then gravitates to the rear of the tank and there may be practically no "head" of liquid existing on, say, the front carburetter of a V-twin and this instrument will be starved in consequence. An adequate breather must also be used on the tank, particularly if this is of the tiny sprint variety. These may seem to be obvious points, but all too often they are overlooked.

It must never be forgotten that the rate at which fuel can enter the float-bowl must always be much greater than the rate at which it is being used. Otherwise the level in the bowl may at some time be much lower than it should be: the position of a carburetter in relation to the tank and the conditions existing during violent acceleration or braking may seriously affect the rate of flow. If, for instance, the down-draught angle is appreciably steepened to obtain a straighter inlet pipe the bowl may be brought so close to the tank that the head of liquid present when the tank is nearly empty is so small that the flow will be inadequate unless two very large taps and pipes and possibly twin float-bowls are fitted. Also under braking conditions, the outlet may be uncovered as the fuel surges forward thereby admitting air into the pipes and this must be got rid of in some way before fuel can again commence to enter the bowl. Lack of attention to these matters has more than once caused trouble which has been wrongly attributed to the carburetter itself.

## Finding Compression Ratios

The graph on this page has been drawn to provide an easy method of finding out the C.R. given by any particular combustion space volume (or vice versa) in conjunction

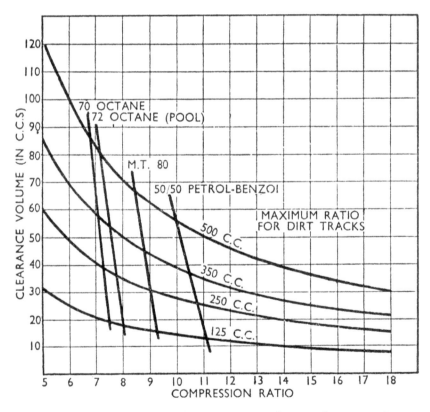

*Relationship between combustion-space volume and compression ratio in the most commonly used cylinder capacities is readily seen from this graph.*

with cylinders of various capacities; these curves represent the most commonly used cylinder (*not* total engine) capacities, the 125 c.c. curve, for example, applies also to 250 c.c. twins or 500 c.c. four-cylinder engines. To find the ratio given by any known combustion chamber volume, read across from the volume figure to the curve of the cylinder capacity concerned and then downwards to the ratio line.

Conversely, to find what compression space is required for, say, 7½ to 1 in a 250 c.c. cylinder, read up from 7.5 on the ratio line to the 250 curve, then across to the volume line, where it will be seen that the required figure is 38 c.c. If it is desired to raise the ratio to 8, for which the volume should be 35½ c.c., the amount of packing (or material which has to be removed from the cylinder base) can be found by reference to the second graph, which will be mentioned in a later paragraph.

The diagonal lines drawn across the capacity curves indicate roughly the maximum ratios which can be used with various grades of fuel, though (except in the case of alcohol) the indication is necessarily only approximate owing to the aforementioned varying factors. An engine with an iron head and barrel and poor finning cannot employ nearly as high a ratio as one with an aluminium head and extensive finning, unless the latter's breathing is so poor that the cylinder does not fill properly at maximum r.p.m., and then its *actual* compression pressure is very much less than the measured value.

For the same reason, reduced cylinder filling, engines which are to be raced at high altitudes, and consequently low atmospheric pressures, will stand a higher ratio than when run at sea-level, which is worth remembering in some countries where competitions are held in mountainous regions. A damp atmosphere also helps to suppress detonation.

### Detonation the Limiting Factor

A peculiar thing about almost all engines is that with any particular fuel there is a limiting ratio above which one

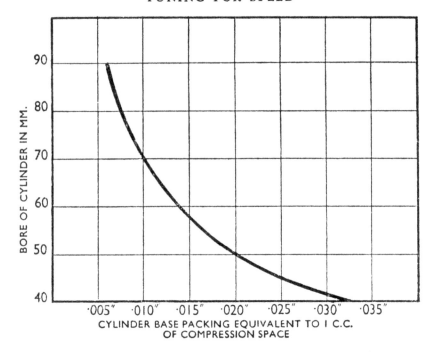

*Here is shown the thickness of packing equal to 1 c.c. for given bore dimensions.*

dare not go without an almost certain risk of piston trouble, yet the ratio at which the engine will run happily is frequently only very slightly lower; dropping from, say, 9.8 to 9.5 may make all the difference between success and failure, with but little or no diminution in performance.

Apart from audible " pinking," the signs that detonation has been occurring are unmistakable when the piston is examined: on the side of the crown remote from the plug some of the carbon film will be burnt away and the surface of the aluminium will be locally pitted and rough, for which condition the colloquial description is that " the mice have been at it."

To some extent detonation due to an excessively high ratio can be suppressed by retarding the ignition and using a jet giving a very rich mixture, but the result will only be diminution of power: in other words, there is nothing to be gained and everything to be risked in attempting to use

56

a ratio higher than the engine is willing to accept. This is particularly true in long-distance races in which the throttle is wide open most of the time; for small tracks and sand racing, it is usually possible to go up a little in the ratio, because as the engine is not running for very long, and in any case is being shut off fairly frequently, the internal temperatures do not have time to become dangerously high.

The graph on page 56 enables the amount of packing which must be removed or added when adjusting the ratio to be determined very easily. Referring to the previous example, it was found that to raise a 250 c.c. cylinder from 7.5 to 8 to 1 the compression space must be reduced from 38 to $35\frac{1}{2}$ c.c. With this second graph, supposing the bore of the cylinder to be 68 mm., if we read across from 68 mm. on the vertical line to the curve, and then down to the horizontal line, we find that .0115 in. is equivalent to 1 c.c.; therefore the thickness of packing must be reduced by 2.5. × .0115 = .029 in., or just under $\frac{1}{32}$ in.

By reading in the reverse direction, i.e., upwards from the horizontal line, then across, the difference in volume effected by removing or adding a known thickness of packing can be read off directly, thus saving a lot of calculation. With the aid of this graph, a series of plates can easily be made up so that the ratio can be altered rapidly to any desired figure.

If the barrel is held down by studs which go through the

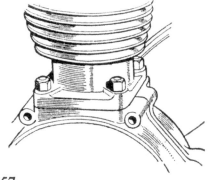

*If the barrel is attached to the crankcase by short studs it is inadvisable to remove metal from the base. When long bolts such as those illustrated on page 128 are used, a small amount of metal can be removed from the base with safety.*

flange only, care must be taken to see that the latter is not made too thin, as it is in a highly stressed locality, and in overhead camshaft engines with the usual Oldham couplings in the vertical shaft there is a likelihood that the small amount of end-float normally allowed may all be swallowed up—a state of affairs which will put excessive end-thrust on the vertical bevel shafts. This point must, therefore, be verified.

On the other hand, if at some future date the barrel is stacked up again with shims by an appreciable amount, it may be necessary to obtain a longer shaft or a pair of coupling-discs of greater thickness. On no account must these couplings be run with the tongues only half-engaged in the slots, as the metal is then subjected to a form of stress which may cause failure.

It goes without saying that the cylinder bore should be in perfect condition, particularly at the upper end, where the heaviest wear invariably occurs. The wear practically ceases about an inch or so below the ridge which forms just level with the top ring at t.d.c., but, in effect, over this short length the barrel is tapered. In their attempts to conform to the varying diameter, the rings have alternately to expand and contract, a feat which may be beyond their capacity above a certain speed.

When this occurs, gas will be able to blow past and also oil can work its way up into the head. Worse still, if the rate at which the rings are being forced in and out corresponds to their natural frequency of vibration, they will get into a state known as " flutter," and after a while will break, usually at a point fairly close to the gap. If the ring design is incorrect, flutter may occur even in a perfect bore, or may be aggravated by barrel distortion of an unsuspected nature, which may be caused either by thermal distortion or through the base flange or crankcase face not being dead flat.

Another snag about altering compression ratios by omitting compression plates or reducing the base flange is that the piston ring will inevitably strike any ring ridge which has formed; occasionally this has even been known to cause the piston ring land below the top ring to break away. Even a change from one type of piston to another may introduce the same effect due to varying ring heights, so it is always wise to remove every vestige of ridge by very careful work with a sharp hand scraper or a ring-ridge remover if any possibility of fouling exists. This point has already been noted in Chapter II but is sufficiently important to warrant repetition.

### Re-conditioning Worn Barrels

Badly worn barrels may be rejuvenated by reboring or by linering, though the first method is rarely applicable for racing, as mentioned in Chapter I; Norton engines of 490 c.c. are one exception as they can be bored out from 79 to 79.6 mm. before exceeding the 500 c.c. limit. Not all barrels are thick enough to stand being linered without danger of fracture at the flange, although the type in which long bolts extend from the crankcase up to the head are much less likely to fail than those with a bolted flange. Also it must be remembered that however well the liner fits, its junction with the barrel constitutes an additional heat-break, though this is of less moment with alcohol than with petrol fuel.

Barrels can be brought back to original size by chrome-plating, though this is a specialized process, as it is necessary for the plating to have a porous surface to provide a multitude of oil reservoirs; the processes are known by various trade names such as "Listard," the Van der Horst patent administered in England by R. A. Lister and Co., Ltd., Dursley, Glos., and "Honeychrome," a speciality of Monochrome, Ltd., Alcester. Laystall Engineering Co., Ltd., London, S.E.1, market a range of liners under the name of "Cromard," these being very thin mild-steel tubes with chrome-plated bores supplied finished to size; all that has to be done is to bore the barrel to the correct size and press the liner into place, no subsequent boring being required. Included in the range is a liner, specially designed for fitting to the speedway J.A.P. engine.

This liner is slightly reduced in diameter near the lower end and the cylinder must be machined with a corresponding step in the bore, so that there is no possibility of the liner, which has no flange at the top, being pulled down into the crankcase should it come loose or if the piston seizes badly. Such an occurrence is nothing short of a calamity and, where possible, liners should always be provided with a flange at the upper end which can be gripped between the head and barrel and thus prevent the liner from moving in any direction.

Other points which must not be overlooked are the drilling of any oil-holes and cutting out any con-rod clearance slots which may be provided in the barrel originally.

If the skirt of the barrel, which projects inwards into the crankcase, is long and of fairly thin section, as it is for instance, in MOV and MAC Velocettes, it is a wise plan to reduce the liner diameter at the lower end so that it is just the same size over the length of the skirt as the bore into which it is pressed. This eliminates the danger of the skirt developing a crack when the liner is pressed into position.

Incidentally, liners in aluminium cylinders should be fairly thick—not less than $\frac{1}{8}$ in., and preferably more—to resist distortion, but when used in an iron barrel they may be made as thin as $\frac{1}{16}$ in. Provided a locating flange is present, an interference fit when cold of .001-.002 in. is sufficient, irrespective of diameter, as the liner is bound to be hotter than the jacket when running, and it will never loosen. In aluminium jackets a greater interference is required, and allowance must be made for the high expansion, on the following basis, according to the alloy used:

High silicon (L.33, "Alpax," "Lo.-Ex"), .0009 per in. of diameter.
Y Alloy, R.R. 50 or 53, "Birmabright," .0011 per in. of diameter
Magnesium Alloys (Elektron, Magnuminium), .0016 per in. of diameter.

After a short period of running, liners in aluminium shells

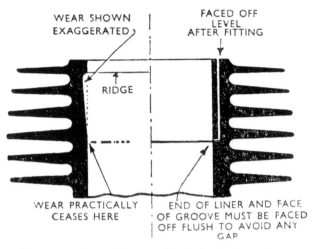

*Short liners may be used very effectively for barrel renovations
without reducing strength near the base flange.*

sometimes bed down a little and exhibit either tight spots
or hollows in the bore; it is therefore a wise precaution to
hone them out initially 2 or 3 thou. small and re-hone
or lap out to the correct size after a short period of running-
in with an old or slightly undersized piston.

Shown above is a simple method of rejuvenating a cast-
iron barrel by boring it out and fitting a short liner, which
can be made from any good grade of cast-iron but preferably an alloyed iron containing $1\frac{1}{2}$ to 3% of nickel. The
important point to watch is squareness of the shoulder and
liner to avoid any semblance of gap; if properly done
the joint will be almost invisible and will remain so in service.

The quickest method of truing up worn or tapered bores
is by means of a cylinder hone which can be rotated and
reciprocated in the bore either under a drilling machine
with a long spindle travel or by means of a slow-speed
electric drill. A copious and continuous supply of kerosene or paraffin oil is vital to prevent scratching the surface, but there is no need to attain a mirror-like finish.
The ideal surface consists of a large number of very fine
criss-cross markings which retain oil and give a quick bed-
in of the rings.

Hand-lapping to obtain a perfect finish or to clean up a slightly damaged bore can be done with a discarded piston, split in halves and expanded by two springs slipped over the gudgeon bosses. Mounted on an old rod or a piece of wood, this device is pushed up and down the barrel by hand and given a partial rotation at each stroke, the abrasive being flour emery mixed with oil if much metal has to be removed, and metal polish for obtaining the final finish. All traces of abrasive must, of course, be finally eliminated by several washings in clean spirit.

If this treatment is applied to side-valve barrels a hollow will sometimes be noticed in the surface adjacent to the

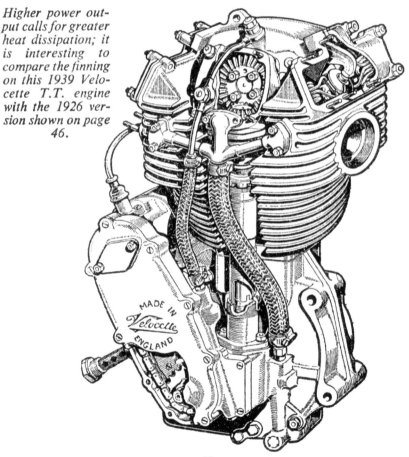

*Higher power output calls for greater heat dissipation; it is interesting to compare the finning on this 1939 Velocette T.T. engine with the 1926 version shown on page 46.*

exhaust-valve port; this is a sign that, when hot, the barrel distorts inwards, and the " bump " so formed has in time been rubbed away by the piston. When cold, of course, the former " bump " now appears as a " hollow," and it is better not to continue lapping in an attempt to eliminate it. If that is done, the bump will reappear when the engine warms up and may cause trouble if full-throttle is applied without a lengthy preliminary running-in period.

Enclosure of side valves in large boxes which eliminate a lot of fin area is bad from the cooling aspect, and in such cases the covers should be liberally drilled and fitted with scoops in order to stimulate a flow of air through the valve chest ; the fins sometimes cast on the covers are not really effective, as the stagnant pocket of air in the valve chest is the real barrier to heat dissipation.

For short-distance events with alcohol fuel—grass- and dirt-tracking and sprint work—deep barrel fins are not necessary (readers will remember the early dirt-track J.A.P. power units, which might almost be called " clean-shaven "), but when road racing, complete with mudguards, barrel cooling becomes worse as the speeds become higher, due to the " dead air " region behind the front-wheel assembly becoming more and more pronounced. Hence the use of fins up to 8 in. in diameter, which would be of prohibitive weight in iron and are, therefore, made of aluminium or, in rare instances, magnesium alloy.

For anyone with a little skill in lathe work there is no great difficulty in making up a bi-metal barrel out of a solid casting, or, better still, a forged bar of light alloy, with the fins turned from the solid. The tapered form of fin has been found to be the most effective, although a little more difficult to machine than the parallel variety. The bore should be finished at as high a speed as the lathe will permit, using for preference a tungsten carbide tool and a feed of about .003 in. per revolution, as successful heat transference between liner and barrel depends very largely upon the perfection of finish of the contacting surfaces.

The actual composition of the alloy is of little moment,

except in so far as the coefficient of thermal expansion varies. High expansion rates are not advantageous, and in this respect the magnesium alloys and the L5 aluminium alloy commonly used for general castings are the worst of the lot at .000026 in. per degree C. High-silicon alloys to specification L33 are the lowest at .000019 in., but do not machine well. "Lo-ex," the alloy from which most motor-car pistons are made, has the same coefficient as L33 but machines quite well, especially if given a low-temperature heat-treatment of 10 hours at 170° C.

The best compromise is afforded by Y-alloy or R.R.50, with a coefficient of .000022 in., while the aluminium-magnesium group—such as " Birmabright " or Hiduminium 40—are only very slightly higher and have the additional advantage of being very resistant to corrosion, even by sea-water.

A process which has lately come into prominence is the "Al-Fin" system, in which a true metallic bond is formed between the iron and aluminium, so eliminating a heat-break at this locality. The process is handled by Wellworthy Ltd., Lymington, Hants, who are prepared to cast solid jackets on to barrels, the fins, of course, having to be sub-sequently turned by the customer. Racing Norton and J.A.P. engines have been equipped for some time with "Al-Fin" barrels, with fins cast to size. The main patents covering the process are held by the Fairchild Aviation Corporation, Farmingdale, N.Y., U.S.A., and there are several licencees operating in that and other countries. A recent development has been the bonding-in of austenitic cast-iron ("Ni-resist") seat inserts in cylinder heads, thereby obtaining better conduction of heat from the insert to the head than with shrunk-in inserts.

After considerable usage, the bores in aluminium jackets sometimes increase in size to such an extent that the grip upon the liner is insufficient; this may show up by the liner turning in the jacket either in service or when being honed. When the engine is at running temperature, the heat conductivity between liner and jacket will be very poor, and, moreover, movement of the liner will be resisted mainly by the top flange instead of by the grip of the jacket. This is likely to cause the flange to break away and the liner to drop down, so if looseness is suspected, then either a larger liner should be obtained or the old one increased in size by copper-plating, after making quite sure there is no sign of a crack around the flange.

Vincent liners can be supplied .010 in. oversize on diameter. Before fitting the jacket should be re-bored to .006 in. smaller than the liner.

## CHAPTER V

## CHECKING PISTON AND RING WEAR

JOINTLY or singly, the piston, rings and gudgeon-pin have a number of jobs to perform. They must prevent leakage of gas from, and the passing of oil into, the working part of the cylinder, and also act as a cross-head to resist the side-thrust of the con.-rod and absorb the minimum of power in so doing. As each is dependent upon the others to a greater or less extent, they can be considered as a little family group in which the behaviour of one affects the well-being of the remainder.

All these components work in highly adverse conditions of high and fluctuating temperatures, high pressures and rubbing speeds and scanty lubrication; it is not surprising, therefore, that nearly half the power lost in internal friction is absorbed by them. Luckily, as no medals are awarded for mechanical silence in racing, the problem of eliminating piston-slap does not arise; thus the clearances which give the best results can be used irrespective of any noise which may occur. Nevertheless, it is a mistake to

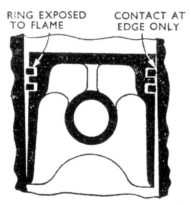

RING EXPOSED TO FLAME    CONTACT AT EDGE ONLY

*A piston with excessive clearance in the barrel tilts at t.d.c., thus exposing the top ring to flame contact and rounding the edges of all rings.*

66

think that ultra-wide clearances are essential or even beneficial; the reverse is the case in fact, for piston rings cannot function properly in a piston with an excessive amount of "slop." Whenever the piston is tilted, the rings, instead of being in contact over their full face-width, will make only edge contact over a large part of their circumference, and so cannot seal properly; in time the rings will wear to a barrel shape, and this will diminish their ability to prevent the upward passage of oil. Also, as the piston alternates in position from side to side of the barrel the rings have a tendency to follow suit (due to the friction between them and the ring grooves), and even if their contact with the wall is not momentarily broken, the action is very prone to initiate ring-flutter.

These effects are governed by skirt clearances, i.e., the diameters measured *at right angles to the gudgeon* just below the lowest ring and at the bottom edge of the skirt. Since there is, or should be, very little oil present above the rings, the lands between them cannot be expected to carry any load at all, and should run just clear of the barrel. As there is a sharp rise in temperature as the crown is approached, the lands must be progressively smaller, but again it is undesirable to make the top land too small, since this would expose the top ring to the full fury of the combustion, whereas a close-fitting land will shield it to some extent.

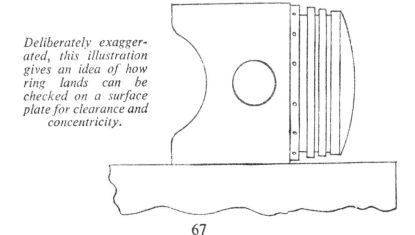

*Deliberately exaggerated, this illustration gives an idea of how ring lands can be checked on a surface plate for clearance and concentricity.*

A correctly fitted piston, after running at racing speeds for some time, should show an even bearing over the thrust faces of the skirt and just the faintest witness of rubbing contact on the ring lands. To obtain this result it is imperative that the relationship between skirt and lands is correct— that is to say, in addition to being the right relative sizes, the lands must be concentric with the skirt, which cannot be determined simply by direct measurement with a micrometer.

It is, of course, possible for a piston which is too small all over to exhibit the appearance just described, but this can be detected by the presence of thick carbon deposits in the plane of the gudgeon pin, or by the skirt showing areas of heavy bearing at the upper and lower extremities and light bearing in the centre, which appearance is caused by the piston running tip-tilted, in turn permitting the ring lands to make contact. Easing down these areas of heavy bearing under the erroneous impression that they are " high spots " will only make matters worse.

Perhaps at this juncture it might be as well to deal with this matter of easing down the high spots, which is frequently misunderstood. Obviously the piston must touch the barrel somewhere, but if every time the motor is down all the rub marks are carefully eased off with a file, the piston will simply become smaller and smaller until it is useless. The thing is to distinguish between the appearance of *normal* and *abnormally heavy* contact areas. The latter are potential sources of seizure, and the surface may be either torn and rough (in which event momentarily seizure has actually occurred) or possess a smooth polished appearance easily visible by viewing tangentially across the curved surface.

Areas of normal pressure have a dull-grey matt surface, possibly intersected by machine marks of trifling depth, and should be left undisturbed, but the polished areas, or true " high-spots," should be eased down with a dead-smooth single-cut, or Swiss file used very sparingly, for it is a simple matter to convert a high spot into a hollow, and, once done, the fault cannot be rectified—it can only be disguised by still further filing. The file must, of course, be used with a circular motion, so that the cut washes out smoothly to zero at the perimeter of the area being worked on.

The appearance of the wear-marks on the skirt is also an indication of whether or not the piston is running true in the bore. If the markings veer to one side just below the oil ring and to the other side at the bottom of the skirt, there is a remote possibility that the skirt was not finish-machined true to the gudgeon-hole, but it is more likely that the con-rod is bent. Filing the skirts to remove the uneven marking is useless in this case, because the original error still remains and there is a likelihood that the ring grooves which should of course be absolutely square to the axis of the piston and of the bore will in fact be lying at a slight angle. This will prevent the rings from seating properly and after a while they will wear barrel-shaped, a condition which is bad both for gas-sealing and oil-control. The only solution is to track down the cause of the error and eliminate it, not to disguise it by relieving the skirts.

As regards the actual clearances, conditions vary so greatly that it is virtually impossible to give any hard-and-fast rules and in case of doubt the manufacturer's advice must be sought. Generally speaking, the temperatures in racing engines, even with 50/50 fuel, are not a great deal higher than those sometimes encountered in touring engines, thanks to the use of open exhaust systems and the fact that the racer is almost always making a pretty fair breeze of its own. As a rule, therefore, an increase of .001 in. to .003 in., according to diameter, will suffice, in most cases when the piston being fitted is the same one or is of the same type and material as the original.

However, it is often advisable to change over to a different design or to use a more suitable material when maximum power is being sought. Alloys such as RR53b or Y-alloy in the fully heat-treated condition are preferable to the medium-silicon, low-expansion varieties known under various trade names such as Lo-ex, Heplex, etc., or the U.S. specification A143, because of their greater strength at high temperatures and slightly less coefficient of friction, but allowance must be made for their greater thermal expansion if a change-over is made. As an approximate guide, the following table gives the clearances *per inch of diameter* which will be found suitable for Y-alloy or R.R. 53 B pistons running in iron barrels:

| | | | | |
|---|---|---|---|---|
| Top land | .. | .. | .. | .0065 in. |
| Second land | .. | .. | .. | .0055 in. |
| Third land | .. | .. | .. | .005 in. |
| Top of skirt | .. | .. | .. | .0036 in. |
| Bottom skirt | .. | .. | .. | .0027 in. |

Bi-metal barrels with shrunk-in liners have a slightly higher expansion rate than plain iron, and the clearances in such cases can be about .001 in. *less* per inch of diameter. These clearances apply to pistons without T-slots (which are not commonly employed in racing), and are measured at right angles to the gudgeon.

All pistons distort to some extent under the influence of heat and load, and pistons of the plain cylindrical pattern (sometimes referred to as the "pot" type) are oval-turned to the extent of .006 in. or .010 in. to give greater clearances on the sides, although the ring lands are frequently circular; when cold, therefore, the skirt clearances progressively increase from the central plane outwards.

Actually, quite a small area is sufficient to carry the con.-rod side-thrust, and this fact led to the development of the slipper piston, which is both stronger and causes less friction loss through oil shear than the "pot" variety, but to some extent the latter can be improved by heavily relieving the sides so that they run well clear of the walls. Owing to the heat-flow down the side ribs and their consequent expansion, the thrust faces of slipper pistons depart from their cold shape quite a lot when hot, and the clearances should be increased perceptibly towards the lateral

70

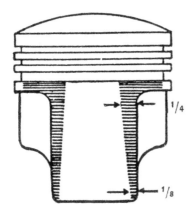

*The shaded portion suggests how the contact faces of a slipper piston can be relieved.*

edges, particularly just below the top ring, as indicated in the diagram on the left.

There are two ways of measuring clearances: (a) by measuring the bore with an internal micrometer or a dial gauge such as the Mercer, and subtracting the various piston diameters as measured by "mike" or vernier; and (b) by direct measurement, using various feeler gauges. The latter is the means which most private owners will have to adopt, and is quite accurate if carefully performed. For the wide clearances round the top lands it is best to use a number of thin feelers rather than one or two thick

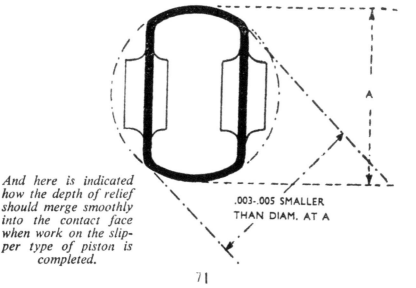

*And here is indicated how the depth of relief should merge smoothly into the contact face when work on the slipper type of piston is completed.*

.003-.005 SMALLER THAN DIAM. AT A

ones, as the latter give a false reading through being too stiff to conform with the barrel curvature.

As mentioned, the ring lands must be concentric with the skirt, and this is easily proved by placing the piston on a surface plate and measuring by feelers the gap between plate and lands, which should be equal for corresponding localities on each side of the piston (*see page* 67).

It is sometimes necessary to reduce an oversize piston to fit a standard bore, or to finish to size a semi-finished piston, i.e. one with all machining completed except the final sizing of the ring-lands and skirt. This job can be done in a lathe using a large 60° cone centre in the open end with a loose pin or blade bearing on the gudgeon bosses to provide the drive, and a regular centre in the tail-stock. Alternatively a soft spigot can be turned in the chuck to fit the register bored in the open end of the piston which is then pulled back on the spigot by a loose pin and bolt passing through the hollow head-stock. In either case the ring-grooves must be checked with a dial-gauge to see that they run free from wobble; with any reputable make of piston, this is an indication that the piston as a whole is running true and finish-turning can commence.

Camming, or relieving, the sides as just described, is best done in one of the piston-finishing machines used by engine re-conditioners. Of the range of cams developed and widely adopted for these machines, type "C" is usually most suitable. It gives .009 in. total ovality and .006 in. reduction in diameter measured at the 45° points. Failing access to one of these devices, camming can be done either by hand or in the lathe by offsetting the piston .010 in. in the direction of the gudgeon and relieving the high side to a depth of .005 in. and then repeating the process on the other side. This will leave about half the skirt on each thrust face still circular and the sides of these areas must finally be merged into the relieved portions by hand filing.

A precaution which must always be taken, even with new factory-made pistons, is to see that the corners of the ring-grooves are slightly chamfered. If not, a fine square file run round the grooves will do the trick. The purpose of these chamfers is partly to provide a small channel for oil distribution, but mainly to prevent the rings being locked into the grooves by metal being pulled over at the corners should the lands happen to run in contact with the cylinder. Locked rings permit local blow-by to occur and destruction of the piston in that area may then occur with startling rapidity.

Another worthwhile idea is to chamfer the open end at 45° almost to a knife-edge. This has the effect of skimming excess oil off the bore and directing it up towards the piston crown, whereas a square shoulder just rolls the oil up ahead of itself, creating oil-drag and increasing the work to be done by the oil-control ring.

The skirt clearances of two-stroke pistons are of great importance because the piston has to act as the pumping element for the induction system. Pressures of up to 8 lb. per sq. in. are involved in the crankcase breathing cycle, and as there is very little oil present and no rings at all on the skirt, leakage can only be prevented by the latter being a close fit all round its circumference. Extreme ovality leads to loss through the transfer ports, round the piston sides and out through the exhaust. Consequently many such pistons are ground circular or with not more than .003 in. camming, and that concentrated in the region of the gudgeon bosses, leaving the last ½ in., or so, of the skirt parallel and with a clearance of .0015 to .002 in. per inch of diameter.

The bores of air-cooled split-singles distort quite considerably on account of the difficulty of cooling the metal between the bores. It pays to make these pistons a fairly close fit, then, after a warm-up period, to give the motor a short burst at full-throttle, shutting off immediately at the first indication of tightening-up. Then dismantle the engine, ease down the areas of high pressure and repeat. This process will give much better results than any amount of running-in at light load and low temperature.

The most satisfactory ring equipment is two narrow pressure rings, and one scraper, usually of the slotted type, which is so effective that a very copious supply of oil can be fed to the barrel. The pressure rings should have .0015 in. to .002 in. side clearance in the grooves, but scrapers perform their work better with about twice that amount. Oil wiped off the bore is thereby enabled to pass through to the back of the ring and out through the drain-holes. Sometimes a row of drain holes is provided below the oil-ring; these should be horizontal and not drilled downwards at an angle, as the rapid acceleration of the piston away from t.d.c. then has the effect of driving any oil in, or near, the holes back through the piston.

On the other hand, the primary job of the upper rings is to maintain gas-tightness, but this is done not so much by the natural pressure of the rings against the walls as by the action of the high-pressure gas passing through the clearance between ring and groove into the clearance space behind, and thus forcing the ring outwards against the cylinder. If the side clearance is insufficient the gas cannot get through sufficiently fast to build up this vital pressure in the very short time available, but if it is greater than .003–.004 in. there is a likelihood of the grooves being quickly hammered out wider still as the rings change rapidly from one side to the other at each end of the stroke with not much oil present to provide a cushion.

To assist in building up gas-pressure almost instan-taneously behind the rings, the grooves should only be .005–.010 in. deeper than the radial thickness of the pres-sure rings, but much more clearance than that should be allowed behind the oil rings to assist oil to leave via the drain holes. A small clearance helps to damp out flutter which sometimes causes top-ring breakage, and in all cases the sides of rings and grooves must be free from waves or ridges. These defects do not often occur in the grooves unless the piston has seen a great deal of service, but are sometimes noticeable on rings; the remedy is to lap the sides on a flat iron plate with flour emery and finally metal

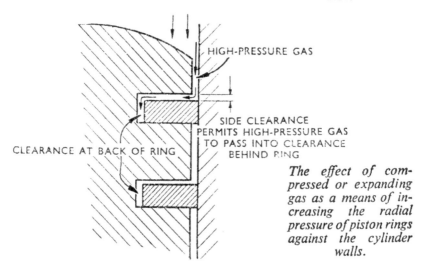

HIGH-PRESSURE GAS

SIDE CLEARANCE PERMITS HIGH-PRESSURE GAS TO PASS INTO CLEARANCE BEHIND RING

CLEARANCE AT BACK OF RING

*The effect of compressed or expanding gas as a means of increasing the radial pressure of piston rings against the cylinder walls.*

polish, using only light finger pressure. Incidentally, it is better to have dead-flat rings running at slightly excessive clearances than wavy ones with the correct amount of side-clearance.

The grooves in pistons which have been run for some time in severe conditions often wear unevenly. When new rings are fitted in such grooves they may feel as if the side clearance is correct because, being of correct radial depth, they are located in the unworn portion of the grooves. However, under working conditions, the top ring in particular is subjected to a severe twisting action, due to lack of support at the outer edge, and it will almost certainly

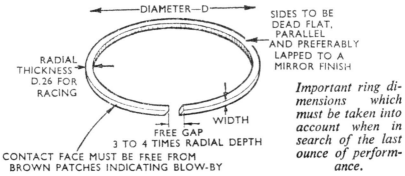

DIAMETER—D

SIDES TO BE DEAD FLAT, PARALLEL AND PREFERABLY LAPPED TO A MIRROR FINISH

RADIAL THICKNESS D.26 FOR RACING

WIDTH

FREE GAP 3 TO 4 TIMES RADIAL DEPTH

CONTACT FACE MUST BE FREE FROM BROWN PATCHES INDICATING BLOW-BY

*Important ring dimensions which must be taken into account when in search of the last ounce of performance.*

fail in short order. The only cure is to skim the grooves out parallel and, if wider rings are not available, to fit two rings per groove by grinding down standard rings by the requisite amount. There is, of course, a limit to how much can be taken from the grooves because the lands eventually become too thin and may break under load. Definite figures are hard to give but, as a general rule, $\frac{1}{16}$ in. would be about the safe minimum land width and then only if the piston is of strong material such as Y-alloy or R.R. 53.

Effective gas sealing is achieved mostly by the top ring, the second acting as a standby should the top one fail, and also as an oil controller. For sprint work, or in very small engines when there is little room for rings, it is possible to omit the second ring and use a single groove, with two narrow side-by-side rings therein as just described. By placing the gaps on opposite sides minute leakages through this point will be almost entirely eliminated.

A recent development is the Dykes ring, which is of "L" section, the horizontal leg providing location in the piston, while a comparatively large clearance at the top of the ring allows a clear path by which high-pressure gas can flow rapidly into the space behind the vertical portion, and thus expand it against the bore. Only one such ring per piston was employed in the 1954 A.J.S. racing twin, and this practice is continued on the 7R and G50 models.

There is little to choose between the various well-known brands of ring, but each maker has perfected types specially suitable for racing, notably the Wellworthy " Thermochrom " and " Limalloy " or Hepworth and Grandage "Phormicast." Whatever the make, it is advisable to obtain rings with lapped sides, since they maintain correct side clearances for long periods, and there is much less friction between the ring and groove when subjected to heavy gas pressure.

The usual radial depth of English or Continental piston rings is $D/30$ ($D$ is the barrel diameter), but lately high-pressure rings of greater radial depth, $D/26$, have come into use. The latter type are less prone to flutter at high speeds, but if

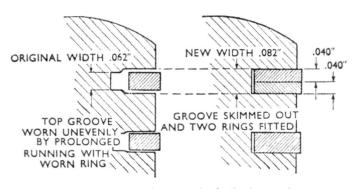

*A piston ring reclaim method which may be
used in cases where spares are not available.*

they are used care must be taken to see that the ring-grooves
are deep enough to accommodate them. If they are fitted in
grooves of normal depth there is a likelihood that they will
stand proud of the ring lands even when forced down to the
bottom of the grooves, and, in service, the ring faces will
then be forced to carry the side thrust which should be
borne by the piston skirt. This condition, although easy to
overlook, is very bad indeed, and must be rectified by
deepening the grooves. Another point about these rings
is that, being stiffer, they will not conform to a worn, or
oval, barrel quite as freely as will the lighter variety, and it
is advisable to lap them in very carefully to ensure gas-
tightness if the barrel is not so perfect as it might be.

In side-valve engines and most two-strokes some barrel
distortion is bound to occur due to unequal distribution of
metal and varying temperatures around the cylinder, and in
these motors it is a good plan to peg the rings so that they
cannot rotate in the grooves. They then bed-in closely to
the shape which the cylinder attains when running and will
maintain good gas-tightness and oil control even when the
cylinder has worn appreciably.

Two-stroke rings are also pegged for another reason—to
prevent the ends springing into the ports and becoming
broken, and they are also generally made wider in proportion
to their depth than four-stroke rings of equivalent diameter

to enable them to traverse the ports with less shock. When fitting new rings care must be taken to clean out the corners adjacent to the pegs very thoroughly, otherwise the rings will be propped up above the lands and either they or the barrel will suffer as soon as the engine is started up. The tiny lips on the ends of the Puch rings are very frail and can easily be broken off during assembly if held proud of the piston by the pegs or by carbon.

Wide ring gaps are advisable, particularly for engines subjected to rapid cold starts; .010 in. per inch of diameter is a good figure to work to. To make a thorough job, after rough gapping, lap the rings in to the barrel with metal polish until they are bedding uniformly all the way round, and finally finish the gaps to the correct width.

Regarding gudgeon pins, it is a great aid to assembly to make these an easy hand-push fit in the piston when cold. Some makers prefer to fit them a little tighter, but this entails driving the pin out with a drift, or warming up the piston with hot water or a bit of meta-fuel in a cocoa-tin lid; as in any case a $\frac{3}{4}$-in. pin will have about .002-in. clearance at running temperature, another .0005-in. will make very little difference. The best way to take a thou. or so out of gudgeon pin holes is with a hone of the Sunnen or Delapena type, using kerosene or paraffin liberally. It is not easy to take out small amounts with an ordinary reamer without leaving small chatter-marks in the bore: indeed, sometimes a better job can be made with a triangular hand scraper.

The main attributes of a gudgeon pin are stiffness and high surface hardness; pins which have become " blued " are softened and should be replaced. Insufficient pin rigidity is a fruitful source of cracked piston bosses, and the most satisfactory designs have a central bore not greater than 0.6 of their diameter. Although this can be tapered out for one-third the length of the pin at both ends, the bore must be left soft and is preferably polished to remove surface blemishes from which cracks may start. A nickel-

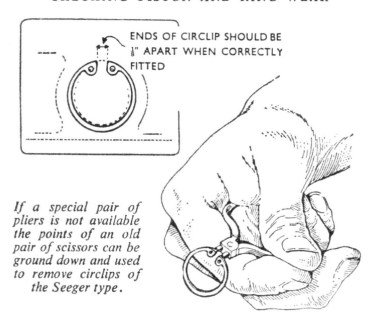

ENDS OF CIRCLIP SHOULD BE
⅛" APART WHEN CORRECTLY
FITTED

*If a special pair of pliers is not available the points of an old pair of scissors can be ground down and used to remove circlips of the Seeger type.*

chrome steel such as K.E. 287, case-hardened, .025 in. -.035 in. deep, is an excellent material for the purpose.

The best form of end location is by circlips, either of the spring-wire type (without bent-in ears, which sometimes break off) or the Seeger pattern, although for fitting the latter variety you must have the right sort of pliers, available quite cheaply from the makers of the circlips. The wire type is perfectly satisfactory provided the ends of the gudgeon pin are chamfered, and the overall pin length is

ENDS CHAMFERED 45°

*Chamfered outer gudgeon pin edges act as circlip retainers, whilst the tapered bore, left soft, reduces weight and is polished so that flaws may be detected.*

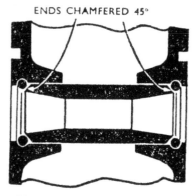

such that the final circlip can just be sprung into place with the pin thrust hard against the opposite one. The chamfers then act as retainers, and there is no likelihood of the circlips ever managing to work out of the grooves. Seeger circlips require flat-bottomed grooves turned to accurate depths in accordance with the table which covers the range of sizes most likely to be met. This type of circlip must never be fitted in the half-round grooves used with wire circlips because, although it may seem to fit correctly, in fact it would only be seating on the corners and in a short period of running the corners dig in, the circlip becomes loose and eventually comes right out of the groove, with disastrous results.

Wire circlips should always be stretched out before re-fitting to make sure that they will fit tightly in place. Occasionally an engine will exhibit a tendency to hammer the circlips loose, more so on one side than the other; in such a case examine the alignment of the small end bush for both squareness and absence of " twist "; the latter is difficult to detect but may be the unsuspected cause of the trouble.

If a spare is not available at all, or the standard article is known to be unreliable, a new piston can be made from a solid bar with only a lathe, a drill, and the usual hand tools. The process is rather too long for inclusion here but as a guide it will help to note that the best material is aluminium alloy R.R. 59, which is specially made for pistons and retains strength very well at high temperatures. The American material to SAE260 specification, and known commercially as 14S also is very suitable. Alloys such as R.R. 77, which are even stronger at atmospheric temperatures, contain zinc and, therefore, are not so good at higher temperatures.

# CHAPTER VI

## THE CONNECTING-ROD AND BIG-END

THE function of the flywheel assembly is to convert the straight-line motion of the piston into rotary motion at the engine sprocket. The crankcase also forms a vital link in this mechanical chain by providing a rigid location for the cylinder and mainshaft bearings, whilst, in addition, housing timing gears, oil pumps and so forth. Referring back to Chapter I, it was pointed out that any areas where undue wear has occurred are open to suspicion and that the cause of the wear (which may be malalignment, lack of lubrication or faulty material) must be investigated with an eye to its cure. This advice should come in useful at this stage, for the main job of work to be tackled in the " basement " will consist of the elimination of friction usually due to malalignment.

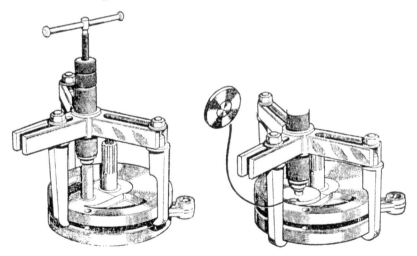

*The Velocette slow-taper crankpin-flywheel assembly calls for the use of a specially modified " Pickavant " hydraulic tool when dismantling (left) or reassembling (right), unless a power press is available.*

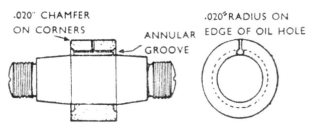

.020" CHAMFER ON CORNERS     ANNULAR GROOVE     .020" RADIUS ON EDGE OF OIL HOLE

*A worn big-end assembly can be renovated by grinding down and fitting a press-fit hardened sleeve to the crank-pin. Where the pin is not drilled centrally for lubrication, the sleeve must be provided with annular grooves and a transverse passage.*

The big-end is the most highly-stressed bearing of all, and if there is any sign, however small, of flaking of the roller track or the crank-pin, that component should be discarded; wear on the areas rubbed by the cage is not of such great detriment as long as it does not encroach on to the track.

Some crankpins (e.g. in certain Velocette, A.J.S. and Matchless engines) are made in two pieces with a hardened sleeve pressed on a tough steel centre, and if new complete pins are unobtainable, new sleeves can be made up, and any pin in which the central portion is considerably larger than the ends can be repaired by grinding down this portion and fitting a similar sleeve. If the outer race in the con.-rod is also worn, this should first be ground or lapped out true—preferably without removing it from the rod —after which operation the pin-sleeves can be ground to the particular oversize necessary to suit the finished outer race diameter and whatever rollers are available.

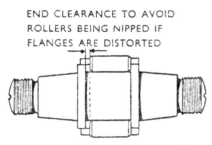

END CLEARANCE TO AVOID ROLLERS BEING NIPPED IF FLANGES ARE DISTORTED

*With the shouldered type of crankpin there must be end-float between rollers and shoulders to avoid danger of the former becoming nipped when the pin is tightened in the flywheels.*

The pin-sleeve should preferably be made from ball-race steel (1% carbon, 1% chromium), which hardens right through by quenching in oil after soaking at 820° C. for half an hour. After quenching, temper for half an hour at 200° C. and cool in air; this procedure relieves internal stresses without materially affecting the hardness, which should be Rockwell C. 60-64 or diamond hardness number 750-800.

If the crankpin is already drilled centrally for oil, a mating hole must also be drilled in the sleeve before hardening. Where the pin is not drilled, an annular groove should be formed at one or both ends of the sleeve to collect lubricant from the flywheel oil-hole, a shallow transverse groove with central hole finally delivering it to the rollers as shown in an accompanying sketch. After hardening, the sleeve must be ground internally to a diameter .001 in. smaller than the pin, then forced into position under a press. Finally, it must be ground externally and on the two end-faces; squareness of the latter is *particularly* important, as the slightest error will be greatly magnified at the mainshafts.

If carbon-chrome steel is not available, a case-hardening variety can be used, in which event the bore can be left soft if desired, thus avoiding the necessity for internal grinding. The scheme is first to rough-turn the blank to grinding sizes and then to carburize for six hours to obtain a case-depth at least .045 in. After cooling, rough-bore then recess the end faces to $\frac{1}{8}$ in. larger diameter than the bore to a depth of $\frac{1}{16}$ in., drill the oil hole and finally heat-treat. After hardening, the sleeve can be finished internally either by boring or grinding, fitted to the pin and then finish-ground exactly as previously described.

Mild steel is not up to the arduous nature of this work, the case being liable to flake away from the soft core; 3% nickel to specification S15 or EN 33, or single-quench 3% or $3\frac{1}{2}$% nickel will be satisfactory for moderately heavy duty, but better varieties are S82, S90, EN 34, 36 and 39, the last three being wartime specifications. The heat-treatment for all these grades is practically the same, viz.: carburize at 900-920° C. Refine by quenching in oil from

850-860° C. Harden by quenching in oil from 760° C. Temper by cooling in air from 150-170° C., except for the 3% and $3\frac{1}{2}$% nickel single-quench grades, in which the refining and hardening can be effected simultaneously by quenching in oil or water from 760-780° C.

Equivalent American specifications are S.A.E. 51100 for carbon-chrome ball-race steel, S.A.E. 2317 for $3\frac{1}{2}$% nickel case-hardening steel and S.A.E. 3316 for $3\frac{1}{2}$% nickel-chrome C.H. steel. If it is necessary to make up a completely new pin, either of the two case-hardening steels mentioned will do. The plain nickel steel, though having less core strength, gives a slightly harder case than the nickel-chrome steel. Steels which harden right through, such as the ball-race steel mentioned or medium-carbon direct-hardening steels must not on any account be used for complete pins, because, when hardened sufficiently on the roller track, such steels are far too brittle in the core and are certain to break in service. In any case the threaded ends must always be left soft and this can be achieved by copper-plating prior to carburizing and hardening. Another method is to rough-turn the threaded portions .100 in. oversize, carburize the whole pin, turn off the carburized skin locally and screw-cut the threads and finally harden. Incidentally, great care must be taken to ensure that the threads are square to the axis, otherwise it may be difficult to maintain tightness of the nuts.

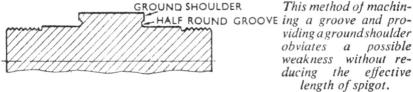

GROUND SHOULDER
HALF ROUND GROOVE

*This method of machining a groove and providing a ground shoulder obviates a possible weakness without reducing the effective length of spigot.*

Breakage of crank-pins of the shouldered type almost invariably occurs in the corner of the shoulder, and it is desirable to have a definite fillet in this corner, even at the expense of reducing the length of bearing in the flywheels. The faces of the shoulders should be slightly concave; on no account may they be convex even to the slightest extent. Unfortunately, with normal grinding equipment, it is difficult to attain this finish, but somewhat the same effect can be gained by turning a shallow undercut in the faces which also provides a little extra room for the vital fillet.

*Details of crankpin design which are likely to cause weakness under high-duty conditions.*

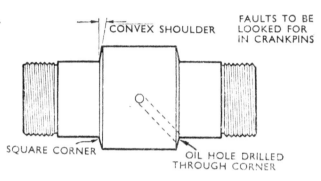

Sometimes the oil-hole in the pin is drilled inwards from the corner of the shoulder, causing a local weakness from which a fatigue crack will start. It is best to modify the drilling to avoid this danger; it may also be necessary to drill another hole in the flywheel to coincide with the new position of the hole in the pin (*see* illustration below).

When reassembling the big-end new rollers should be fitted for preference, but old ones can be used, provided they are absolutely free from flats or other surface blemishes (which can be detected by examining them through a magnifying glass under a fairly strong, oblique light) and are all of the same diameter to within one or two tenths of

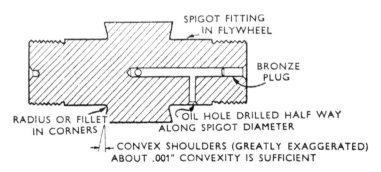

a thou. One or two oversize rollers will rapidly ruin any roller bearing, this being the reason why new and old rollers should *never* be run together.

Caged rollers are maintained in parallel by the spacing bars, and, if the pin is of the shouldered type, the rollers can have several thou. end clearance—in fact, this is advisable, otherwise if any deflection takes place the shoulders may close in a trifle and nip the rollers endways. If the pin is without shoulders, the bars of the cage should be relieved on the internal diameter so that the cage bears on the pin only outside the roller path, for although the cage is soft it will wear away the pin surface much faster than will the rollers. In engines running at 7,000 r.p.m. or more, this form of wear can become very serious, and it may be advisable to hard-chrome-plate the rubbing areas; .001 to .002 in. thickness will be ample, but the deposit must be finally ground to a dead-smooth finish and must on no account be allowed to encroach on the roller tracks. Useful as it is in other ways, hard-chrome cannot stand up to the action of heavily loaded rollers and will inevitably flake off if applied to the tracks.

What makes the life of a big-end so strenuous is not so much the speed or the loading but the fact that the roller assembly does not rotate round the pin at a steady speed, as it does in a main bearing. Instead, it has alternately to speed up and slow down because at or near t.d.c. the swing of the connecting-rod is in opposition to the motion of the pin, whereas at bottom dead centre the two motions are in the same direction though of course not at the same speed. Like all objects possessing weight, the roller assembly objects to this process and relatively heavy loads are created between the rollers and the bars of the cage and a certain amount of sliding motion takes place in addition to normal rolling, when the engine speed exceeds a figure at which the friction between rollers and tracks is insufficient to overcome the inertia of the roller assembly.

The lighter the assembly, the less its inertia, and for that reason racing cages are made of one of the strong wrought aluminium alloys such as R.R. 56 or 24 S. Some cages are made from cast aluminium which, though light, is relatively weak and for serious work should be replaced by parts made of bar or tube. Factory-made cages have the slots formed by broaching, a method which is not available to everyone; an alternative process is to end-mill the slots and then machine the ends out square. A cage with relatively long slots to accommodate long rollers such as $\frac{3}{16}$ in. by $\frac{9}{16}$ in. (a very useful size) or three short rollers placed in each slot can easily be made by milling the slots with a standard Woodruff key-seat cutter, and finishing the ends out by hand using a square file ground to width so that it does not damage the machined sides. The blank should be turned with a shoulder or groove at each end to mark the length of the slots, which is not vitally important. What is important, however, is that the slots must be dead parallel to the axis, otherwise the whole roller assembly will run over to one side and, therefore, accurate setting-up of the milling machine and dividing head is essential.

Large uncaged rollers are not good for high-speed work because of the heavy pressure between them due to centrifugal force. This force can be reduced to an acceptable figure by using rollers which are small in diameter and

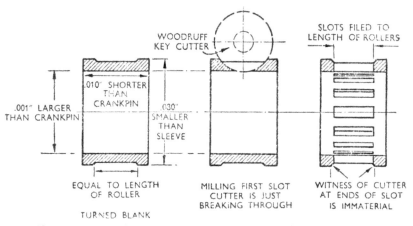

*Three stages in the fabrication of a big-end roller bearing cage, using bar or tube material.*

consequently light. The Vincent big-end uses three rows of rollers 3 mm. diameter by 5 mm. long per rod, separated by parallel rings which prevent the rollers skewing; the total end clearance must be held to limits between .004 in. and .008 in. if skewing or binding endways is to be avoided. The 250 Guzzi also used small rollers of 3 mm. diameter by approximately $\frac{5}{8}$ in. long with no cage, but in this instance the big-end is split, just as if the rod had a plain bearing. Plain big-ends have been successfully used for some time now on high-speed engines though they are necessarily smaller and more heavily loaded than their counterparts in the automobile world. Rigidity of the metal surrounding the big-end is of more importance than lightness, therefore no attempts at lightening or altering the design of plain rods should be attempted without consultation with the makers, who in some instances supply rods of different design for racing. The correct clearance for plain big-ends is .001 in. to .0015 in. per inch when the rods are cold though a much greater clearance is permissible provided the oil pressure is maintained above the allowable minimum figure as quoted by the makers.

In any design of roller bearing there is bound to be a certain amount of rubbing going on, which, at ultra-high speeds, will generate sufficient heat to cause seizure unless it is carried away by the lubricant. For reasons of strength, the oil-holes are never very large, and care must be taken to check that they are clear by feeding oil through them with a force-feed oil can. Incidentally, when doing up a " vintage " model, it is often possible to obtain a more up-to-date big-end which will fit the old pattern wheels with little or no modification.

After assembling the rollers with oil (*not* grease, which is likely to block the oil-holes) the con.-rod should just slide into place. If it has to be pushed or screwed on, the fit is too tight; if there is more than .002-in. diametral clearance it is too loose. The best way to get an exact fit is by means of several sets of rollers graduated in steps of .0001 in. but if these are unobtainable the outer race can be lapped out with flour emery and a mild-steel lap, but on *no* account must any attempt be made to ease a tight big-end by rotating it with abrasive applied to the rollers; such a procedure will almost certainly lead to rapid breakdown in service. A piece of hard wood turned to size makes quite an effective lap for emergency use, but when many rods of the same diameter have to be handled, it pays to make up an expanding lap. This tool can either be held in a vice and the rod turned by hand or it can be used in a drill; in either case the rod should be allowed to "float" on the lap and be frequently removed and reversed to avoid tapering the bore.

When spun round with the pin held horizontally, the rod should not show the slightest sign of working over to one side; if it does, either the pin or the outer race is tapered or the slots in the cage are at a minute angle. Reversing the rod may effect a cure, in which event mark the correct position of pin, rod and cage; if not, the cause should be located and rectified. Sometimes deep grooves are formed in the flywheels through rods running over, and if these are present they should be skimmed out to accommodate phosphor-bronze or hard-steel washers of suitable thickness. The correct amount of side-clearance varies according to the design, but is rarely of great importance, .010 in. to .020 in. being about right in most cases.

If not already done, it is a good idea to polish the con.-rod all over, since the removal of the rough outer skin greatly diminishes the chance of fatigue-cracks developing.

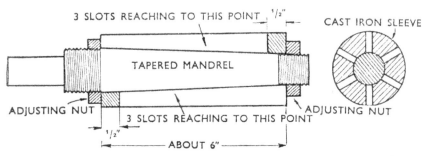

*Details of a lapping tool of the split-adjustable type suitable for the cleaning up of the big-end eye.*

Although rare, cracks of this nature usually occur at the junction of the shank and small-end. They can be detected by immersing the rod in hot paraffin for some time, and, after drying, dusting the surface with french chalk; if any cracks are present they will be indicated by the chalk adhering to the paraffin retained in them. Cracks may also be detected by the Magnaflux, or similar methods, which are commonly employed in aircraft manufacturing or maintenance establishments and it is a good idea to avail oneself of such facilities if they are easily accessible.

Shot-peening the surface is of great value in preventing fatigue-cracks—the system is to bombard the surface with steel shot, projected at high velocity by compressed air through a nozzle. This process must not be confused with shot-blasting, which uses sharp-edged grains and removes a certain amount of metal. The *smooth* shot used in shot-peening removes no metal at all but, through its compacting action, places the surface skin of the metal in compression.

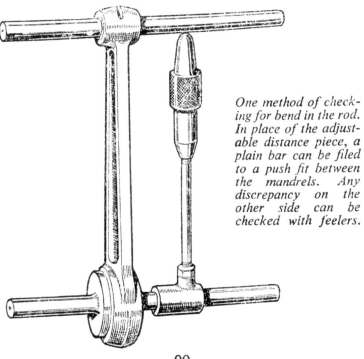

*One method of checking for bend in the rod. In place of the adjustable distance piece, a plain bar can be filed to a push fit between the mandrels. Any discrepancy on the other side can be checked with feelers.*

Obviously, shot-peening must be done *after* polishing, as any work done on the surface after peening will remove the compressed layer and destroy the effectiveness of the process.

Experiments in lightening rods extensively are *not* advisable, unless the maker's advice has been obtained. There is sometimes a fair amount of excess metal round the small-end due to taper in the forging dies and manufacturing tolerances and much of this can safely be removed by filing. As the stress concentration falls mainly on the extremities of the small-end, these should be left untouched. It may be possible to obtain a lighter rod made specially for racing from higher-grade steel; as one example, the early KTT Velocette rod can be used in the push-rod MOV engine. "Manx" Norton rods can also be used in "International" angines, and Vincent rods, with the big-ends narrowed cen be used in speedway J.A.P.s.

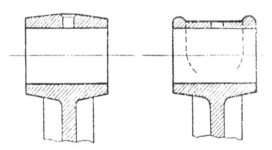

*A guide to the amount of material which may be removed from the small-end eye for lightening purposes.*

Rods must be tested carefully for alignment in all planes. Checking off the sides of the big-end, the small-end should be central within .005 in. to .008 in. The big-end and small-end bores must be dead parallel; although it is possible to carry out an approximate check for this by using the crank pin and gudgeon pin as mandrels, a better way is to make up a pair of bars, at least 6 in. long, which are a tight push fit in the respective bores. For preference, they should be hardened and ground, but soft ones will suffice if carefully handled. Commercial bright-drawn bar is usually .003 in. less than nominal size and quite effective mandrels for use

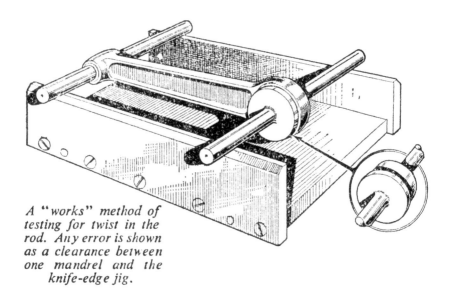

*A "works" method of testing for twist in the rod. Any error is shown as a clearance between one mandrel and the knife-edge jig.*

in small-ends can be made from such material, hard-chrome plated up to finished size.

With these mandrels in place, the distance between them measured at the extremities should not differ by more than .002 in. In the absence of the necessary measuring equipment, a steel bar can be filed so that it will just fit between the mandrels at the tightest end; the gap at the larger end can then be measured by feeler gauges. The bearings must also be free from " wind " or twist, i.e., the mandrels should be parallel when viewed along the length of the rods. Accuracy in this respect can be checked quite easily on a surface-plate by the use of blocks and a dial gauge or feeler gauges.

It is quite likely that at least one of these errors will be found, possibly all three. To avoid pulling the rod about unnecessarily, the three checks should first be made and the situation carefully weighed up, otherwise one may cure one error by making another worse. As a general rule, first eliminate any " twist " and then set about getting the centrality and parallelism of the small-end correct. If it is central but inclined, bend the rod close to the small-end;

if off-centre and inclined in the same direction, bend near the big-end. The rod should never be gripped by the big-end sleeve when being "set"; this action might just cant the sleeve in the bore and in service it would revert to its original position. Setting should preferably be done in a straightening press, but failing that a strong vice and three bolts can be used, two being placed on one side of the rod and one between them at the point where the bend is required; the bolts should be of large diameter and soft to avoid local damage to the rod. Alternatively, narrow strips of thick brass can be used with much less possibility of damage.

If these errors are in opposite directions, the rod will have to be set at both ends, but do *not* use the checking mandrels for the purpose and bend these as well. Since the side clearance between small-end and piston bosses can be fairly generous, it is permissible to face off one side of the small-end if all the errors cannot be corrected otherwise.

Considerable patience may be needed, but it is vitally important that the con.-rod be absolutely true; even the slightest error can have a serious effect at very high r.p.m.

Rods which have been set only slightly often show a tendency to revert to their original position, so the best

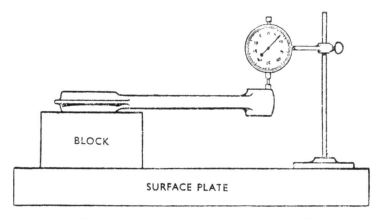

*A third method of checking for bend in the rod. Dial gauge should show same reading when rod is reversed.*

plan is to set the rod too far and then correct the amount of overset to bring the alignment right. Rods treated in this manner are unlikely to lose alignment again.

The small-end bush for racing must not have less than .001 in. clearance, but more can be allowed without detriment except for the noise caused. Nortons can be permitted up to .005 in. before replacing the bush. Phosphor bronze is the usual material but any of the light alloys, such as R.R. 56 or R.R. 59 or Duralumin H, which retain strength at high temperatures, make very good bearings and save perhaps an ounce of reciprocating weight.

It occasionally becomes advisable to make up a completely new connecting-rod, and at the same time to redesign for greater rigidity. In this connection, the best design is the simplest; the flanges of the I-section should be tangential to the small-end boss, and taper outwards to a width equal to the bore of the big-end eye. Circumferential rigidity of the big-end is most important, and to obtain this without excessive weight there should be either one or two deep ribs running right around the eye. For material, "Vibrac" V 30 is extremely good, and for best results the rod should be rough machined in the soft state, then heat treated to 85 tons tensile. All polishing of the exterior should then be completed and the big- and small-ends finally ground to size. Rods which are not likely to be run at ultra-high revs, do not require a steel of this nature, and carbon-manganese steel to Spec EN 16, heat-treated to 65 tons tensile, gives a very good result; it is a standard steel used in many English machines built after 1945. It can be machined in the fully heat-treated state and, therefore, does not require to be ground in the bores after hardening, which makes the manufacture somewhat simpler.

Where extreme lightness is sought, the weight of the big-end sleeve can be saved by making the rod from 5% nickel or $3\frac{1}{2}\%$ nickel-chrome case-hardening steel, case-hardened to a minimum of .045 in. in the big-end eye only, the rest of the rod being kept soft by copper plating before carburizing. Many two-stroke rods are made on this

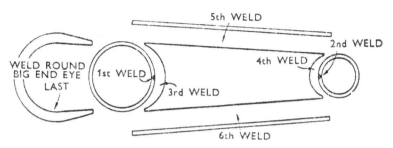

*The author's idea of a connecting rod built of high-tensile sheet steel and fabricated by welding.*

principle and it was standard practice in Rudges for many years and is to-day on many Italian engines.

Although it seems a rather revolutionary suggestion, the writer sees no reason why it should not be possible to fabricate a rod from high-tensile alloy steel sheet, united by welding. If the small and large ends are composed of strips cut along the grain of the steel and bent to shape, and the flanges of the I-section are carried round as shown in the diagram, the grain flow in every part of the rod would be ideal, which is not always the case with one-off hand forgings. The joints could be made with filler rod of the same analysis as the components and the whole assembly heat-treated before finally machining the rod to size.

Aluminium rods are not normally fitted with small-end bushes, but if badly worn, the holes can be opened out and fitted with aluminium or B.R.56 bushes; bronze bushes almost invariably come loose in time.

Some steel rods have been made without small-end bushes, the eye being either hardened and ground or simply left soft. This idea is satisfactory up to a point, but if a seizure occurs, it may be almost impossible to extract the pin. A good way to avoid this without incurring the extra weight of a bush is to adopt a system developed for the heavily-loaded articulated con.-rods of radial aircraft engines, which consists of silver-plating the small-end bores with silver to a thickness of .002 in.

CHAPTER VII

# TRUING AND BALANCING FLYWHEELS

THE maximum of rigidity in the flywheel and crankpin assembly is essential to avoid power-wastage through internal vibration. This is obtained partly by providing heavy sections of metal in the regions of maximum stress, and partly by the manner in which the assembly is held together.

Some years ago it was common practice to grind fairly steep tapers on the pin, and to pull these into the wheels by fine-thread nuts. This method of construction makes a good job, provided that the tapers fit really accurately; thus, in doing-up such an engine (particularly if a new pin is being used) the fit should be checked by means of prussian-blue smeared on the pin, which is then lightly rotated in the holes. If contact is not made over the whole internal surface of each hole the parts can be lapped together, using a fine-grit abrasive, but great care must be taken to see that the holes are not lapped out-of-square, in which event the second state will be worse than the first. This process will cause the wheels to come a little closer together and the side-float of the con.-rod will be reduced by a like amount, thus the clearance must be checked carefully on final assembly. The tapered crank-pins used in J.A.P. Speedway engines are supplied in three lengths, standard, plus $\frac{1}{32}$ in., and plus $\frac{1}{16}$ in., to allow for any enlargement that may, in time, occur in the holes. By selecting the correct length of pin, the con.-rod side-clearance can be maintained within the correct limits of .015 in. to .030 in.

It is now more usual to pull the wheels up against substantial shoulders on the pin, rigidity being gained more by this action than by the actual fit of the reduced portions of

96

the pin in the wheels. If parallel, these are usually made a light drive fit (i.e., about .001 in. larger than the hole), and if for any reason the fit is much looser than this, the pin can be hard-nickel-plated and ground to correct size. Early Velocette pins are ground with an almost imperceptible taper of .001 in. per inch length, and should push in by hand for half the depth of the flywheel hole; the nuts will then do the rest, but if the pin will not go in so far as that, the shoulders may not be pulled up into hard contact with the flywheel as intended by the makers and not only will the assembly lack rigidity but there will be a grave danger that the crankpin will break in service.

Whatever the form and fit of the pin, the whole assembly eventually depends upon the nuts, which should be examined for possible damage or distortion of the threads and scrapped if there is any doubt about them. The abutting faces must be square to the threads and can be checked and, if necessary, rectified by turning up a mandrel with a thread tightly fitting the nuts, which are then screwed on and skimmed up dead flat. If it is necessary to make new nuts because spares are unobtainable, mild steel is not good enough: nothing less than 45-ton tensile steel should be used, and alloy steel of 55–65 tons such as K.E. 805 is better still for racing. Most English crankpin nuts are tapped either 20 or 26 threads per inch, Whitworth form, the commonest sizes being $\frac{3}{4}$ in., $\frac{7}{8}$ in. and 1 in. and, therefore, it is often possible to utilize nuts of another make if genuine spares are not available.

Recently there has been a growing tendency to do away with nuts altogether and rely simply upon a press fit. This system was introduced on Velocette and Villiers two-strokes, and has been adopted for the 86 mm. four-stroke Velocettes. In this case, the pins are tapered .008 in. per inch and should push a little less than half-way by hand; 4 tons pressure should then be required to force the wheels hard against the shoulders.

An excellent method of eliminating nuts which is worth consideration by experimenters is the S.K.F. system of using

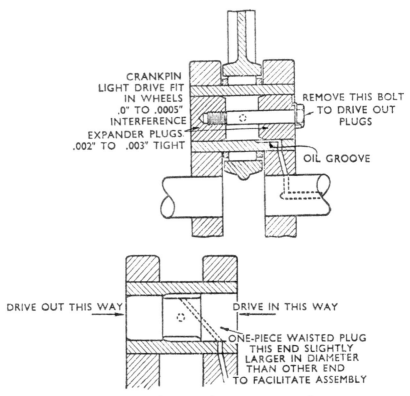

CRANKPIN
LIGHT DRIVE FIT
IN WHEELS
.0" TO .0005"
INTERFERENCE
EXPANDER PLUGS.
.002" TO .003" TIGHT

REMOVE THIS BOLT
TO DRIVE OUT
PLUGS

OIL GROOVE

DRIVE OUT THIS WAY

DRIVE IN THIS WAY

ONE-PIECE WAISTED PLUG
THIS END SLIGHTLY
LARGER IN DIAMETER
THAN OTHER END
TO FACILITATE ASSEMBLY

*Two types of expander-plug fitting to supersede a conventional crankpin.*

expander plugs in a hollow pin or shaft. The scheme is to make the shaft a tight push fit in the hole so that initial assembly is easy with no danger of scoring. Then a hard steel expander plug is forced into the bore, which is about one third to one half the diameter of the shaft, and the latter is thereby expanded and locked firmly in the flywheels. Diagrams show two methods by which this scheme could be applied. A somewhat similar idea was used in the 1954 A.J.S. racing twin though, in this instance, the expander plugs had a fairly steep taper.

Regarding the flywheels, there is very little point in going in for a big course of weight reduction; in fact, it is possible to reduce rather than increase the performance by such a proceeding, except perhaps for speedway work. Some riders find they get better results with light flywheels on short tracks where acceleration out of the corners is of paramount importance, but for road work, where full use can be made of the gearbox and clutch, there is not much in it. However, a general cleaning-up of all surfaces will not be a waste of time and is of decided benefit on the rim surfaces, as oil-drag is perceptibly reduced by a high polish.

Another method of reducing oil-drag is to chamfer the outside diameter of the rims, leaving only a narrow land next the inner faces running in close proximity to the edge of the crankcase scraper. As the majority of the oil to be skimmed off travels down the inner faces of the flywheels, the scraping action is not unduly impaired but remember that, during assembly, the wheels cannot be roughly aligned by a straight-edge across the rims if this modification is performed.

The correct fit of the main-bearing inner races on the shafts varies according to type; in no circumstances should there be any actual slack present, but if the races are locked up endways in some manner, they can be quite an easy fit. If not so retained, there must be sufficient interference between bore and shaft to prevent " creep " which, once it commences, will cause the shafts to wear, particularly if

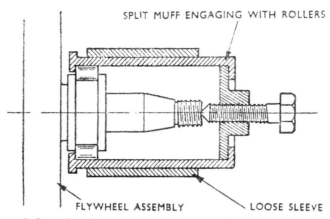

*Split puller for removing inner main-bearing races.*

99

they are not case-hardened; a light drive fit is the ideal at which to aim.

One snag about these tight-fitting races is the difficulty of removal without damage; applying two levers to the roller-cage will almost inevitably distort it, thus nipping one or two rollers endwise, and this defect should always be looked for in old engines. The best scheme is to make up a split puller which cannot harm the cage, but, failing that, two sharp-edged chisels ground to a narrow taper may be driven in from opposite sides between the race and flywheel until there is a gap wide enough to insert a pair of levers. Of course, before reassembling, any burrs raised on the faces must be filed off flush.

On all models, Velocette mainshafts have an almost imperceptible taper of .001 in. per inch on the bearing seats; the inner bearing races are also ground to the same taper and to a diameter such that they have to be lightly driven on for the last quarter-inch, or so. If looseness develops, the inner race may appear to fit correctly if it is reversed on the shaft but this must *not* be done on any account, as the race is then only in contact at one end and will rock about under load.

If slackness is found, do not adopt the barbarous process of centre-punching or chiselling the shaft, which, however good it may seem at the time, ceases to be effective after a very short while. Building-up the shaft by nickel-plating or metal-spraying with zinc are both effective and lasting repair methods and are necessary for these and similar shafts which are forced into the flywheels and permanently locked by grub-screws. Though the course is not advisable, Vincent shafts can be pressed out after driving out the Mills pin fitted through at an angle. The correct interference fit is .003 in. and this must be verified before pressing-in the new shafts. On the drive side, press in the new shaft hard up to the shoulder, with the angle-hole about 60° away from the original position, then drill back through the shaft at 45° with a $\frac{3}{16}$ in. drill, and fit a new Mills pin.

Where the main bearing rollers run direct on the shafts, as

in J.A.P. engines, renewal is the only course open if wear shown by pitting of the roller tracks is present. As previously noted, chrome-plating cannot be used as a reclaiming process for roller races. Take particular care to line up the oil-holes in shaft and wheel accurately on the timing side, and, as a precaution, check that the axial distances of the hole from the face of the wheel and from the shoulder of the shaft are the same, otherwise the oil flow may be restricted. If any error is found, full flow-area can be obtained by grooving in the required direction with a half-round chisel.

It is essential after new shafts have been fitted, and advisable even if not, to check, the truth of each wheel before final assembly commences. One method is to apply a dial indicator to the outer side of the wheel near the rim with the shaft supported between lathe centres; another is to rotate the flywheel with the shaft running in an accurately-bored bush, or even in its own bearings. If there is more than .003 in. run-out, the shaft will have to be set in the requisite direction; it will be impossible to line both shafts up accurately, if one, or both, are not dead square to their own wheels.

Strictly speaking, any balancing which is thought to be necessary should be done at this stage so that each wheel can be dealt with individually; it is, however, easier to work on the wheels after they are assembled, so unless two odd wheels are being made into a pair the job can safely be left until later, on the assumption that they were individually balanced by the makers in the first place.

After all work on the components has been completed, assembly is a straight-forward job, although it is easy to overlook the obvious precaution of ensuring that the oil-holes in the crankpin and timing side wheel are accurately in line. This precaution is not required when fitting pins with annular oil grooves, which should be placed with the hole leading to the rollers at the 3 o'clock position, looking towards the drive-side with the pin at the top, this being the position of least load. Cleanliness is essential, not only for the sake of the bearing but also to ensure that no particles of foreign matter are trapped between the

101

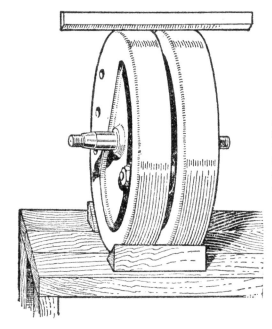

*A simple method of rough-aligning the fly-wheels with the aid of two wooden chocks and a straight-edge before final checking and tightening.*

abutting faces to the detriment of mainshaft alignment.

If the pin is of the solid type, it can be inserted and the nut fully tightened on one wheel only before assembling the rest, but if it is of the two-piece variety with a pressed-on sleeve, it is not advisable to tighten either nut fully unless the other wheel and nut are in place, otherwise the pin may be pulled over too far to one side, leaving insufficient thread for the nut on the other end. Great care must be taken with tight parallel-fitting pins to avoid damaging the hole when fitting the second wheel, which is liable to cant over due to its overhung weight. The temptation to pull the wheel on with the nut as soon as a couple of threads project through must be resisted, as so doing will overload, and very probably damage, the thread inside the nut.

The Velocette pressed-in pin is best fitted first to the drive-side wheel and forced home under a press with a ring supporting the flywheel as sometimes the pin may project a little. After fitting the con-rod, the other wheel is then partially pressed on and the wheels lined up as accurately as possible with the end of a straight-edge laid across

*Where a pair of centres is not available, the flywheel assembly may be supported on a pair of bearings in a simple wooden jig. A steel base plate makes for added accuracy.*

the rims. Similarly, with other designs, initial lining-up is facilitated if the second nut is not quite fully tightened. Final tightening or pressing home is done after correct alignment has been achieved.

The best way to move the wheels relative to each other is to hold the assembly in both hands and bump the rim of one wheel on a heavy lead block or the end grain of a hardwood post; the inertia of the wheels does the trick and no damage is done to the rims, as there might be if they were struck with a hammer.

For final tightening a properly fitting box-spanner with a strong tommy-bar at least 2 ft. long is essential; the normal type of tubular spanner is not really up to the job (unless reinforced by a brazed-on ring turned to clear the crankpin nut counterbore), but if made from chrome-molybdenum steel tube, this type will do. The best spanners, of course, are those made from solid steel with integral tommy-bars, which can be purchased from any good small-tool factor.

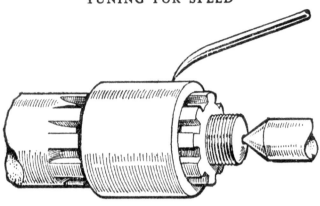

*When checking a splined mainshaft for truth with a scriber
or dial gauge, an externally ground sleeve, which is a push
fit on the shaft, will prove of great assistance in making
accurate measurements.*

Real strength must be put into the final tightening, something of the order of 400 pounds-feet being necessary.

The final check must be made on the main shafts, using
an indicator reading to thousandths of an inch. If a lathe
or a pair of centres is available, the assembly should be
mounted thereon, taking care that the wheels are not
deflected inwards by excessive pressure applied to the centres.
Next apply the indicator to each shaft as near as possible to
the ends, as all too frequently the centres in these shafts
get knocked about; any defect will immediately be shown
by the indicator, and must be rectified by scraping, lapping
or re-turning the centres until concentricity is obtained.
A number of engines have one or both shafts splined, and
in such cases a tightly fitting, accurately ground concentric
sleeve fitted over each spline will greatly assist matters.

The next move is to check the shafts close up to the
wheels; this will probably show one shaft to be " high "
and the other " low " in a direction at right angles to the
crankpin. If this is the only error present the situation is
good, because bumping the wheels in the appropriate
direction will (albeit after quite a number of shots) eliminate
it entirely, but if in spite of all your efforts both shafts are
" high " in the *same* direction, the whole assembly is in
effect " bent " in the centre.

This may be due to swarf between wheels and pin, lack of parallelism between the outer faces of the pin shoulders, or similar causes. If not due to dirt, the trouble can sometimes be cured by refitting the pin in a different position should the oil-hole arrangements permit. Failing that, some very careful work can be done with a scraper applied to the flywheel faces, but most people adopt the easy way of nipping the rims in a vice, in the plane in which both shafts are " high." This process is all right if the wheels are of steel and the pin is robust, but is not to be recommended if the pin is of light section or the wheels are cast iron.

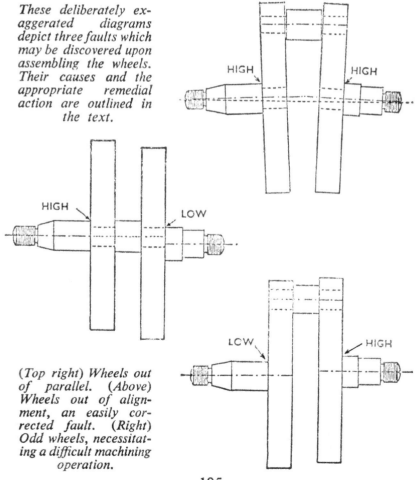

*These deliberately exaggerated diagrams depict three faults which may be discovered upon assembling the wheels. Their causes and the appropriate remedial action are outlined in the text.*

*(Top right) Wheels out of parallel. (Above) Wheels out of alignment, an easily corrected fault. (Right) Odd wheels, necessitating a difficult machining operation.*

105

There is a third error which is rarely met with unless the wheels were not originally a pair, and that is when one shaft is high and the other low in the plane of the crankpin. This is almost certainly due to the radius of the pin-hole in one wheel differing slightly from that in the other and can only be remedied by a machine shop operation.

If a pair of centres is not available, or the shaft-centres are too badly damaged to be usable, another method of checking is to support the assembly by its own or a similar pair of main-bearings resting in V-blocks. Alternatively, if there are only two bearings the crankcase itself can be utilized, although it is rather laborious having to separate the whole issue in order to bump the wheels whilst carrying out the truing process—needless to say, it is a bad plan to attempt to shift them while supported in their own bearings. If there are two fairly widely spaced bearings on either side of the case the job is a little easier, as then one shaft can be run in these bearings, leaving the other wheel and shaft completely exposed for checking. These last two methods are, however, only suggested as makeshifts where facilities for employing one of the others are unavailable. Another workshop method is to bore out a block to a close running fit on the shafts and rotate the assembly with one shaft fitting in the hole and the other in the air, a dial gauge fitted to an arm attached to the block indicating the truth or otherwise of the free shaft. One shaft is first tried, and then the other, and this method is just as good as doing the job between centres except that one cannot check both shafts at the same setting.

The question now arises—how true should the shafts be? Well, the correct amount of error is zero, but this is rarely attainable, and if the sum of the errors indicated on both shafts comes to less than .002 in. there is nothing much to grumble about. Two-bearing assemblies can run with a greater error than those with three or four, particularly where the latter are housed in a very stiff crankcase. Having made the shafts as true as they can be made, the nuts must be given a last nip-up, and the shafts finally rechecked. If all is well, a couple of squirts of oil up through the holes drilled in flywheel and pin to clear out any possible grit will finish the job off, unless for any reason, such as a big change in piston weight, you wish to rebalance the engine.

## The Balance Factor

The lower half of the rod can be considered as rotating weight, and it, together with the crankpin, can be completely balanced by an equal and opposite counter-weight, or by removing metal from the crankpin side. But it is not possible to do this with the reciprocating weight in a single-cylinder or parallel-twin engine for, if an equal and opposite weight were added, the balance would be good in the direction of the cylinder axis, but just as bad as before along a line at right angles to the cylinder. Hence a compromise must be effected by adding only a certain percentage of the reciprocating weight, this figure being termed the balance factor.

It is quite useless to postulate any particular balance factor as being the ideal; so many considerations enter into the matter that it varies with almost every design of engine, or even the type of frame in which engines of the same kind are mounted. That being so, do not be misled into rebalancing your engine just because one of your pals with an entirely different machine thinks he has some magic formula of his own.

The only source of reliable information is the parent factory but, failing advice from that direction, a factor of .66 of the reciprocating weight usually gives reasonable results. Strangely enough, some makers use a smaller factor for racing than for touring, while others do the reverse; the idea in all cases, however, is to get an engine which runs most smoothly in the speed-range at which it is intended to operate for the majority of its life. It does not matter much if the engine feels "rough" at 4,000 r.p.m. if it is to be raced and feels smooth at 6,000, whereas such an engine would be very undesirable for fast touring, where much of the running is done at the lower r.p.m. Altering the balance factor will usually succeed in moving the rough period, if any, well away from the most-used speed.

The aforesaid balance-factor applies, of course, to the reciprocating parts only—i.e., piston, rings, gudgeon pin and *the top half* of the connecting rod. A lot of weighing and measuring can be eliminated by dealing with the complete flywheel assembly only, thus-wise. Arrange it on a level surface so that the con.-rod (minus piston) is lying *horizontally*, with the small end resting on one side of a pair of scales, or supported by an accurate light-spring balance. If the balance pan is other than flat the rod must be supported in the plane of the gudgeon pin. This is best done by passing a short bar through the bush and resting the former on the edges of the pan. First, a few nuts and washers can be placed in the other pan to counterbalance the short bar and then there is no likelihood of getting confused with the other weights used to find the weight of the small end, which we will suppose is found to be 6 oz. Next weigh the complete piston assembly, which comes to, say, 15 oz. Thus the total reciprocating weight is 15 + 6 = 21 oz. and employing a factor of .66 the amount to be balanced is, therefore, 14 oz.

The wheels are already bound to be balanced to *some* percentage, and if they are placed with the shafts resting on a pair of accurately horizontal metal straight-edges they will eventually come to rest with the crankpin vertically upwards, although they may show a tendency for the pin always to be slightly to one side of the dead centre-line. This indicates that the bob-weights are off-centre, a fault which must first be rectified by drilling equal-sized holes into the side of each rim, in a position at right angles to the pin and, of course, on the " heavy " side of the vertical centre line.

When symmetrical balance has finally been obtained, attach to the small end a weight equal to the amount to be balanced *minus* that of the small end; using the figures quoted above, this would be 14 − 6 = 8 oz. The manner of

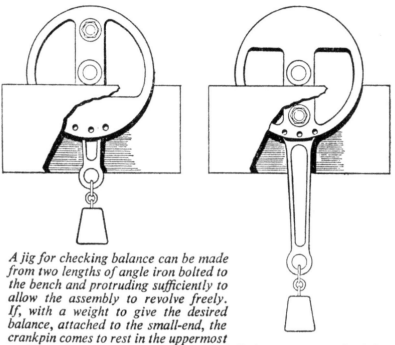

*A jig for checking balance can be made from two lengths of angle iron bolted to the bench and protruding sufficiently to allow the assembly to revolve freely. If, with a weight to give the desired balance, attached to the small-end, the crankpin comes to rest in the uppermost position, the counterweights must be drilled as shown on the left. If the crankpin stops at the bottom the wheels must be drilled adjacent to the pin.*

making up this weight or of attaching it to the small end is purely a matter of choice—it can be, for instance, a bag full of oddments, or a bolt with the requisite weight of washers. If the balance-factor does actually correspond to the figure desired, the wheels will roll freely along the straight-edges and show no tendency to settle in any one position; if not, the pin will go to the top or bottom according to whether the bobweights are too heavy or too light.

Correction is usually made by drilling the rims in the appropriate positions, being careful to take equal amounts out of each wheel and on each side of the centre plane, but it can equally well be done by tapping and plugging existing holes. If a bit of experimenting to find the best balance is part of the tuning programme, it is a good idea to drill or tap a few holes of, say, $\frac{3}{8}$-in. or $\frac{1}{2}$-in. diameter, into which plugs of the required weight can subsequently be fitted or removed. In some engines it is possible to drill a hole somewhere in each crankcase wall below the main-bearings, and tap it $\frac{1}{4}$ in. gas (or more correctly, $\frac{1}{4}$ in. B.S.P.), thread which is the size commonly employed for drain plugs, and drill several holes in the flywheels at the same radius, tapping these out $\frac{1}{8}$ in. B.S.P. Plugs of various lengths in steel or bronze can then be inserted or removed from the flywheels through the crankcase holes in a couple of minutes without disturbing the engine and experiments to find the most satisfactory balance can be very rapidly conducted. This is a very good scheme to employ when adapting engines for use in 500 c.c. racing cars, because the different method of mounting as compared to a motorcycle very often leads to trouble in obtaining smooth running.

In closing, a word or two about those " horizontal straight-edges." For permanent workshop use it is nice to make up a proper jig, but there is no necessity to go to such lengths. There are plenty of other ways: for instance, two lengths of angle iron can be bolted to the bench-top over-hanging the latter by about a foot. The only vital qualification is that the top edges must be flat, smooth and absolutely horizontal and level with each other when the wheels are resting on them. A good spirit level is the best aid to check-ing this point, but failing that a dead-round bar such as a piece of silver steel will prove the point, since it will obviously tend to run towards whichever is the lower end. Most machine-shops equipped with cylindrical grinders possess a pair of straight edges on which the grinding wheels are balanced and, with a little blandishment exercised in the right quarters, it is often possible to obtain the use of such equipment.

On A.J.S. 7R and G50 models, special circular nuts are used, which must be split (and are thus destroyed) to re-move them. Replacement nuts must always be on hand if the big-end is to be inspected; these are made with a reduced hexagonal portion which must be sawn off after the wheels are fully tightened.

## CHAPTER VIII

## WORK ON THE CRANKCASE

THE primary duty of the crankcase is to provide a rigid mounting for the main bearings and a foundation for the cylinder sufficiently solid as to maintain that component square to the mainshaft axis at all times, irrespective of temperature changes or cyclic load variations. The rigidity of the bearings is settled by the original design; thus in the search for speed little can be done other than to see that the outer races are a good fit in the case when the latter is hot. If they are not, the races will show signs of " creep " indicated by a polished appearance of the outer surface. If there is any doubt about the matter, each side of the case, complete with bearings, can be immersed in boiling water, after which the bearing rings should not be free enough to turn by hand.

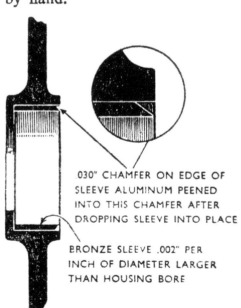

*How worn main-bearing housings may be renovated by the insertion of a shrunk-in bronze liner. (Inset) How the edge of the liner is chamfered to permit of peening the aluminium surround.*

.030" CHAMFER ON EDGE OF
SLEEVE ALUMINUM PEENED
INTO THIS CHAMFER AFTER
DROPPING SLEEVE INTO PLACE

BRONZE SLEEVE .002" PER
INCH OF DIAMETER LARGER
THAN HOUSING BORE

Several methods are available for curing loose races, of which the easiest—tinning the surface—is not to be recommended, as it is almost impossible to get an even coating, and in any case it inevitably gives away after a while. Chromium or nickel-plating the races is satisfactory, provided that the finished outer surface is absolutely circular and true to the bore; if only about .001 in. thickness of deposit is required to restore the fit it will not need to be finished to size if the job is done by a competent plating shop, but deposits of greater thickness will need to be finally sized by grinding owing to the tendency of these metals to build up more thickly at the edges than at the centre. Copper-plating on the other hand does not show this tendency and can easily be cleaned up to size with a file whilst the race is rotated in a lathe chuck. Owing to its softness, copper plating does not always last very long but is such a convenient method that it is often utilized.

Probably the best method of effecting a permanent cure is to bring the housing back to its original size by boring it out and fitting a bronze sleeve about $\frac{1}{16}$ in. thick and .002 in. per inch of diameter larger than the housing. Having heated up the crankcase to 200° C. (400° F.)—which can be done with the aid of a domestic oven—the sleeve can be dropped into place, and after peening the aluminium over the edge as shown in the diagram, the sleeve is then finish-bored to .001 in. per inch smaller than the race. A job such as this requires to be done extremely accurately; the crankcase must be set up in the lathe with the joint face and spigot diameter both running dead true. In some instances, one or more of the outer races are clamped endways, either by plates or ring nuts, in which event they cannot turn or work out sideways, and, provided there is no actual looseness perceptible, the diametral fit need not be so tight. "Manx" Norton bearing sleeves, besides being retained in this manner are machined with grooves on the sides, into which the metal of the retaining plate is punched to form keys to prevent rotation. When refitting these sleeves they must be

112

placed with the grooves visible and the retaining-plate punched in to them in the prescribed manner.

## Main Bearing Clearances

If any bearings need replacement through excessive wear or pitting of the race tracks, remember that the outer races close in by approximately half the amount of interference between them and the case. Consequently, the bearings should have a slight amount of slackness in them before fitting, otherwise the rollers or balls may be subjected to a damaging overload, even though the inner races may still *seem* to turn quite easily. Some makers supply bearings with various amounts of diametral clearance to allow for the tightness of shaft or housing, and mark the races accordingly. Two small polished circles on the edge of a Hoffmann outer race, for example, indicate that it has the right clearance if the outer race is tight, but the inner a push fit; three circles are visible if both races are intended to be tight. Apart from this indication, the inner assembly of a roller bearing should just slide into place by hand if the fit is correct, and ball-races, when free of oil, should spin for several turns. Most ball-bearings, rotated dry, emit slight noise but, if the noise sounds irregular or rough, the condition of the bearing is open to suspicion and its replacement is the wisest course. The inner tracks of roller bearings can be examined by prising a roller out of the cage.

Another important matter is the alignment of the bearings, particularly if there are two in either or both halves of the case. The only check of any real value is to turn or grind a mandrel to a size (or sizes) which will just push through the inner bearings without shake, and then insert this through the whole set of bearings with all the crankcase bolts tightened up. The mandrel should push through without effort and turn freely when in place; if not, the error must be tracked down and eliminated.

Sometimes in old engines the spigot on one half-case is a poor fit in the register in the other half, and relative move-

THIS FACE TO BE DEAD FLAT
DIMENSIONS A AND B MUST
BE EQUAL

*The studs should be removed, the case placed mouth downwards on a surface plate and the distances A and B then checked for equality with a mandrel. The end diameters of the mandrel must be of equal size.*

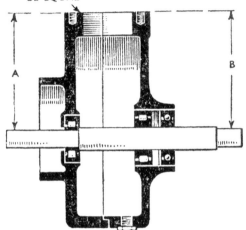

ment which would alter the alignment can take place. This can be prevented by reaming out two existing bolt-holes to accommodate special oversize bolts acting as dowels; before reaming, the cases must be tapped lightly this way and that until the best position is attained, as indicated by the freeness of the test-mandrel.

Fortunately, since it is a difficult fault to eradicate, incorrect bearing alignment is a rare disease, but it should be looked for just the same.

If plain bearings are included in the make-up and have been renewed, it is best to leave the bores a few thous. undersize and finally line-ream with the reamer piloted in the bearing on the opposite side. When a bearing of this type is used to transfer the main oil supply to the crankshaft the fit is particularly important and the maker's instructions regarding clearances must be rigorously followed. Naturally any communicating oil-holes must be accurately lined-up and checked by injecting oil through them from a pressure can.

The test-mandrel also comes in useful for checking the cylinder-base, which must be parallel to the main-shaft centre line in addition to being flat and free from any step at the joint. Presupposing that it is accurate as to flatness, parallelism can be checked by inverting the case on a sur-face-plate and measuring the distance on each side between the plate and mandrel. Should the bearings be of differing bores on each side, a short length of the mandrel at each end can be turned to exactly equal diameters—which avoids having to make allowance for varying sizes. If the face is not flat it must be re-machined or trued up with file and scraper until it is correct in all respects. Lack of flatness is bad; it permits oil leaks, allows the barrel to rock about under load, and can be an unsuspected cause of barrel distortion or cracked base-flanges.

At this stage it is as well to cast a critical eye over the cylinder studs—particularly if the compression ratio is being raised considerably, because the gas pressures will be greatly increased thereby; the accompanying graph shows the actual rise of compression pressure with increase of ratio, and as explosion pressures are some $3\frac{1}{2}$ to 4 times

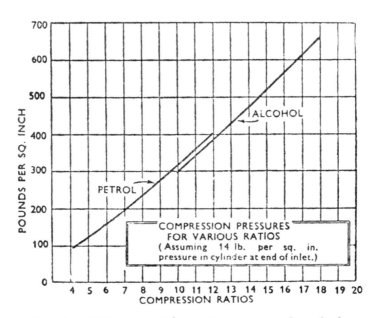

*A study of this graph will reveal the reason why cylinder studs should be examined when the compression ratio is raised.*

115

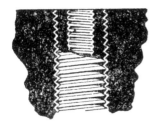

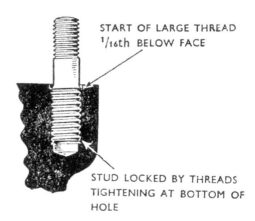

START OF LARGE THREAD
¹/₁₆th BELOW FACE

STUD LOCKED BY THREADS
TIGHTENING AT BOTTOM OF
HOLE

*If cylinder studs are loose, internally and externally threaded sleeves will effect a good repair. Alternatively, double-diameter studs can be made up.*

the compression pressures, it will be appreciated that a good deal depends upon the cylinder fixing in an ultra-high compression motor.

Almost invariably the studs are tapped direct into the aluminium. As the latter metal is relatively weak, the length of thread in engagement should preferably be twice—and certainly at least one and a half times—the stud diameter. In addition, the threads should tighten at the *bottom* and not at the top of the hole; in the latter case the run-out of the stud thread exerts a powerful wedging action on the surrounding boss, which may be the cause of a crack making an unwelcome appearance either at the first onset or later on when the engine is put to work.

Should the crankcase threads appear to be damaged or partially stripped, there is usually enough metal present to permit drilling and tapping to a greater depth. If not, two courses are available. One is to re-tap to a size $\frac{1}{16}$ in. larger and fit a double-diameter, or "bull-headed", stud; for example, a stripped hole previously $\frac{5}{16}$-in. Whitworth can be re-tapped to $\frac{3}{8}$-in. Whitworth, having first opened it out with a letter N drill. In other cases it may be preferable to retain the existing size of stud by tapping out the hole to take a bronze or steel bush, screwed inside and out to the appropriate sizes, this being particularly advisable if there

TAPPING SIZES FOR VARIOUS THREADS

| SIZE | PITCH THREADS PER INCH | CORRECT DRILL SIZE | NEAREST FRACTIONAL DRILL SIZE |
|---|---|---|---|
| 2 B.A. | 31.4 | No. 23 | 5/32 in. |
| 1/4-in. B.S.F. | 26 | No. 5 | 13/64 in. |
| 1/4-in. Whit. | 20 | No. 8 | 13/64 in. |
| 5/16-in. B.S.F. | 22 | Letter G | 17/64 in. |
| 5/16-in. Whit. | 18 | Letter F | 1/4 in. |
| 3/8-in. B.S.F. | 20 | Letter O or P | 21/64 in. |
| 3/8-in. Whit. | 16 | Letter N | 5/16 in. |
| 1/8-in. B.S.P. | 28 | 11/32 in. | — |
| 1/4-in. B.S.P. | 19 | 29/64 in. | — |
| 3/8-in. B.S.P. | 19 | 37/64 in. | — |
| 7/16-in. B.S.F. | 18 | 3/8 in. | — |
| 7/16-in. Whit. | 14 | 23/64 in. | — |
| 1/2-in. B.S.F. | 16 | 27/64 in. | — |
| 1/2-in. Whit. | 12 | 13/32 in. | — |
| 9/16-in. C.E.I. | 20 | 33/64 in. | — |

is any future likelihood of the studs being removed and replaced at intervals.

For the external threads on these sleeves, either $\frac{1}{4}$-in. or $\frac{3}{8}$-in. gas threads—both having 19 threads per inch—are very suitable. The table on this page, which may come in useful for other jobs, gives the tapping sizes and drill designations for a number of pitches.

Still another scheme is to instal Armstrong or Cross wire inserts, which somewhat resemble springs made from steel wire of diamond section, and are screwed into an oversized tapped hole and finally locked in by punching or "staking" the end coil.

## Timing-side Mechanism

It is now time to give a little attention to the mechanism contained in the timing-side case, to wit, the timing-gear and oil-pump. Despite their relatively small size and heavy loading, the camshaft bearings in push-rod engines give very little trouble, and unless they are in a very bad state it is best not to disturb them. Provided the surfaces are not torn or worn into ridges, clearances up to .005 in. are permissible, and if new bushes are needed they should be reamed to .002 in. clearance, except in the rare instances where they form part of the lubrication system, when slightly less clearance is necessary in order to prevent the escape of too much oil.

The modern tendency is to provide fixed spindles upon which the cam-wheels rotate, the spindles being drilled for lubrication, and it is an easy matter to make sure that all oil-ways are clear and that the wheels spin freely. Designs in which the outer cam-bearings are located in the timing cover are not so easy to check or to rectify if incorrect, the chief difficulty being to get both pairs of bearings in line simultaneously.

If the cover is attached only by set-screws its location may not be sufficiently positive as to ensure that it remains in the correct position indefinitely when under the influence of irregular load and severe vibration. This contingency can be entirely prevented by fitting a couple of dowels, which need only be quite small—$\frac{1}{8}$-in. diameter will do if there is no room to fit a larger size—the holes being drilled and reamed after the cover has been worked into a position where the cam-wheels are at maximum freeness *with all screws tight*; with journals and bushes free from oil, either wheel should spin for several turns if given a sharp flick with the fingers.

The dowels should be a light drive fit in one component and a good push fit in the other, otherwise it is difficult to get the cover off subsequently. If there is no room to fit dowels, two of the existing holes can be modified to accept screws with close-fitting plain shanks, which will serve the same purpose.

Replacement bushes are almost invariably bored slightly undersize to allow for reaming. This operation must be done with a piloted reamer to ensure alignment, and occasionally a special jig-plate is really required to do the job properly. Failing this device, which is only worth having if it is extremely accurately made, the bushes, after being fitted with the crankcase or cover heated, can be reamed a little on the small side, and then eased out with a scraper, using prussian blue on the shafts to show up the tight spots. Do not attempt to lap the shafts in with emery powder, as this will embed itself into the soft bearing metal and subsequently cause rapid wear of the shafts. In the matter of end-play, it is better to err on the generous side rather than have too little, except when the gears have helical teeth, in which event only .001 in. to .003 in. should be allowed. Excess play in the timing gears of Velocette engines is the frequent cause of harsh, noisy running.

Several modern engines, the A.J.S., Matchless and Vincent for example, employ porous-bronze bushes for camshafts and also at other localities. These bushes should never be reamed if at all possible; the correct method is to size them, after fitting, with a planishing broach—i.e. one with no cutting edges—or else bore them with a sharp single-point tool. The ordinary shop reamer almost invariably smears the surface instead of cutting and thus blocks up the pores in the metal, though a very keen reamer will not do much harm if the amount of metal to be removed is very slight.

### Increased Lubrication

Lubrication of the timing-gear is not always well carried out, and can frequently be improved by chiselling extra V-grooves leading to oil-holes in the bushes, or by arranging an extra oil-feed to the timing-chest. In dry-sump engines an easy way to accomplish this is to take a lead off the pipe which returns oil to the tank and couple this up to a union and internal jet in the timing-case placed where it will do the most good—preferably so that the oil drops directly on to the cams. Naturally there is a limit to how much oil can be re-circulated in this way, and the flow needs to be restricted, otherwise the scavenge pump will be overloaded.

A fixed jet with an orifice about .030 in. in diameter should suffice to start with, or alternatively an Enots adjustable drip-feed can be used. Small jet orifices are rather prone to blockage when return-oil is being fed through them, but this can be largely overcome by using a larger hole into which a loose wire or split pin is fitted. This scheme is used by Vincents in the rocker-feed jets, but, for racing, the restrictor wires should be removed from the exhaust valve feeds and also from the inlet-valve feeds if the valve guides are in good condition.

If the lubrication is of the total-loss type, it may be worth while fitting an additional sight-feed pump, or if the existing pump is of the single-delivery type, to replace it by a duplex pattern, the aim being to let one pump feed the big-end while the second takes care of the timing gear. Each supply can then be adjusted to suit its own department without risk of swamping or starving other parts of the motor. This of course is the system used on J.A.P. Speed-way and 8-80 engines which are intended for short-distance work, but full dry-sump systems are used on these engines for long-distance racing and Formula III cars.

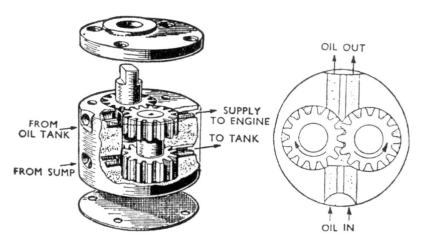

*The efficiency of a gear-type oil-pump depends upon the minimum possible side clearance between wheels and case. The case faces can be rubbed down when clearance becomes excessive.*

The oil-pump in dry-sump engines is usually housed directly in the crankcase, and in most o.h-camshaft designs is tightly fitted into a recess bored in the back of the timing-chest. To remove, it is necessary to heat up the case and tap it, timing-chest down, on the bench-top. It may sometimes be necessary to run a tap into two of the retaining screw holes, so that a couple of screws can be inserted by which the pump can be pulled out. The internal bore of the housing must never be enlarged to make refitting of the pump easier, as this is almost certain to lead to leakage between the pressure and scavenge side of the pump. As a rule, gear-pumps give very little trouble, unless a piece of metal has found its way in and damaged the teeth or the gear-pockets, but in time side wear will develop and reduce the delivery rate.

It is sometimes thought that backlash between the teeth affects the pumping, but it makes no difference at all—in fact, for smooth functioning at least .005 in. backlash should be present. The side clearance, however, should not exceed .001 in. (particularly if the gears are thin in relation to their diameter), and if more is present the faces of the pump body should be very carefully dressed to the required amount. Should a paper packing be a standard fitting, the simplest course is to lap the pump-face on a surface-plate with the gears in place until the whole surface, including that of gears, is flat and level; the paper packing will subsequently provide the requisite clearance. All push-rod Velocettes have double-gear pumps, somewhat similar to those in the o.h. camshaft models, but driven at a much slower speed by a single-start bronze worm-wheel engaging with a straight-cut pinion on the pump spindle, the pump housing being bored at a small angle to give correct engagement between worm and pinion teeth. On later models the pump speed was doubled by using a two-start worm and helically-cut pinion; and it is possible to utilize the later design of gearing to increase the oil-flow of earlier engines.

In those pumps which have a plunger which rotates and

121

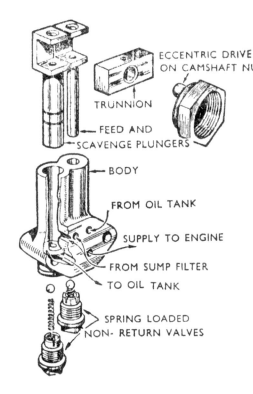

ECCENTRIC DRIVE
ON CAMSHAFT NUT

TRUNNION

FEED AND
SCAVENGE PLUNGERS

BODY

FROM OIL TANK

SUPPLY TO ENGINE

FROM SUMP FILTER

TO OIL TANK

SPRING LOADED
NON- RETURN VALVES

*As in the case of the double-gear wheel pump, the plunger type employs a scavenge outlet with a capacity larger than that of the feed pump.*

reciprocates, the points to note are the condition of the gear-teeth, the fit of the plunger portions in their respective housings at each end, and the state of the small driving peg which is screwed into the crankcase and engages with an inclined groove machined in the plunger. As these pumps turn at a relatively low speed, wear is very slow as a general rule; it is a wise plan, nevertheless, to verify that all is as it should be, for even a momentary shortage of oil at maximum revs. is fraught with the most expensive, and sometimes physically painful, consequences. The driving worm, if renewable, should be replaced without hesitation if the teeth have worn thin, and, when the design has been changed from bronze to hardened steel, as in Vincent engines, it is desirable to instal the new design in any event.

Rotary plunger pumps are not designed for working against pressures of more than a couple of pounds or so to the square inch, and if any blockage should occur in the outlet passage or pipes from either the pressure or scavenge ends, either the worm drive or the driving peg which engages with the cam-slot in the plunger will fail in a fairly short time. Therefore this point must be carefully watched both inside the engine and in all the external connections.

Apart from that eventuality, this form of pump lasts for a long time and has the merit that it does not allow oil to syphon back through it whilst standing, which is an annoying defect of the gear-pump.

When plain big-end bearings are used, it is essential to maintain a high oil pressure, consequently they are lubricated either by a gear-pump or one with purely reciprocating plungers as used on Triumph and some Ariel engines. These also give little trouble but the trunnion block should be examined for wear and care taken to see that the plungers, ball-valves and springs are all operating correctly.

Should an engine ever suffer the misfortune of having a piston break up badly, or have a hole burnt in the crown, the resulting mass of aluminium particles penetrates into every nook and crevice with astonishing rapidity, and is likely to congregate in odd corners or pockets such as exist where two drilled oil passages meet, or where unions are screwed into bosses. Flushing-out cannot really be guaranteed to get rid of them all and the only safe way is to remove all plugs and unions and make a thorough job of the cleansing process. When replacing these parts, remember that the slightest trace of an air-leak on the suction side of the scavenge pump is certain to lead to poor scavenging and, even if the engine does not oil plugs as a result, it will be down in speed due to oil-drag. Consequently, too much care cannot be taken to see that every joint, or plug, is completely air-tight and locked up so that it will remain so indefinitely, this remark applying also to the driving-pin of a rotary pump which, after being fully tightened, should have metal punched into the screw slot as an insurance against loosening.

## CHAPTER IX

# REASSEMBLING CRANKCASE COMPONENTS

WITH the exception of the cam-followers and overhead gear, practically all the components within the engine which demand attention or possible modification have by now been dealt with sufficiently thoroughly to indicate the lines upon which to proceed.

If everything has been done to your own satisfaction—and the more self-critical you are the more likelihood there is of your beating other and more easily satisfied rivals—a spot of assembly work can now be put in hand prior to getting down to the vitally important matter of valve and ignition timing.

It is probably unnecessary to mention the point again, but, to be on the safe side, let me remind you that before commencing this work the bench and its surroundings must be swept clean of all foreign matter—dust, filings, cigarette butts—and the crankcase halves, flywheels, bearings, and so forth laid out, preferably on sheets of paper, after having been thoroughly cleaned.

The first step is a trial assembly of the flywheels in the crankcase in order to verify the centralization of the con.-rod and the amount of end-float, if any, on the mainshafts. Lateral location of the flywheel assembly is normally effected by one of two main methods : either one of the mainshafts is clamped endways in its bearings (usually on the driving side), or, alternatively, the main bearings on both sides of the wheels share the duty between them, each preventing movement towards its own side of the engine.

In the first-mentioned category the question of getting the amount of end-float correct does not arise, since it is fixed and limited to a very small amount by the design of the location bearing. Care must be taken, however, to see

124

that any distance-pieces or washers, either next to the wheels or between the various bearings, are in place in their correct order; otherwise, there is a risk that some bearing not intended to take end-thrust may be subjected to loading of this nature, which, in addition to causing stiffness, will rapidly destroy the bearing involved.

In the G3L Matchless, for instance, two ball bearings, with a pair of spacing washers separating their inner races, are fitted on the drive side, and should these spacers be inadvertently omitted, the pressure of the shock-absorber spring will put very heavy thrust-loads on the bearings, and may ultimately cause the whole flywheel assembly to move out of position in the direction of the chain. In this design, as in quite a number of others, the end-thrust of the shock-absorber spring is ultilized to clamp the drive-side mainshaft in its bearing or bearings; thus, when verifying the flywheel location, the spring should be lightly tightened with the sprocket and face cam (or an equivalent distance piece) in place.

In this condition there should be no measurable side play

*It is an easy matter to mislay or misplace essential washers or packing pieces which vary considerably with individual makes. This drawing shows the correct method of assembling drive-side bearings used for many years for the Matchless G3L series.*

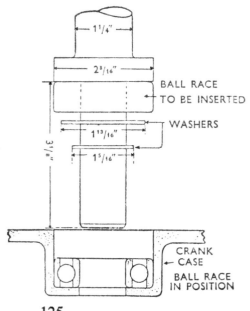

125

present, but if the spring is then removed, there should be a perceptible amount; if not, the bearing on the timing side is too close in and appropriate measures must be taken to obtain, say, .005-in. float and thus avoid the possibility of undesirable end-thrust being placed on the bearing.

In other designs such as the post-war Vincent singles and twins, a distance-piece is used between the inner and outer main bearings. If this is inadvertently omitted, the shaft will be locked up solid when the main shaft nut is tightened up, an operation which may not take place until the motor is almost completely assembled. It is therefore a golden rule *always* to assemble all relevant components on the mainshaft and tighten the nut fully early in the piece just to make sure that all is in order. There is never very much clearance to spare in this locality and it may be that a new crankpin is a fraction longer than the original and fouls the crankcase, though this might otherwise have escaped notice. In some engines, the crankpin nut runs so close to the bearing housing that a portion has to be cleared away with a chisel and this naturally must be done before proceeding further.

In those designs in which the bearings on both sides of the wheels assist in their location, it is not uncommon to allow up to .010-in. end-float, except in the case of o.h.c. Velocettes, in which the mesh of the bevel timing gears is partly controlled by the position of the mainshaft. These engines, and also those push-rod models equipped with taper-roller main bearings, *must* be adjusted so that there is precisely 4 thou. "nip" or negative clearance when the crankcase is cold. This is checked by noting with feeler gauges the gap between the two halves when tightness in turning the wheels becomes apparent, and shims to the requisite thickness must be placed behind either or both outer rings to ensure the correct "nip".

In o.h.c. Nortons, the assembly is located by the timing-side ball-race in order to limit the amount by which thermal expansion can affect the bevel mesh. Centrality adjustment is made by fitting shims between bearing and flywheel and

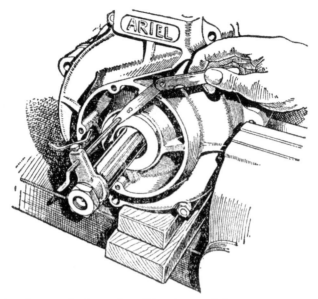

*Another method, employed in the Ariel factory, is to fix a pointer on the drive-side mainshaft just touching the crank-case when the wheels are pushed fully over to the timing side. The wheels are then pulled in the opposite direction and clearance between case-face and pointer checked with a feeler gauge.*

should be verified with all timing side components fitted and the retaining nut pulled up tight.

With the wheels placed correctly in the case and the latter tightly bolted up, the small end of the connecting-rod ought to be exactly central in the cylinder-barrel register, but as in almost every design $\frac{1}{32}$ in. or more side clearance is allowed between the small-end bush and the piston bosses, a little latitude in centrality is permissible. There is always a certain amount of side play of the rod itself if the big-end has been correctly fitted up, and so the simplest method of checking centrality is by callipering the distance between the register and each side of the small end, with the rod lightly held over in the opposite direction. The two measurements should not differ by more than .010 in. when checked by this means.

If the difference is perceptibly greater, it is *not* a good idea to attempt to correct it by bending the rod over; such a

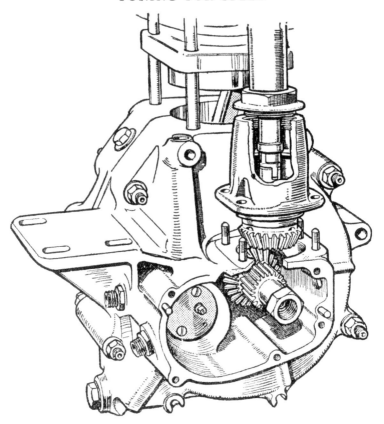

*The overhead-camshaft engine differs from the o.h.v. and
side-valve types in that end-float in the flywheel assembly
must be avoided, otherwise the bevel gears will tend to
mesh incorrectly, thereby permitting backlash. Full details
of the correct treatment are given in the accompanying text.*

procedure would simply undo the value of the work
previously carried out in truing up the rod. Instead,
correction must be effected by altering the lateral location of
the flywheels—hence the reason for the trial assembly before
finally adjusting the end-float. Should the latter be excessive,
obviously the side on which it is taken up should be the one
which will tend to centralize the small end.

There are various methods of adjusting end-float, but
most of them entail the use of shims, which, if not available
from the makers, can be cut from shim-steel stock or, alternatively, use can be made of the shim-washers commonly

employed for adjusting the end-float in the steering knuckles of cars. The location of the shims varies, but the golden rule is never to put them between two parts which rotate relatively to one another, but only between faces which are relatively stationary. Thus, they can be placed on the mainshafts between the inner races and flywheel bosses, or between the bearing outer rings and the inside of their housings.

The latter entails rather more work in fitting, but in some designs is the only suitable place. For example, Velocette mainshafts are ground with a very narrow taper, and the races are designed to fit tightly thereon when hard up against the flywheels; obviously, if shims were interposed the fit of the inner races would be slack, so the shims must be placed behind the outer races.

Again, in many J.A.P. models the rollers run direct on the hardened shafts and end play is fixed by the clearance between the faces of the outer rings and the flywheel bosses. If this is too great, these rings must be shimmed up from behind. At the same time, it is wise to verify that the rollers have sufficient end clearance between the flywheels and the hardened washer placed at the other side of the outer race, otherwise they cannot rotate freely and will rapidly destroy the shaft surface. In the racing twins of this make, phosphor-bronze thrust washers are interposed between the flywheels and bearing sleeves and side-float can be regulated by using shims of varying thickness.

When building up an old engine with new parts, it will occasionally be found that there is no end play; there is, so to speak, negative clearance. In that event, first heat the case, drop out the main bearings, remove any shims there may be, and then try again. If this treatment is of no avail, the only thing to do is skim the requisite amount of metal off the flywheel bosses—the amount being determined by measuring the distance between the main bearings with the case bolted up and subracting this from the width over the flywheel bosses. For this job a large pair of external and internal callipers (or an internal micrometer) are required.

*The use of inside and outside micrometers will determine the amount of end-float; the minor reading is subtracted from the major one. This is a good method for camshaft engines which employ "nil" clearance, but the amateur who has no such elaborate equipment will find a pair of inside and outside callipers a reasonably satisfactory substitute.*

Having finally obtained a state of perfection in which the rod is central and the end-float correct, the flywheels should spin with the greatest ease as the rod is pumped up and down with the fingers, and there should be no perceptible difference in " feel " with or without the sprocket and shock absorber in place. If there is, the cause must be tracked down and eliminated forthwith and not glossed over in the hope that it will run off shortly in service. If all is well, the crankcase joint can be coated with the preferred form of jointing compound and reassembled. The author's preference is for one of the non-hardening cements such as "Gasket-goo", which does not dry quickly so that there need be no undue haste to slap the case together before the compound hardens. Make absolutely sure that nothing has been omitted which should be fitted at this stage, particularly in unit-construction engines in which certain gearbox components may have to be in place before the case goes together. Even though some may have to be refitted subsequently, it is preferable to fit and tighten all the crankcase bolts at this stage, but at all events it is very bad practice to put in a few in the region of the cylinder, leaving the bottom ones out because they are not easy to get at just at the moment. Subsequent joint leakage may be traced to this cause.

Some crankcase bolts are drilled for cylinder-base oil-feeds and care must be taken not to overstress them. As part of the checking routine, inject oil with the pressure can through every oil passage there may happen to be to make absolutely certain all are clean and to wash out any foreign matter. Sometimes an oil hole may be blocked with excess gasket cement and it is better to clear it at this stage than after some mechanical damage has been wrought later on.

The next step is to fit the piston, minus rings, as a preliminary to checking its " lie " in the barrel. If the piston is new or undamaged, the bottom edge of the skirt should

*An error in workman-ship may necessitate setting of the connecting rod; this can safely be attempted if a block of metal is first placed between crankcase and connecting rod, with the latter at bottom dead centre.*

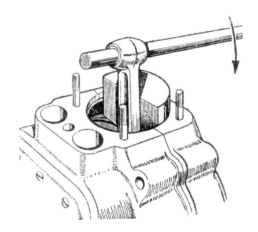

be parallel to the crankcase face in a direction parallel to the mainshafts, but, owing to the various amounts of side play present and the shape of the bottom edge, which is frequently by no means flat, this is not an easy matter to check with real accuracy. In any case, it does not matter a great deal; what *does* matter is whether the piston lies centrally in, and parallel to, the barrel.

This is checked by lightly bolting the cylinder in place and viewing the piston from the open end of the barrel under a good light. It is then quite easy to see just where the piston does lie, and if it shows any undesirable tendency to work over to one side when the flywheels are rotated.

If it does so, it is a sign that an error—or, more likely, a multiplicity of small errors all tending the same way—is causing trouble. Sometimes reversing the piston will effect a cure, although this method, of course, cannot be adopted (except as a temporary method of checking) with a piston which has unequal-sized valve clearance pockets in the crown, or with the split-skirt pistons fitted to a few sports models which must not be run with the split towards the rear, or thrust, side.

Even if the top lands appear to be central, this provides no guarantee that the piston as a whole is lying parallel. This can best be verified by turning the engine over several times after coating the cylinder bore with a very light (almost imperceptible) smear of prussian blue. Both thrust faces of the piston should then be symmetrically marked, but if differences of only a minor nature exist, a little careful work with a dead-smooth file will usually rectify matters. Severe cases call for a little more drastic treatment, and it may be necessary to set the small end slightly, although this will be a reflection on the quality of the previous work. To perform this operation, position the rod at bottom dead centre and select a block of metal which will just jam into the space between the crankcase mouth and the shank of the rod about half an inch below the little end. Insert a mandrel (*not* your checking mandrel!) into the small-end bush and bend in the requisite direction, remembering that only a very small amount is required to make a big difference to the position of the piston, owing to the latter's relatively greater length.

Once the piston is really true, it ought to be possible to make it reciprocate (without rings) at least half a dozen times by giving it a smart push with the thumb downwards from t.d.c. and it should always come to rest at b.d.c., because the flywheel counterbalance weight is less than that of the piston and rod.

Before finally completing the assembly, temporarily fit the barrel and head and pull the nuts down to correct tension to verify that no barrel distortion is thereby brought about. If distortion is present, it will be shown up by the engine not being quite so free to turn as it was before. Lack of flatness or squareness at the cylinder-base flange or crankcase face is the most probable cause, and this can sometimes be detected by observing the effect of loosening the bolts one or two at a time. Final fitting is dealt with at the end of Chapter X.

The golden rules during assembly are *always to check everything you do as you go along, and not to assume anything is correct without verifying it.* Many hours of hurried midnight toil would have been avoided time and again had these simple precautions been observed.

CHAPTER X

## " TOP-HALF " REASSEMBLY

WE have now proceeded to the point where the barrel is ready for final bolting-down, provided that there is no further work to be done either upon it or the piston.

If, however, larger valves or a high-domed piston have been fitted, or the barrel shortened to any extent, it is essential to verify that the valve pockets in the piston crown are sufficiently deep, and if not, to deepen them, which will mean that the barrel must come off again in order to carry out the re-machining or to get rid of swarf if the pockets are deepened with the piston in place. Another matter which can be attended to at this stage is the head joint, a vital factor which will be touched upon later.

Reverting to the question of valve clearances, in themselves piston recesses are no earthly use—in fact, they are detrimental, inasmuch as they break up the crown contour and create pockets of gas in which detonation may take place. In extreme cases they may even render a considerable portion of the valve-opening area inoperative for a few degrees before and after t.d.c., so reducing the effectiveness of high-overlap valve timing at an exceedingly important period of the cycle.

Although this is only likely to be serious if ultra-high compression ratios are being sought after, the tendency to masking of the valve heads can be reduced by milling flats on the crown—to, say, half the maximum depth of the pocket —and counterboring into the flats to make up the rest of the clearance required.

Another point to be watched is the thickness of metal between the corner of the pocket and the top ring groove; this can be quite thin on the inlet side, down perhaps to $\frac{1}{16}$ in., but on the exhaust side as much metal as possible

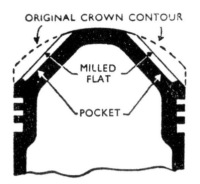

*The masking effect of deep recesses may be offset by milling down the original crown contour and forming flats.*

must be left. Insufficient thickness at this point allows an excessive amount of heat to pass through to the top ring; moreover, the upstanding rim of metal will become very hot and consequently weak and liable to crumble away if for any reason the carburetter is delivering a weak mixture.

This brings up the question of how deep the pockets really need to be, to which the answer depends to a large extent on the type of engine and the conditions of racing. In o.h. camshaft designs (provided the springs are of the correct strength) the valves follow the cams very closely up to a certain designed speed. Provided, therefore, the revs. are studiously kept below the danger mark by the use of a rev. counter, the clearance need be only a little greater—say, $\frac{1}{16}$ in.—than that necessary just to clear the valve-heads at the point at which the valves and piston are in the closest proximity. *This is not necessarily at t.d.c. but may be a few degrees to either side*, depending entirely upon the cam contour and timing in relation to the piston movement. The danger points can be determined by temporarily setting up the head with light springs on the valves and checking the amount of clearance under each head at 1° intervals of crank rotation, measured by a degree-plate on the mainshaft, and with both valves correctly timed.

Another method is to fill the pockets of an old piston with deep recesses with plasticine and rotate the engine so that the valves form impressions in the soft material. These will be the minimum depths, but thermal expansion of the piston, any rocking of this component in the barrel

135

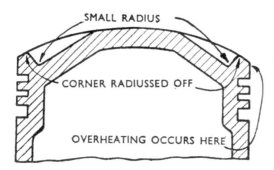

SMALL RADIUS

CORNER RADIUSSED OFF

OVERHEATING OCCURS HERE

*Recesses in the piston crown should be radiused off. If they are too deep the top ring land will tend to overheat.*

and take-up of bearing clearances, all tend to reduce the measured clearances, and the actual pockets should be cut 30 to 40 thou. deeper.

Owing to the greater possibility of whip or spring in push-rod mechanisms, particularly if the rockers are not too well supported, a little more clearance is desirable in o.h.v. units, even for road racing work where the rev. counter can be kept under observation. In other varieties of racing, particularly scrambles or sprint events where, in the heat of battle, engines are liable to be grossly over-revved, it is best to play safe and to cut the pockets sufficiently deep to clear both valves at their full lift.

Failing the use of a milling machine, the common method of deepening the pockets is to file cutting-teeth on the heads of an old pair of valves and, after bolting the cylinder head on with the piston locked at t.d.c., to rotate those valves with the aid of a tap-wrench or similar tool clamped on the stems. This scheme has the merit that the actual clearance can be measured as the work proceeds ; but, of course, the radius of the pocket thus formed is exactly equal to the valve head. It is obvious that in running conditions the rim of the valve head will almost certainly scrape the pocket sides, therefore it will be necessary either to use valves (or, better still, a proper cutter, which can easily be made from a piece of hardened tool-steel) about $\frac{1}{16}$ in. larger in diameter than the real valves, or else to remove the necessary amount of metal by scraping, a laborious and not very easy job to do nicely.

If you are intending to experiment with compression ratios and have provided for one or two packing plates beneath the cylinder, it is advisable to arrange the valve clearances to suit the highest obtainable ratio.

As a final touch the edges of the pockets should be rounded off and the piston crown polished, preferably on a power-driven cloth mop with Tripoli compound; small mops or " bobs " which can be fitted in a drill-chuck, or to a

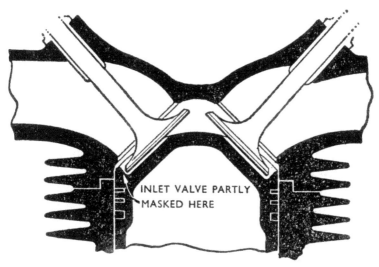

INLET VALVE PARTLY MASKED HERE

*Unduly deep recesses tend to decrease the effective area of the inlet valve.*

flexible shaft as used for port-grinding, can be purchased for a shilling or two, and this form of polishing gives a surface superior to anything which can be obtained by hand with the aid of metal-polish.

The value of crown polishing, like that of port polishing, is a debatable point, as some engines do not give of their best until a perceptible film of carbon has formed. The sequence of events is actually this: a bright, highly-polished surface absorbs less heat than a dull black one, and as less heat is extracted by it from the burning mixture, more is available for conversion into mechanical work. This is the state of affairs when the engine is first run, but shortly after, if using fuel other than alcohol, a film of carbon forms which greatly increases heat absorption, thereby reducing power and increasing the piston temperature. Carbon, however, is a very bad conductor of heat; therefore, as the thickness increases the heat able to pass through the deposit to the metallic surface becomes less, and so the power returns almost to its former figure.

If using alcohol a polished crown will remain bright for a long time, and, whatever the fuel used, is much easier to decarbonize. Generally speaking, a high degree of polish is preferable.

When an extremely high dome is used in an endeavour to obtain a very high compression ratio, there is a danger that the plug will be badly masked. The close proximity of the crown to the plug points blocks the rapid spreading of the flame-front which is vital to good power production at high speed, and this masking may commence quite a long way before t.d.c. measured in crankshaft degrees, particularly if the shape of the head approximates a hemisphere rather than being flat. The result will be that engine power will fall off badly at high r.p.m. unless the ignition is advanced an excessive amount, and even this expedient is no real cure as it is merely trying to eliminate one error by putting in another.

Sectioning a wax cast of the combustion space as recommended in Chapter IV will clearly show the true state of affairs which can be improved by forming a local depression in the crown near the plug, or even making the whole crown unsymmetrical. In any event, it is better to use a lower compression and obtain good combustion than to aim only at maximum compression ratio.

### Cylinder-head Joints

Next, attention can be given to the head joint, which can be made gas-tight in a variety of ways. The " double-ground " variety in which simultaneous contact is made between two areas (but at different pressures) is widely used, and is particularly good if the head is not very robust and therefore liable to be distorted by the tension of the head-bolts.

This design takes the form of a recess in the head which fits over a spigot on the barrel, recess and spigot being of substantially equal depths. To form a gas-tight joint the two components are ground together, with *fine* grinding paste between the spigot faces and *coarse* paste between the broad outer faces through which the bolts pass. The result of this method is to leave a minute gap between the broad faces when the spigot faces are in actual contact; thus when the bolts are tightened heavy pressure is applied to the latter to form the gas-seal, but distortion is prevented by the broad faces coming into contact.

During grinding the coarse paste should be continuously renewed, but as the spigot faces approach perfection the fine paste can be gradually reduced in quantity by wiping the barrel spigot clean and adding a drop or two of oil, after which attention the process is continued until the spigot and its recess acquire a bright, smooth finish over their entire area. The broad faces will have (when the coarse paste is cleaned off) a matt surface which ought to be continuous, although one or two small patches of indifferent contact will not be seriously detrimental.

In the final assembly no jointing compound is necessary — in fact, it is undesirable. Besides being gas-tight, this type of joint permits a good flow of heat from the underside of the exhaust valve seat to the barrel, and so assists in keeping this region of the cylinder head cool. On the other hand, feeding heat back locally into the barrel is not good practice, since it is liable to cause distortion therein.

This snag is avoided in some of the later designs (employing aluminium heads with thick basic sections and particularly effective finning) by permitting the two components to be in contact only over a small area, preferably at the top of the barrel register, since this method eliminates the small annular gap which would be present if contact took place on the outer faces.

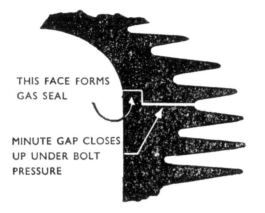

THIS FACE FORMS
GAS SEAL

MINUTE GAP CLOSES
UP UNDER BOLT
PRESSURE

*The principle of the "double-ground" head joint, to be found in several successful racing designs.*

For this type of joint laminated copper gaskets are excellent, but they should always be annealed every time they are fitted. Annealing of copper is done in precisely the reverse way to steel—i.e., the gasket is supported on a flat metal surface, heated to redness, and then dropped, *edge-on*, into cold water, from which it emerges in a dead-soft condition.

In cases where long bolts extending from head to crank-case are used, and particularly if the head and barrel are of light alloy, the bolt tension with the engine hot is considerably greater than when cold, possibly to such an extent that unsuspected distortion may take place, or the bolts may actually yield and become permanently elongated. These conditions should be suspected (a) if the engine does not hold its compression as well when hot as when cold; (b) if the head-bolts frequently have to be re-tightened.

If the engine on which you are working is known to possess these faults, it may be as well to make up a new set of bolts in high-expansion austenitic steel such as K.E. 965 or Jessop's G2—which conform to Specification D.T.D. 49B—or the " 18/8 " grade of stainless steel to Specification D.T.D. 176A.

Each of these steels has a tensile strength of 37 tons or more, but all are a little difficult to machine due to their work-hardening propensity. A tip to remember when working on them is to use keen-edged tools with 8° to

140

10° top rake, a slow cutting speed and a comparatively heavy feed. On no account must the tool be allowed to rub or skid on the work; if this happens the surface will immediately become hard and impossible to cut unless the tool is run back and then dug in under the skin.

The coefficient of expansion of the steels mentioned is .000017 in. per in. per deg. C., but there is another type — the Firth-Brown product called N.M.C.—which has a coefficient of .000022 in. per in. per deg. C., nearly equal to that of many aluminium alloys.

Owing to space limitations the head studs on KTT Velocettes are only $\frac{5}{16}$ in. in diameter and, being tucked away under the rocker boxes, necessitate a special short-headed T-spanner, which must be handled with care to avoid overstressing the studs, which if replaced must be of high-tensile steel. Early-pattern Vincent engines are fitted with large hollow bolts, through which pass the smaller bolts that carry the frame stresses. The large bolts have large nuts but must not be tightened to more than 30 pounds-feet torque, otherwise they may break when the cylinder expands; the later-pattern solid bolts are not subjected to this restriction.

In some engines it is necessary to fit the head before assembling the rocker gear, but in others it is more convenient to reverse the procedure. In view of work described in Chapter XI, dealing with valve mechanism as a separate subject, let us suppose your engine to be in the first category and that it is, therefore, now ready to have the barrel and head bolted on.

The procedure is quite straightforward. First, just make sure that the gudgeon circlips are all in place, then, with clean fingers, smear the rings and skirt of the piston with oil of the same grade you intend to use for racing, making sure that the ring grooves are full, for this will provide a store of oil to cover the starting-up period. Smear the whole surface of the barrel likewise, then slip it over the piston, easing the rings into place with their gaps staggered round the circumference; do not omit the base gasket or packing washers if any are to be used.

On some engines it is not easy to handle the rings as they enter the barrel, due perhaps to the presence of a forest of studs, and none of the conventional ring compressors are much use either. The simplest and handiest tool is a strip of thin sheet metal, about $1\frac{1}{2}$ in. wide, bent to the circumference of the piston and pulled up with a small bolt through the ends. The top-edge is lightly crimped with pliers to prevent jamming in the chamfer of the barrel, and after the piston has entered half-way, the strip can be pulled off simply by removing the bolt. All piston rings, and slotted oil rings in particular, are fragile, but as one cannot tell whether they are broken or not once the barrel has gone on, the operation cannot be carried out too carefully. Afterwards rotate the engine a few times to spread the oil evenly and wipe excess from the piston crown.

Next, after making sure the contacting faces of head and barrel are clean, bolt the head down by carefully tightening each bolt a fraction of a turn in rotation in order to obtain an equal amount of tension on each.

Finally, check your compression ratio exactly and enter it up, together with any relevant details such as type of piston, number of packing plates and so forth, in your notebook, and one more stage will have been completed.

CHAPTER XI

# LIGHTENING THE VALVE MECHANISM

IRRESPECTIVE of any air of finality about the reassembly work comprising the last part of Chapter X, if cams giving a modified timing are to be used it may pay to make a trial assembly with only a single spring on each valve, or to put in only one rocker at a time when checking the opening and closing points. Otherwise it may be difficult to measure the top overlap with exactitude, because near t.d.c. the exhaust valve, as it closes, tries to turn the camshaft forwards, thus taking up all the backlash in the drive in the wrong direction.

The best sequence of operations for any particular engine depends entirely upon the design, but in any case the points to watch closely in connection with the rocker gear are similar. In addition to operating correctly in relation to the valve stems, all the moving components must be as friction free as possible and all sources of lost motion, such as flexure in the rockers or rocker supports, must be eliminated.

Friction in valve gear comes into a different category from that of friction in the rest of the engine. The latter, while being very undesirable, simply subtracts from the amount of power the engine is potentially capable of developing at any speed. The former, even though seemingly insignificant in amount, can have the much more serious effect of limiting the maximum revs. by lowering the speed at which the valve gear can be returned from full lift by the springs, which have to overcome any friction present *before* they commence to close the valves.

At low speeds the inertia of the valve gear is small, and there is plenty of excess spring-force available to overcome friction, but as the speed rises towards the peak the excess of spring-force over inertia becomes progressively less. The

**143**

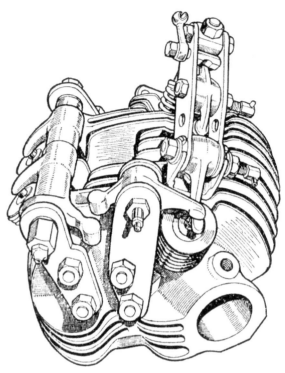

*Wear may be occasioned by cross-loading on the rocker mechanism of semi-radial-valved Rudge and Python engines.*

ill-effect of friction thus becomes proportionately greater and either or both valves cease to follow the cams on the closing side at a much lower speed than one would think without giving the matter some consideration.

Rockers and cam-followers must, therefore, be absolutely free on their pins and have enough end-float to ensure that they cannot possibly bind at running temperature. Occasionally spring washers are fitted to take up end-play and eliminate a possible source of rattle, but for racing it is better to replace these by distance pieces of the appropriate thickness. Felt washers are sometimes used to retain oil, and these can be an unsuspected cause of binding if they are too thick or made of insufficiently resilient material.

Radial-valve Rudge and Python engines have an unusual form of rocker layout which puts a certain amount of cross-loading on the bearings of those rockers which act at right-angles to each other. After a while wear occurs on the sides of the central bosses and the hardened washers against

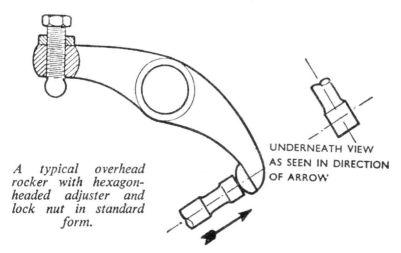

UNDERNEATH VIEW AS SEEN IN DIRECTION OF ARROW

*A typical overhead rocker with hexagon-headed adjuster and lock nut in standard form.*

which they bear. In addition to causing noise, this wear diminishes the valve-lift and should be taken up by renewing the washers and shortening the hardened central roller-race until the side clearance is reduced to .001–.003 in. The length of the needle rollers must also be reduced if necessary so that there is no chance of their being nipped endways when the rocker pins are fully tightened.

Lightness is a very desirable quality in valve gear, but it is fatal to achieve it at the expense of rigidity. Where the latter is lacking at high speeds, when the loads are heaviest,

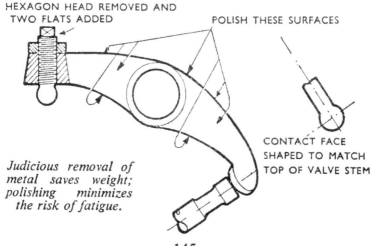

HEXAGON HEAD REMOVED AND TWO FLATS ADDED

POLISH THESE SURFACES

CONTACT FACE SHAPED TO MATCH TOP OF VALVE STEM

*Judicious removal of metal saves weight; polishing minimizes the risk of fatigue.*

145

the motion of the valves will be quite different from the theoretical figures; in fact, the rockers in some racing engines are actually made heavier than those in their touring counterparts to ensure maintenance of power at high r.p.m. In this connection one of the main advantages of the double o.h. camshaft layout is the elimination of places between cams and valves where flexure or lost motion might occur.

Broadly speaking, the arms of a rocker are subjected to bending loads which are heaviest close to the point of support and fade out to zero at the points of contact at each extremity. The central part of the Z-shaped rocker usually fitted to push-rod engines is subjected mainly to torsion or twisting of constant value from end to end.

The only safe places to remove metal are those at which stress is clearly low or non-existent, paying most attention to the ends of the arms, since these portions move at the highest speeds. It is often possible to grind a sizeable amount off the faces which contact the valves, or to reduce the weight of the screwed adjusters sometimes fitted. Although reducing the section of the arms is *not* to be recommended, it is a good plan to polish the whole rocker in order to minimize the chance of fatigue cracking.

Flexure may occur in the rocker mounting unless this is bolted very firmly to the head. Anyone tuning one of the older engines with the rockers held between sideplates should verify that the attachment bolts are a really good fit

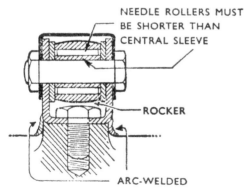

NEEDLE ROLLERS MUST BE SHORTER THAN CENTRAL SLEEVE

ROCKER

ARC-WELDED

*The U-shaped rocker-brackets of Rudge and Python radial-valve gear can seldom be kept tight with the standard bolt. An effective cure is to weld them to the head.*

in the mating holes. Some editions of the Python engine were poor in this respect, the cross-rockers being held in a steel pressing attached to the head by rather inaccessible set-screws which were both difficult to tighten and inclined to work loose. The sovereign remedy is to have the pressings electrically arc-welded to the head, this process being preferable to acetylene welding because of the absence of distortion risks.

Push rods are normally made either from Duralumin or high-tensile steel tube. It is important to check that they are absolutely straight (by rolling them along a surface plate) and also that they have not been badly bent and re-straightened, because a rod which has been so treated is always liable to go again. If spares are not obtainable, light-alloy tube to specification 4 T 4 is the correct grade, the usual size being $\frac{3}{8}$-in. diameter by 16 S.W.G. This is a handy gauge because the bore is slightly under $\frac{1}{4}$ in. and can just be reamed out to that size to take the end-fittings. Whether these are fitted internally or externally, they must be tight, otherwise the ends of the tube will hammer away quite rapidly. If the tube is steel instead of light alloy the end-fittings should be securely sweated in place with tin-man's solder, completely penetrating the whole joint.

In some designs the push rods are of considerable length, and it may pay to experiment with tubes of larger diameter or heavier gauge; unsuspected buckling may take place at high speeds, and this will have the same bad effect as flexure in the rockers.

Tappets or push-rods are occasionally on the heavy side, due to the presence of adjusters. If you are well acquainted with the engine's habits when cold and hot with regard to correct valve clearances, something is to be gained by making up a set of non-adjustable components, finally setting the clearances either by adjustments to the push-rod length or by using hardened caps of the appropriate thickness fitted to the ends of the valve stems. These components are very often fitted as standard to minimize stem wear, but for making them up individually K.E. 805 steel hardened in oil at 830° C. and tempered by quenching in oil from 550° C. cannot be bettered.

The top cups on Velocette Venom and Viper pushrods are a sliding fit in steel sleeves, clearance being measured by feeler-gauging the gap between the components. A slight saving in weight can be gained by keeping the original pair for checking and making up a new pair with fixed cups, without the sleeve, for running. The scheme is very easy to apply to side-valve engines with their flat-topped tappets; the method is to use the existing adjustable pair, set to the correct length, as gauges from which to obtain exactly the length of the non-adjustable pair, which can be made up out of silver steel, hardened on the ends by quenching in water from a bright red heat.

Sometimes shims of the correct thickness for placing under the valve stem cap are not available when making adjustments to o.h. camshaft engines which employ this system. Satisfactory substitutes can, however, be made by cutting discs from a set of feeler gauges, this material being sufficiently hard to withstand the rigorous duty entailed.

### Camshaft Drives

Even in o.h. camshaft engines, motion can be lost in the valve gear unless all is as it should be. If bevels are used they must be in correct mesh, which means the minimum of backlash consistent with absence of whine. Fortunately, neither these gears nor their bearings wear very rapidly, but if the adjustment is faulty it may not be possible to rectify it by moving only one of a mating pair of gears. As an approximate guide, the inner ends of the teeth on each pair of gears should be just level with each other as they pass through the point of intersection.

If this is not the case, one or both gears must be moved in the appropriate direction, either by adding shims or skimming a small amount off the face of the vertical shaft bush housing, or the bush itself. Since the camshaft, and hence its crown wheel, is usually located by a ballrace some distance

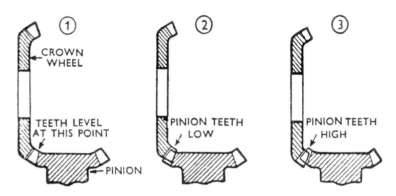

(*1*) *Pinion and crown wheel in perfect mesh, with slight backlash.*
(*2*) *If excessive backlash, raise pinion. If no backlash, move crown wheel to left.* (*3*) *If too much backlash, move crown wheel to right. If no backlash, lower pinion.*

from the gears, thermal expansion has the effect of increasing the backlash by a small amount, and it will often be found that a slight whine, noticeable when the engine is cold, will cease as running temperature is attained.

Another point to notice is the fit of the tongues of the Oldham couplings in the bevel-shaft slots; they should be just free enough to slide, but have no trace of clearance sideways. If any shake has developed, new couplings are required, or, alternatively, the originals can be built up with hard nickel plating or chromium plating.

Conversely, a small amount of end-clearance must be present in the vertical shaft assembly. If this is not provided, severe thrust load will be applied to the bevel shafts when the head is bolted down, and this point must be closely watched if the barrel has been shortened appreciably. If no clearance exists it is possible to gain a little by grinding a small amount off the ends of the bevel shafts and vertical shaft. This process, however, must not be overdone or the area of contact of the coupling tongues will be seriously reduced. If at a future date the barrel is packed up again on compression plates, it will be necessary to obtain either a longer shaft or some couplings with thicker centres, otherwise the uppermost tongue will not run fully in engagement

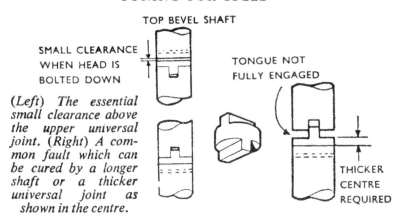

TOP BEVEL SHAFT

SMALL CLEARANCE
WHEN HEAD IS
BOLTED DOWN

TONGUE NOT
FULLY ENGAGED

THICKER
CENTRE
REQUIRED

*(Left) The essential small clearance above the upper universal joint. (Right) A common fault which can be cured by a longer shaft or a thicker universal joint as shown in the centre.*

with the top bevel-slot. This condition is likely to lead to failure as the metal in the tongue will be subjected to a destructive combination of shear and bending loads instead of pure shear as intended by the designer.

There is a small opportunity for saving weight in the vertical tube and its retaining ring-nuts by making these in light alloy, using Duralumin or R.R. 56 for the tube and any reasonably strong alloy, such as L 1 or D.T.D. 423, for the nuts and possibly the bevel-shaft housings.

### Attention to Cam Followers

Coming back to push-rod and s.v. motors, freeness of the cam followers is important. The procedure with lever followers is similar to that for the overhead rockers; in addition, if any of the rocker bearings or pins show patches which are unduly rubbed or worn, indicating lack of lubrication, an additional oil hole or a nick ground into the end face of the bush may improve matters.

A little weight may be saved by judicious reduction here and there, but it is a mistake to remove too much from the region of the follower-foot, as this may lead to local overheating with consequent softening and rapid wear. Depending on the shape of the cam and the foot, there is a certain minimum area over which rubbing contact takes place, and it is an advantage for the foot to be appreciably longer than

150

this, as the excess portion acts as a lead-in for oil and thus improves lubrication at a vital spot.

Followers which are only slightly worn can be reshaped to their original curvature by hand with an oil-stone, but if wear to a depth greater than .030 in. is present, there is very little of the original hard case left and new rockers are required — unless the originals can be re-casehardened and ground, a process which some service departments are willing to carry out.

If it is desired to embark on the project of making a new set of followers, $3\frac{1}{2}\%$ case-hardening nickel steel is an excellent material; the hardening should be .045 in. to .055 in. deep on the contact faces, but the remainder of the surface should be kept soft by copper-plating before hardening. An even better job can be made by using $5\%$ air-hardening steel to Specification S 28 with a coating of "Stellite" welded to the contact faces.

Following the application of the "Stellite" the component is heat-treated by cooling in air from 830° C., after which the faces are finally ground to shape. Welded " Stellite " is not very hard but will withstand very arduous treatment without appreciable wear as, unlike case-hardened steel, it does not soften under the influence of heat. " Stellited " faces must be finished by polishing to a dead-smooth surface, otherwise the cams will suffer undue wear.

### Points to Bear in Mind

When reconditioning or making new followers (or o.h. camshaft rockers) with curved feet two things must be borne in mind. One is that the radius of curvature does *not* alter the timing at all, but that it *does* affect the rate of acceleration; in other words, if you substitute a radius of $\frac{1}{2}$ in. for one of $\frac{3}{8}$ in. the opening and closing points measured in degrees will remain the same, but the initial acceleration will be greater with the larger radius. The second point is that the distance between the rocker pin centre and the line of contact with the cam *does* affect the timing. A difference in length of .004 in. makes one degree difference with a cam base circle of 1 in. diameter; obviously, therefore, the presence of a flat due to wear at this point will lengthen the period of opening in proportion to its width. This matter will be gone into in greater detail later, when valve timing comes up for discussion.

## Varying Types of Follower

A few designs employ lever followers with flat feet and with these the rate of wear is usually lower owing to the greater area over which the rubbing action is spread. Eventually grooves will appear near the middle of the faces but except in extreme cases the parts can be reconditioned simply by smoothing on a flat oil-stone, taking care that the faces are maintained parallel with the rocker-pin holes.

The only other common variety of lever follower is fitted with a roller in place of a solid foot, and as the bearing in the roller is necessarily very small, heavily loaded and not too well lubricated, wear develops after a period. Replacing the pins usually effects a cure, but while the parts are dismantled it is advisable to check the roller holes for ovality. If they are out of round they can be lapped out with a mild steel bar and emery paste, after which oversize pins will be required of a size giving .002-in. clearance in the lapped-out holes.

The holes in the follower itself must be enlarged to a light drive fit on the new pins, which can be made from silver steel hardened and tempered to a straw colour in the centre but blued at the ends to enable them to be riveted over after assembly. Some racing J.A.P. engines employed rollers running on needle-roller bearings which were quite an improvement over the plain variety.

If some serious defect, such as extensive flats or pitting of the circumference of the rollers, is in evidence it is best to replace them. If spares are unobtainable the 1% carbon–1% chrome steel known as ballrace steel (Spec. EN 31) is about

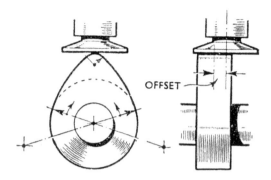

*Wear is minimized by offsetting this direct-contact tappet in relation to the cam, thereby imparting a rotary motion to the rubbing surface.*

the best material from which to make new ones; heat-treat by quenching in oil after heating to 820° C. for one hour, then temper at 200° C. for half an hour and allow to cool in air.

"Direct attack" tappets bearing on the cams without the intervention of followers are used in many s.v. and a few o.h.v. designs. They are usually of the mushroom type offset from the cams a little so that a slow rotation is continually taking place, this distributing wear over the entire surface of the head, which in consequence remains flat almost indefinitely. Non-rotatable patterns wear, of course, in just the same way as lever followers, and require the same reconditioning treatment.

Working loads on the stems and tappet guides are heaviest at the ends and become zero in the central portion; thus a small reduction of weight can be effected by heavily relieving the tappet in that region. Another scheme, applicable only to non-rotating tappets, is to grind two flats on the central portion leaving a rectangular section to take the load. It is worth noting that on most valve-gear one ounce of weight creates an inertia force of thirty pounds or more at top speed, so there is much to be gained by reductions which seem trifling in themselves.

The exhaust lifter is not required for racing. In the case of standard A.J.S. and Matchless the control lever in the timing case can be disposed of, and after extracting the guide and tappet from the crankcase, the valve-lifter collar can be removed through the slot cut in the side of the guide; a small point, but one which illustrates further how the odd fraction of an ounce of unwanted weight can be saved.

In any case, it is wise to verify that the exhaust lifter is not holding the follower off the base-circle or fouling the cam nose if any change on cam form or type is made. As an instance " Lightning " cams when fitted to a Vincent " Rapide " or " Shadow ", foul the exhaust lifter levers : the latter must therefore be filed away to clear the cam-nose, though it is probably better for most racing to remove the entire lifter mechanism and block up the hole through which the lifter rod passes with a $\frac{1}{4}$ in. B.S.P. plug, the same as that used in the crankcase drain hole.

Frequently, there is not overmuch clearance between the pushrod end of the rocker and the inside of the rocker housing or cover. If cams giving a higher lift are installed, it is essential to check that no fouling occurs here at full lift, otherwise the pushrods will be bent or the cams and followers seriously damaged.

# CHAPTER XII

## ADJUSTMENTS TO VALVE GEAR

THIS and the next chapter are closely related and may well be studied in a single reading. The aim is first to deal with standard valve settings and, in Chapter XIII, to indicate adjustments which may result in improved performance.

Newcomers to speed work would be well advised to stick to the maker's timing for a start, and it is also a wise plan for more experienced riders to follow the same course if major modifications have been made elsewhere to the engine. As a general rule, it is a bad policy in experimental work to alter more than one thing at a time, otherwise it is difficult to assess the value of any single modification.

Engines usually have their timing gears clearly marked by dots on the mating teeth or lines inscribed on the rims of the gears. When taking notes on the engine before commencing the initial dismantling, a diagram of these marks should have been included, together with any information relating to the position of the small timing pinion on the mainshaft, since it is a common practice to use a number of keyways, any one of which may be selected, in order to provide a fine variation of timing at this point. If this is the case, it is usual to mark the " standard " keyway in some manner, though this may not be visible when the pinion nut is in place.

By no means do all engines employ a keyed-on pinion. In Rudge and Python power-units, for example, the pinion fits on a plain taper, and thus can be set readily in any position desired.

Marks or no marks, before finally fitting the timing cover it is best to play safe and to check the setting with a timing disc and pointer set to zero with the piston at top centre. It is not too easy to detect exactly where this occurs to within a degree or two just by feeling the movement of the piston

155

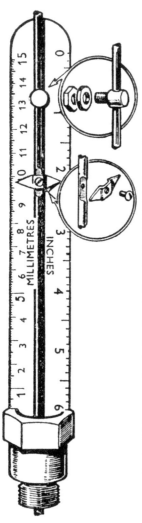

*An excellent timing stick for engines fitted with a central plug can be made up from an old plug body, a steel rule marked in inches or millimetres, a piece of rod, a bicycle brake draw bolt and a simple pointer.*

crown through the plug hole, but it can be determined quite accurately by means of a depth gauge of such a length that it contacts the crown a few degrees—the precise number is immaterial—before top centre. If the pointer is correctly set to zero, the readings at which the crown touches the gauge on the upstroke or downstroke on each side of top centre will be equal, except in the unlikely event of the cylinder being "offset" or "desaxé". Another method is to apply a film of thick soap solution over the plug-hole, or better still over a small hole in a dummy plug body; the point at which the film balloons out to its maximum extent as the piston is rocked over centre will clearly be t.d.c.

With this important matter settled, the timing can be determined and compared with the maker's figures, if this knowledge is available, not forgetting that many makers specify valve clearances for checking which are wider than those at which the tappets are eventually set for running. This is done because with some cam contours the rate of lift over the first few degrees is so gradual that it is very difficult to determine the precise instant at which the valves open or close. As was pointed out in Chapter I, this must be borne in mind when making comparisons between the timing diagrams of various makes. Nortons reverse this practice and specify closer clearances for setting than for running, giving the appearance of greatly increased overlap compared to some other makes. On the short-stroke editions from 1956 onwards, the timing is not quoted in degrees, but in the amounts by which each valve is lifted at t.d.c. and b.d.c.

When the inlet and exhaust cams are separate so that the overlap can be varied either on purpose or accidentally, care must be taken to see that the valve-heads clear each other at part-lift. If the timing is altered from standard, or oversized valves fitted, one valve may quite possibly foul the other, and at least 40 thou. clearance should be present at the closest point to avoid this happening at speed. Except on overhead camshaft models this point is difficult to check and is often overlooked in consequence.

Whatever clearances are used, it is very rarely that the figures obtained will agree *absolutely* with those quoted by the maker, so that a little common sense has to be used to obtain the closest approximation. Generally speaking, the least important point is the exhaust valve opening, and the most important is the relationship between inlet opening and exhaust closing with reference to t.d.c. Sometimes it may be found that the timing is several degrees out on one or more points at the specified clearance but the error is reduced if the clearances are set a trifle wider; whilst not being a hard-and-fast rule, this at least gives an indication that the error is not so serious as it appeared and may even be disregarded. It is often difficult to get an equal timing diagram for both cylinders of a twin unless some allowances of this nature are made, particularly if some wear has taken place in the cams or cam followers. It is as well, while the timing disc is fitted, to obtain some more figures for future reference, and as an aid to getting a clearer picture of the valve-lift diagram, without which any subsequent experimenting will be simply like taking leaps in the dark.

The more obvious additional things to measure are the amount each valve is open at top and bottom dead centres; the actual amount of lift (which is not necessarily the same

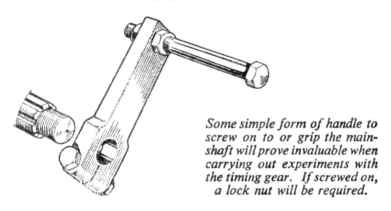

*Some simple form of handle to screw on to or grip the main-shaft will prove invaluable when carrying out experiments with the timing gear. If screwed on, a lock nut will be required.*

as the height of the cam on account of leverage-ratios which may exist in the rocker gear); the crankshaft angles at which the valves reach full lift, and the dwell at full lift, if any is present—" dwell " representing the number of degrees of movement during which the valve is on full lift.

The best way to measure lifts is by means of a dial-gauge rigged up in contact with the valve-spring collar. With this simple apparatus a really painstaking individual can draw a complete lift-curve for both valves by taking readings at intervals of, say, two or five degrees. These results are plotted on squared paper as vertical measurements, crankshaft degrees being measured horizontally. The graph so obtained can be made to give quite a lot of information, as will be shown later on.

There has been such an enormous number of engines manufactured in various types and editions that it is not possible to quote all their timing figures, even if they were available, but on pages 163–165 is a list of quite a few, not all of which are modern. Included are a number of figures for both sports and racing engines of the same make, the object being to show how the timings vary according to the type of performance required.

The checking and running clearances are also given—it being understood that " running " means " as set for running " with the engine *cold*, although at operating temperatures the clearances will probably be very different. As a general rule when hot, the clearances of both valves in push-rod engines tend to widen, though more on the inlet than the exhaust. On camshaft engines both clearances close up, though more on the exhaust than the inlet, and in side-valve engines the inlet widens, whereas the exhaust closes up — the latter point in particular must be watched carefully if a K.E.965 valve has been fitted in place of one of silchrome or some other steel with a much lower expansion coefficient.

It is best when measuring valve lifts, to set the clearances to zero; the readings will then indicate whether the cams are ground with quietening ramps or not. The actual timing can then be shown by drawing lines on the graph parallel to the base-line at heights equivalent to the running clearances.

Each valve should be measured separately, with the other one rendered inoperative by leaving out its pushrod or rocker so that the backlash in the drive is not taken up in the reverse direction by the cam not under consideration.

The rockers on Matchless/A.J.S. twins and KSS/KTT Velocette units with fully enclosed valves are mounted on eccentric spindles, as a means of adjusting the clearances, and either rocker can be removed, even if the valves are fully assembled, simply by unscrewing its spindle, the rocker in the process partially lifting the valve at each revolution. When finally setting the clearances, care must be taken to see that the plane of eccentricity lies in the right direction, otherwise the timing will be badly out and the rockers will not contact the valves properly. Arrows are stamped on the

*A dial gauge, contacting with the valve-spring and cap, read in conjunction with the timing disc, will enable the tuner to prepare an accurate valve-opening diagram.*

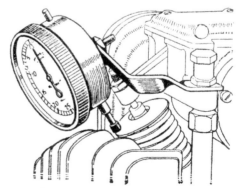

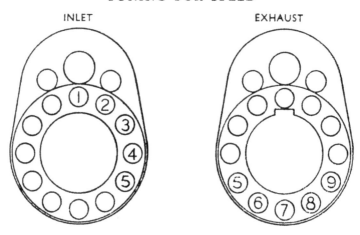

*By a series of hole-and-peg locations, Norton "Manx" cams can have vernier setting in five different positions.*

rocker spindle ends to indicate their correct positions, but any doubts can be settled by checking that the rocker-ends contact the valve stems centrally; if not, the error will be quite noticeable and can be cured by moving the pins half a turn in either direction.

A glance at the timing data shows that there is fairly close agreement between the timings used by various makers for fast main-road work or for racing, and an engine which does not figure in the list is bound to perform reasonably well if timed in a similar fashion. A closer study shows that, on the whole, not only is the overlap on engines intended for use with a silencer much less than on those made mainly or wholly for racing, but it is also split up differently.

In the latter case, the crank angle at which the inlet valve opens before t.d.c. is usually several degrees greater than the angle at which the exhaust valve closes, whereas in sports engines the angles are more nearly equal; indeed, in some cases the inlet angle is a few degrees less than the exhaust. The reason for this is that better low-speed performance and fuel economy are thereby obtained, and, of course, in standard production machines these aspects, although perhaps not so important as flat-out performance, have to be given a fair degree of attention.

160

Engines with "short" timings will respond to some extent to the fitting of an open exhaust system and an inlet pipe of the correct length, but they cannot be expected to perform as well as those with racing timings in conjunction with the correct pipe lengths. Conversely, if maximum performance with a road silencer fitted be the aim, there is nothing to be gained—in fact, a good deal may be lost in speed, economy and acceleration from low speeds—by attempting to utilize cams of the T.T. variety. If it were

*How to convert degrees to linear measurement. First describe a circle the diameter of which equals the length of piston stroke. With a compass set to the length of the connecting rod between centres, strike arcs on the vertical line from top and bottom points on the circle. Next strike arcs from valve opening and closing points and measure distances between these arcs and top and bottom-centre arcs respectively.*

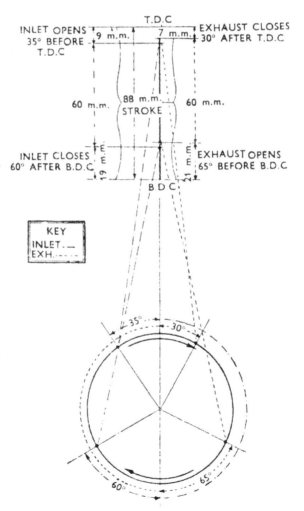

otherwise, manufacturers would not go to the trouble of developing different cams for various types of engine.

In road-racing, engine speeds can almost always be kept high by proper use of a multi-speed gear-box; good torque at low speeds is not essential though it is very desirable on short circuits where time lost in gear-changing may become too high a proportion of the actual running time. In scrambles and trials in which a speed test is incorporated, conditions are very different because one needs an engine which is fast but can put up with large variations of speed because of the fairly wide ratio gear-boxes which have to be used. On speedways it is also essential to have an engine with good pulling power from 3,000 r.p.m. upwards, and for all this sort of work overlaps are not generally greater than 80°, and may be much less for competition models where flexibility is as important as sheer power.

Engines with separate inlet and exhaust cams, as for instance the Triumph twin and the double o.h.c. Norton, lend themselves well to variations in the respective cam settings. In fact the Norton is specifically made so that the inlet cam can be set to the best position for the exhaust system in use by means of a vernier device; as shown in the table, the inlet cam is set to open 10° earlier (and close earlier by the same amount) when a megaphone is fitted than it is with a straight-through pipe.

Actually, the timing figures given do not convey any real information as to the efficacy of the opening diagram—which varies, of course, with the valve lift and the steepness of the cam contours—but assuming a reasonable degree of similarity in the height of lift in relation to the capacity of the cylinder between various designs, they *do* indicate the lines along which to proceed in the search for speed.

It is frequently possible to utilize cams from one type of engine in another type of power unit from the same stable and thus obtain either a longer timing or higher lifts, or both. As an example, the "45°, 65°, 70°, 35°" cams used in the 350 c.c. and upwards racing J.A.P.s can be fitted to the 250 c.c. model. Again, some of the push-rod,

162    [continued on page 166]

## SPECIMEN VALVE SETTINGS WITH COMPLEMENTARY DATA

| MAKE | MODEL | INLET | | EXHAUST | | CLEARANCES | | | | IGNITION ADVANCE |
|---|---|---|---|---|---|---|---|---|---|---|
| | | | | | | CHECKING | | RUNNING | | |
| | | OPENS | CLOSES | OPENS | CLOSES | IN. | EX. | IN. | EX. | |
| A.J.S. | 1930 Camshaft | 40 | 63 | 70 | 35 | — | — | .014 | .022 | 40° |
| | o.h.v., 250, 350 and 500 | 20 | 67 | 78 | 28 | .016 | .016 | nil | nil | 37° |
| | 7R 48-52 | 62 | 71 | 74 | 44 | .005 | .014 | .005 | .014 | 40° |
| | 7R, 1953-54 | 49 | 71 | 70 | 47 | .007 | .012 | .008 | .012 | 38° |
| | 7R 58-62 | 55 | 78 | 78 | 45 | .008 | .012 | .008 | .012 | 34° |
| Ariel | 250, 350 and 500 Red Hunter | 22 | 70 | 70 | 25 | nil | nil | nil | nil | 5/16 in. max. |
| | 250 Model LG | 22 | 70 | 70 | 25 | nil | nil | nil | nil | 5/16 in. max. |
| | 350 Model NG, 500 Model VG | 15 | 55 | 60 | 20 | nil | nil | nil | nil | 5/16 in. max. |
| | 1949 NG, NH, VG, VH | 18 | 68 | 63 | 23 | .010 | .010 | nil | nil | 3/4 in. |
| | Competition | 50 | 65 | 65 | 50 | .010 | .010 | nil | nil | |
| | 650 Twin (Home) | 30 | 70 | 65 | 25 | .010 | .010 | .010 | .010 | 11/32 in. |
| | 650 Twin (Export) | 42 | 62 | 67 | 37 | .010 | .010 | .010 | .010 | 3/8 in. |
| B.S.A. | 500 Empire Star | 35 | 75 | 70 | 40 | .004 | .006 | .004 | .006 | 37½° |
| | 500 Gold Star | 25 | 65 | 65 | 25 | .003 | .003 | .003 | .003 | 37½° |
| | B31, B32, B33, B34 | 25 | 65 | 65 | 25 | .003 | .003 | .003 | .003 | 38½° |
| | B32 Gold Star Touring } International Trials | 43 | 73 | 64 | 34 | .018 | .018 | .008 | .010 | 34½° |
| | Scrambles | 50 | 80 | 70 | 45 | .018 | .018 | .008 | .010 | |
| | Racing, 50-50 fuel | 60 | 85 | 80 | 55 | .018 | .018 | .008 | .010 | |
| | Racing, alcohol | 43 | 73 | 70 | 45 | .018 | .018 | .008 | .010 | |
| | B34 Gold Star | As for B32, Ignition approx 3° earlier | | | | | | | | |
| | A7ST, A10SF | 42 | 62 | 67 | 37 | .010 | .010 | .010 | .010 | 3/8 in. |
| J.A.P. | 175, 250 and 350 s.v. | 15 | 50 | 50 | 20 | .004 | .006 | .004 | .006 | 40° |
| | 500 and 600 Sports s.v. | 16 | 65 | 65 | 25 | .004 | .006 | .004 | .006 | 40° |
| | 1,100 s.v. A/c 60° twin and 1,100 s.v. W/c 60° twin | 16 | 65 | 65 | 25 | .004 | .006 | .004 | .006 | 38° |
| | 1,100 o.v.h. W/c twin 8/45 Std. | 16 | 65 | 67 | 27 | .002 | .002 | .002 | .002 | 38° |
| | 175, 250 o.h.v. Std. and Racing | 27 | 67 | 67 | 27 | .002 | .002 | .002 | .002 | 45° |
| | 1,000 o.h.v. Racing, 1932-34 | 15 | 60 | 63 | 23 | .002 | .002 | .002 | .002 | 45° |

SPECIMEN VALVE SETTINGS WITH COMPLEMENTARY DATA—*continued*

| MAKE | MODEL | INLET | | EXHAUST | | CLEARANCES | | | | IGNITION ADVANCE |
| | | | | | | CHECKING | | RUNNING | | |
| | | OPENS | CLOSES | OPENS | CLOSES | IN. | EX. | IN. | EX. | |
|---|---|---|---|---|---|---|---|---|---|---|
| J.A.P. contd. | 1,000 o.h.v. Racing, 1935–37 | 25 | 66 | 65 | 23 | .002 | .002 | .002 | .002 | 45° |
| | 350, 500, 8/75 o.h.v. Racing | 45 | 65 | 70 | 35 | .002 | .002 | .002 | .002 | 38° |
| | 350, 500, 8/80 Speedway | 45 | 65 | 70 | 35 | .002 | .002 | .002 | .002 | 38° |
| Levis | 350 (high-lift cams) | 25 | 60 | 60 | 25 | — | — | .002 | .002 | 40° |
| | 500 (high-lift cams) | 30 | 78 | 66 | 30 | — | — | .002 | .002 | 35° |
| Matchless | 350 G3L (early) | 20 | 67 | 78 | 28 | .016 | .016 | nil | nil | 7/16 in. |
| | 350 G3L (late) | 32 | 63 | 65 | 30 | .016 | .016 | nil | nil | 7/16 in. |
| | G80 | 32 | 63 | 65 | 30 | .016 | .016 | nil | nil | ⅛ in. |
| | G3CS, G80CS (1959) | 59 | 69 | 69 | 48 | nil | .005 | nil | .005 | 39° |
| | G80R (1959) | 67 | 85 | 83 | 62 | nil | nil | nil | nil | 40° |
| | G9CSR | 24 | 65 | 63 | 25 | .006 | .006 | .006 | .006 | 37° |
| | G12CSR, 600 c.c. twin | 34 | 67 | 67 | 34 | .006 | .006 | .006 | .006 | 37° |
| | G12CSR, 650 c.c. twin | 38 | 78 | 73 | 42 | .012 | .012 | .008 | .006 | 37° |
| | G45, 500 Racing twin | 35 | 68 | 70 | 44 | .004 | .004 | .004 | .008 | 38° |
| | G50, 500 o.h.c. | 55 | 78 | 78 | 45 | .008 | .008 | .012 | .012 | 34° |
| New Imperial | 250 and 350 Grand Prix | 28 | 62 | 60 | 30 | nil | nil | nil | nil | 14 mm. |
| Norton | 350 and 490 International | 47½ | 70 | 85 | 42½ | nil | .004 | .010 | .020 | 42½° |
| | 490 Mod. 18, ES2; 588 Mod. 19 | 25/30 | 43/48 | 60/65 | 25/30 | nil | nil | nil | nil | 42–47° |
| | 30M, 40M, o.h.c. straight pipe | 47½ | 70 | 85 | 42½ | — | — | — | — | — |
| | 30M, 40 M, o.h.c. megaphone | 57½ | 60 | 85 | 42½ | — | — | — | — | — |
| | 30M, 40M, Double o.h.c. long-stroke | 60 | 67½ | 85 | 45 | — | — | .012 | .024 | 36° |
| | 30M Short-stroke, 1954–55 | 74 | 94 | 72 | 64 | .005 | .005 | .014 | .028 | 35° |
| | 40M Short-stroke, 1954–55 | 82 | 95 | 94 | 74 | .005 | .005 | .014 | .028 | 36° |
| | 30M Short-stroke, 1956–58 | 70 | 100 | 82 | 64 | .002 | .002 | .014 | .028 | 36° |
| | 40M Short-stroke, 1956–58 | 74 | 85 | 89 | 70 | .002 | .002 | .014 | .028 | 36° |
| | 30M, 1956–58 } lift at t.d.c. | .278 | .342 | .280 | .180 | .002 | .002 | .014 | .028 | 35° |
| | 40M, 1956–58 } lift at b.d.c. | .280 | .315 | .280 | .160 | .002 | .002 | .014 | .028 | 40° |

SPECIMEN VALVE SETTINGS WITH COMPLEMENTARY DATA—*continued*

| MAKE | MODEL | INLET | | EXHAUST | | CLEARANCES | | | | IGNITION ADVANCE |
| | | | | | | CHECKING | | RUNNING | | |
| | | OPENS | CLOSES | OPENS | CLOSES | IN. | EX. | IN. | EX. | |
|---|---|---|---|---|---|---|---|---|---|---|
| Norton *contd.* | 30M, 1959 | 67 | 98 | 85 | 64 | .005 | .005 | .010 | .028 | 34° |
| | 40M, 1959 | 74 | 97 | 90 | 78 | .005 | .005 | .010 | .028 | 38° |
| | 30M, 1959 } lift at t.d.c. | .330 | .342 | .280 | .260 | .002 | .002 | .010 | .028 | — |
| | 40M, 1959 } lift at b.d.c. | .330 | .310 | .280 | .260 | .002 | .002 | .010 | .028 | — |
| Rudge* | Ulster measured on stroke | 10 mm. | 13 mm. | 16 mm. | 10 mm. | .020 | .020 | nil | .003 | 15 mm. |
| | 350 Replica " " " | 9 mm. | 14.4mm. | 14.4mm. | 9 mm. | .008 | .008 | nil | .003 | 16 mm. |
| | 500 Replica " " " | 9 mm. | 14.4mm. | 14.4mm. | 9 mm. | .010 | .010 | nil | .003 | 18 mm. |
| Sunbeam | Model 90 (Wolverhampton) | 30 | 60 | 60 | 30 | .002 | .012 | .001 | .012 | 44° |
| Triumph | 250 and 350 o.h.v. single | 36 | 70 | 70 | 36 | .001 | .001 | .001 | .001 | 3/16 in. |
| | 500 o.h.v. single | 26½ | 62½ | 75½ | 20½ | .001 | .001 | .001 | .001 | 9/16 in. |
| | Speed Twin and Tiger 100 | 26½ | 69½ | 61 | 35 | .001 | .001 | .001 | .001 | 3/16 in. |
| | Grand Prix, 1948 | 31 | 42 | 47 | 32 | .020 | .020 | .002 | .004 | 37° |
| | T100 (Racing Kit), 1950 | 52 | 70 | 72 | 50 | nil | nil | .002 | .004 | 42° |
| | T100, T110 Racing Kit | 35 | 56 | 56 | 35 | .020 | .020 | .002 | .004 | 42° 39° |
| | Cub Racing Kit | 59 | 81 | 85 | 55 | nil | nil | .002 | .004 | 40° |
| Velocette | KTT., 1931 | 43 | 70 | 68 | 48 | .012 | .012 | .012 | .022 | 42° |
| | KSS. (iron head) | 39 | 69 | 60 | 40 | .012 | .020 | .012 | .020 | 42° |
| | KTT. Mark IV and V | 51 | 57 | 71 | 43 | .020 | .020 | .015 | .025 | 35° |
| | KTT. Mark VI | 55 | 65 | 75 | 45 | .020 | .020 | .015 | .025 | 32° |
| | KSS. (aluminium head) | 34 | 47 | 64 | 29 | .025 | .025 | .012 | .012 | 38° |
| | MOV., MAC. | 50 | 60 | 70 | 40 | .010 | .015 | .003 | .006 | 40° |
| | MSS., early, iron head | 50 | 60 | 70 | 40 | .015 | .020 | .003 | .006 | 40° |
| | MSS., iron head | 30 | 60 | 60 | 30 | .025 | .025 | .005 | .010 | 40° |
| | MSS., Viper, M17/7 cams | 19 | 49 | 49 | 19 | .030 | .030 | .005 | .005 | 38° |
| | Viper, Venom, M17/8 cams | 55 | 65 | 75 | 45 | .030 | .030 | .006 | .006 | 38° |
| Vincent | Rapide, Shadow, Comet | 42 | 68 | 72 | 30 | Valves lifted .005 off seats | | nil | nil | 40° |
| | Lightning, Flash | 56 | 68 | 72 | 50 | | | nil | nil | 38° |

165

Velocette cams are interchangeable, although the helical teeth gears, unique to this make, have been made with two or three different angles of helix and may not, therefore, be interchangeable. However, the camwheels are a press fit on the cams and can therefore be pressed off and changed over; if each pair is marked before being separated by scribing a line radially inwards from the marked tooth, and then refitted with the marks in line, the timing should be correct. Vincent camwheels are also pressed on, but in this instance the holes are parallel and not tapered as in the Velocette. Slight variations in shaft or bore diameters may lead to insufficient tightness if shafts and wheels are interchanged; the interference fit must be *at least* .001 in. requiring 1 to $1\frac{1}{4}$ tons fitting pressure. If less than this the shaft should be nickel or chrome-plated up to the requisite size, otherwise the wheel may move on the shaft when running and damage to the valve gear will result. Rudge cams are yet another example of interchangeability, in this instance for the 500 c.c. and 350 c.c. capacities.

The flexibility and low-speed pulling of side-valve engines is due in large measure to the " slow " timing usually employed, but there is no reason why quite an appreciable amount overlap should not be used. Here, again, it is often possible to substitute the original cams by a pair from a corresponding o.h.v. engine. Many years ago, I remember fitting the cams from a " big-port " A.J.S. into a 350 side-valve of this make with really remarkable results.

Owing to the comparatively poor breathing and lower compression ratio inseparable from any side-valve design, its volumetric efficiency is low at high revs, and it pays to hold the inlet valve open a few degrees longer than on an o.h.v. unit, since it is no use closing this valve until *true* compression actually begins. That does not occur, if the cylinder filling is not too good, until the piston is well up on the compression stroke. This subject of cam design is very complex and will be dwelt upon at greater length in the next chapter.

If the timing has been altered from standard, or there is any reason to doubt the markings, set the engine by means of the degree plate with the crankpin in the position corresponding to the " inlet opening " point. The tappet clearances having previously been set to the amounts specified for use when checking the timing, the cams (or cam, if two separate shafts are used) are rotated until the clearance is just taken up, and the half-time pinion is then fitted to the main shaft in the appropriate position by means which vary according to the detail design. On J.A.P. engines there are five keyways in the pinion and the most favourable position for it is found by trial and error, using each keyway in turn.

A similar scheme is used on Vincent engines, the key in this instance being parallel so that it can be tapped into place after the best position for the pinion has been found. Normally the key is fitted in the keyway marked with a punch-dot.

B.S.A. cams are listed, paired up by part numbers, with the appropriate pinion to give the correct timing, but pinions are also supplied which advance the whole timing by 10°. See Table on page 169 for details.

If the design allows of but one position for the pinion, variation in timing can be accomplished only in steps of one tooth at a time, which is usually far too great. An exception, however, is found in some Velocette push-rod models; very fine-pitch helical teeth, of which there are 48 on the half-time pinion, provide a variation of $7\frac{1}{2}°$ per tooth.

One method of surmounting this difficulty is to make up some stepped keys, remembering that at 1 in. radius 1° equals .017 in.; from this data the amount of " step " to be filed on the key for any particular diameter of shaft and angular variation required can be worked out by direct proportion. Keys so filed must, of course, fit the keyways in both shaft and gear closely, otherwise looseness may eventually develop.

If the engine has separate camshafts for inlet and exhaust, next turn the flywheels until the crankpin is at the "exhaust opening" position and insert the exhaust camshaft so that the valve is just about to lift (or at the nearest tooth to this position), and slip the timing cover into place to steady the outer ends of the camshafts—a precaution which is not necessary if the shafts run in the modern manner on fixed shafts though it is advisable to fit the steady plate temporarily to eliminate spring.

The complete timing figures can now be checked. It will probably be found that they do not come out exactly as anticipated owing to small differences here and there in the mechanism, or because an error has been made in positioning the half-time pinion. Usually a compromise has to be effected, bearing in mind that the *overlap points* are more important than the others. In this connection it is better, in most instances, to have the inlet valve opening earlier rather than later than intended.

Several attempts may have to be made to obtain the most favourable figures, particularly if the cams have been modified. The stepped-key dodge may be very helpful in such cases. For future reference, make a careful record in the notebook of the timing eventually obtained, together with any remarks, such as clearances used at the time of checking, the valve lifts, and so forth.

Then oil all bearing surfaces copiously and fit the timing cover, after making dead certain that everything is correctly in place. At this juncture it is all too easy to omit perfectly obvious things, such as distance pieces or thrust washers on the rocker spindles, any rubber washers for the transfer of lubricant, or perhaps the small spring-loaded jet which feeds oil to the big-end of certain J.A.P. models, or even to overlook the elementary precaution of fully tightening the half-time pinion nut and locking it by whatever means are provided in the design.

If you have gone to the trouble of dowelling the timing cover in correct alignment, it can now be put in place with the appropriate gasket or any good-quality jointing cement thinly applied, and the screws or bolts finally tightened. If not dowelled, the cover may have to be juggled about a little to ensure that the cam spindles are not binding. Incidentally, although brown paper is commonly used for gaskets, a higher-grade material, such as "Oakenstrong," is to be preferred for high-class work, as it is less likely to require renewal if the engine has to be worked upon when far away from its rightful garage. If the joint faces are in good condition, perfectly oil-tight joints can be made by omitting the gasket and using only a thin application of "Gasket-goo."

B.S.A. CAM PART NUMBERS AND TIMING, AT 0.018 IN. CLEARANCE

| | | Opens | Closes | Lift | Total crank angle |
|---|---|---|---|---|---|
| Inlet | 65-2454 | 50° | 80° | 0.415 in. | 310° |
| Inlet | 65-2446 | 63° | 72° | 0.400 in. | 315° |
| Inlet | 65-2442 | 65° | 85° | 0.442 in. | 330° |
| Exhaust | 65-2450 | 70° | 45° | 0.385 in. | 295° |
| Exhaust | 65-2446 | 80° | 55° | 0.400 in. | 315° |
| Exhaust | 65-1891 | 85° | 60° | 0.428 in. | 325° |

Normally used with mainshaft pinion 65-692. 65-696 advances timing by 10°.

CHAPTER XIII

IMPROVED CYLINDER FILLING

ONE reason for providing much longer periods of valve opening on racing engines, as shown in the tables in Chapter XII, is purely a matter of mechanics, for the loads in the valve gear are diminished (or, alternatively, higher speeds can be attained with the same stresses) if the angular periods of opening and closing are increased. Provided that the lift is kept the same, an increase in speed from 6,000 to 7,000 r.p.m. puts up the loads in the ratio of 36 to 49, an increase of 36%, but if the angular periods are increased in the same proportion—for example, by increasing the duration of opening from 260° to 303°—the loads in the gear will be brought back to their original values and the higher revs. can be attained with the same valve springs with no potential loss of reliability, as might be incurred if the spring strength were to be increased from, say, 120 lb. to 150 lb.

Lightening the valve gear, of course, reduces its inertia and consequently the force required to operate it, but this can be done only to any marked extent *in the design stage*. Apart from the minor savings which have been previously described, a really desperate attempt to reduce the weight of a well-designed mechanism by one-third would, in addition to introducing a distinct risk of failure, almost certainly defeat its own object by bringing in a much greater amount of flexure under load.

Despite their seeming lightness, all gases possess quite appreciable weight (as a matter of interest, the air in a room 10 ft. square and 10 ft. high weighs 80 lb.) and consequently also possess inertia; that is to say, they resent being rapidly accelerated, and when they are on the move are reluctant to

170

stop. The effects are similar to the inertia of the valve gear, inasmuch as they become increasingly serious at high speeds. Fortunately, the expedient of lengthening the valve-opening period, used to reduce the valve gear stresses, is also of the greatest value not only in overcoming the adverse effects of gas inertia, but in turning it to good account.

When the exhaust valve opens, the pressure in the cylinder is quite high, somewhere in the region of 80 lb. per sq. in. (the exact figure depending, of course, upon the characteristics of the engine), and the bulk of the exhaust products are entering the pipe as a "slug" of gas at well over atmospheric pressure. Towards the end of the exhaust stroke, i.e. as the piston is slowing down, the column of exhaust gas tends, under the influence of its own inertia, to continue travelling along the pipe and to draw the gas still remaining inside the cylinder out through the valve. Superimposed upon this so-called extractor action is an even more valuable effect created initially by the "slug" of high-pressure exhaust gas.

This "slug" forms the starting-point of a pressure-wave which travels down the pipe at the speed of sound, until it reaches the open end. Here it is reflected back up the pipe but is reversed in the process, becoming a wave of low pressure instead of high. This low-pressure wave travels back to the valve and augments to a considerable extent the extractor action already mentioned, provided that it reaches the port at the right time, which is of course at or near top dead centre. It is possible for the wave action to create negative pressures of up to six pounds per square inch in the port and almost all of the residual gas can be evacuated from the cylinder head if the exhaust valve is still open by a considerable amount at t.d.c. and does not close until 45° or 50° after. Furthermore, the inlet valve can commence to open long before t.d.c. without fear that the spent gases will try to get out of the cylinder by flowing back through the inlet tract: in fact if everything is correctly proportioned the depression created in the exhaust port by the combination of column inertia and wave action will even cause a fresh charge to start moving into the cylinder before the piston begins to move downwards on the induction stroke. The inlet valve can be lifted $\frac{1}{8}$ in., or more, off its seat at t.d.c. and can attain full lift nearly as soon as the piston reaches its maximum speed, near mid-stroke, without undue stress in the cam gear such as would be caused if the valve had not commenced to lift so soon.

The speed of sound in exhaust gas surroundings varies with the temperature and pressure, but, for practical purposes, can be taken as 1,500 ft. per sec. — considerably faster than its speed in air, which is 1,100 ft. per sec. The time taken for a wave to travel down any given pipe and back again to the port is practically constant, so that the effect of the wave action just described is most beneficial only over a limited range of speeds. At other times the effect will be absent or can even be adverse, when there is a pulse of high pressure instead of the required low pressure in the exhaust port at t.d.c. Such a pulse will cause a back-flow of gas out through the inlet valve and may upset the carburation to such an extent that the engine cuts out completely.

Altering the natural frequency of vibration of the exhaust system by altering the pipe length, or diameter, or adding a plain or lipped megaphone, will alter both the maximum power range and the minimum usable speed. Shortening the pipe and, to a lesser extent, reducing its diameter, raises the frequency. Adding a megaphone accentuates the wave effect considerably but tends to narrow down the usable range of speed. High-revving, road-racing, or record-breaking engines, therefore, employ short pipes with megaphones, but, where greater flexibility and a somewhat lower peak power speed are required, a longer, straight pipe is better. For extremely high r.p.m. the correct pipe length may be too short to be practicable or it may not comply with regulations, and it is then necessary to use double the optimum length.

The whole subject of wave formation in exhaust systems

is very complex and not a great deal has been written about it. Dr. Schweitzer's book, *The Scavenging of Two-stroke Cycle Diesel Engines*, published by The Macmillan Company of New York, provides some very useful information, and in Volume XXXIV of the *Proceedings of the Institution of Automobile Engineers* there is a very informative paper on exhaust systems written by J. G. Morrison.

By mid-stroke the incoming charge is rushing through the inlet pipe at several hundred feet per second, and it will continue to do so until the piston has commenced to travel upwards again on the compression stroke. If the valve and inlet pipe areas are inadequate in size, or of poor aerodynamic shape, the cylinder will not be completely filled by the time b.d.c. is reached, and holding the inlet valve open for a further 60° gives a little more time for filling to be completed. But, of course, as the piston has by then risen some distance, the amount of new charge taken in will be considerably less than the swept volume of the cylinder—in other words, the volumetric efficiency will be low.

On the other hand, if the valve area and pipe size are large enough the cylinder should be very nearly filled at b.d.c., and after this the high-speed column of gas will continue under the influence of its own inertia to travel into the cylinder. It is possible by making full use of this "ramming" effect to obtain a small, but very useful, amount of supercharge at certain speeds.

The distance from the valve seat to the outer end of the air-intake of the carburetter has a large influence on this, and on most racing machines is of the order of 10 in. to 13 in. This is several inches longer than is usual on ordinary o.h.v. and s.v. engines—particularly the latter, in which the whole inlet tract is frequently very short—whereas readers with long memories will recollect the much greater induction length used on fast side-valvers such as the long-stroke Sunbeam. The excellent results which used to be obtained from fitting a Binks " mouse-trap " or " rat-trap " carburetter were possibly attributable as much to their extra length as to the variable choke-tube which was the main feature of these instruments.

This may seem somewhat of a digression from the subject of cylinder-filling, but it has to be mentioned because filling and pipe design are to a large extent interdependent.

If all the factors involved are mutually in harmony a very large amount of overlap can be employed, and the long valve-opening periods so obtained will, in turn, permit higher lifts to be used without unduly stressing the valve gear, thus leading the way to a further increase in volumetric efficiency. The extent to which one may go is well illustrated by the 500 c.c. Norton timing diagram, originally published in an I.A.E. paper read by Mr. J. Craig during the war. The Norton diagram also shows very clearly the higher lift, longer duration of opening and larger port diameter of the inlet valve in comparison with equivalent figures for the exhaust. It is also noticeable that the exhaust opening point is a little earlier and the inlet closing point a few degrees later than usual, but the outstanding features are the 115° overlap and the amount by which each valve is away from its seat at t.d.c. Since that time, further research plus the ability to run at still higher r.p.m., gained by using larger valves in "square" engines, have permitted even longer timings to be employed. Reference to the valve-timing tabulation in the previous chapter shows that the inlet valve on the 76 mm. by 76.7 mm. "Manx" Norton model 40M, after allowing for clearance, opens at 75° before t.d.c., which is actually when the piston is just half-way up on the exhaust stroke, while the exhaust valve does not close until the piston is nearly half-way down the inlet stroke. It would be impossible to get an engine to run at all on such a timing unless full advantage were taken of correctly proportioned inlet and exhaust systems.

Diagrams of this nature are most easily obtained without loss of mechanical reliability on engines with valve gear of the double overhead camshaft type—and at the other end of the scale, in side-valve engines—where the best possible combination of lightness and rigidity is attained by reducing

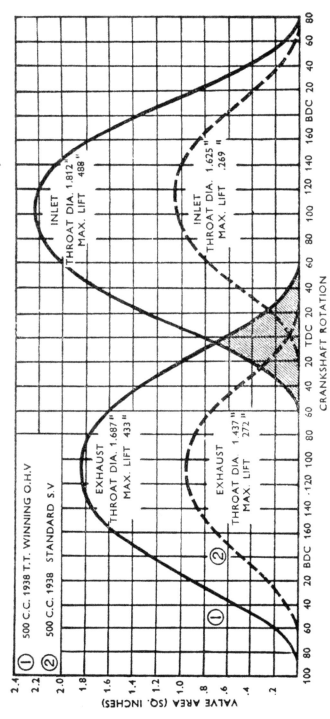

*This double graph, originally published in Mr. Joe Craig's paper, "Progress in Motorcycle Engines," read before members of the Institution of Automobile Engineers, illustrates in an extremely clear manner the increase in valve area and overlap timing possible with a racing power-unit in comparison with an engine of the touring type.*

175

the number of components between each valve and its cam to a single tappet in direct compression. With such a layout the actual motion of the valves follows very closely the motion theoretically imparted to them by the cams, whereas in designs where flexure exists, even to a limited extent, this is not the case and the valve-motion departs more and more from the theoretical as the speed rises.

Extremely good results can be obtained from push-rod engines if this fact is recognized, and legislated for in the cam design or timing, by making allowance for the loss in motion which occurs most noticeably at the commencement of opening of each valve. This can be done by (a) advancing one or both cams by, say, 5°; or (b) modifying the cam contour to give a slow initial rate of lift commencing 10° or 15° before the actual point at which the valve is desired to open. Scheme (a) has the merit of being simple to carry into effect, and comparative tests with various cam settings are easily conducted, but there are limits to what can be done in this direction, since any alteration in the opening points automatically changes the closing points by an equal amount.

However, an engine with "30, 60; 60, 30" timing will almost certainly perform better at high speed with an open exhaust if the inlet can be advanced 5°, making the timing "35, 55; 60, 30," particularly if the inlet porting has been improved and the compression raised, for with the improved volumetric efficiency given by the two latter factors the inlet valve should not require to be held open for so long as it was before such improvements were effected.

Scheme (b) is standard practice with some makers whose engines are notable for their good all-round performance; it has the effect of taking up all clearances, and part of the unavoidable flexure, comparatively steadily and before the valve has lifted off its seat by any appreciable amount. At low speed the valve will leave its seat a little earlier than it does at high speed, but the actual area of opening is so small that there is scarcely any adverse effect on the low-speed performance.

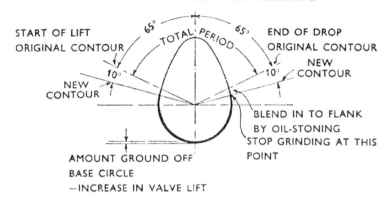

*(Above) A method of increasing simultaneously the valve lift and period of opening by grinding the cam base circle. (Below) To obtain increase in lift whilst retaining the original opening period.*

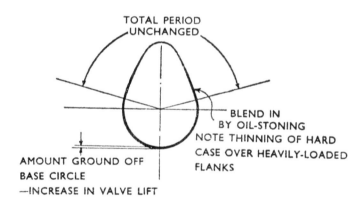

Cam design is, in fact, quite a complicated business. Apart from determining the most suitable lifts and opening points, the contours of the cams and followers need to be very carefully worked out in order to give the minimum stresses in the gear consistent with the type of valve-lift diagram required; the most that the majority of private owners can do is to experiment with different settings or to obtain a set of racing cams.

There are, however, one or two simple methods of modifying the timing diagram with ordinary workshop equipment,

177

although experiments of this nature must, of course, be conducted solely at "owner's risk"!

One of these methods, which has as its objects increasing both the lift and the angular period of the valve opening, is to reduce the radius of the cam-base circle, a process which needs to be done very accurately to achieve good results, and requires the use either of a proper cylindrical grinder or a lathe equipped with a tool-post grinding attachment. The base circle is reduced a thou. or so at a time in successive cuts, the cam being partially rotated by hand between the centres of the grinder or lathe.

To avoid grinding too far in either direction, and thereby ploughing a hollow into the flanks, it is advisable to determine beforehand—by rotating the cam in contact with a dial-gauge—the points at which the cam-flanks join the base circle, and to mark these in some manner which will not subsequently become obliterated. Being dead-hard, it is next to impossible to mark the surface with a scriber. The best method is to make up a solution of copper sulphate (or " bluestone ") in water and apply it to the cam surface. Instantly a very thin film of copper will make its appearance, and scriber lines will show up on this surface very clearly.

A carrier should be attached to the cam spindle and two rigid stops rigged up so that the wheel cannot grind beyond its allotted area—in fact, it is necessary to run out the cut some distance *before* the marks are reached, and subsequently to blend the new base circle into the existing flanks by handwork with an oil-stone—an operation requiring no little skill to carry out in such a manner that a gentle rise is obtained without forming any suspicion of a flat or hollow at the new junction of the flanks with the base circle.

Many workshops are now equipped with tap-grinders which form the lead-in portion of the tap with the correct cutting clearance. These machines can be adapted without much trouble to modify cams and can even be used to grind on new cams completely from master-cams by fixing a disc, which is the same size as the grinding-wheel, to the bed of the machine and mounting the cam to be copied and the rough cam-blank on a mandrel held in the swinging head normally used to carry the tap when it is being sharpened. The master-cam then rotates against the fixed disc, and moves the head in and out as the spindle is rotated with the blank in contact with the grinding wheel. This process gradually forms the new cam, with a high degree of accuracy if the work is not rushed.

A simple method of generating cams with longer timing is to cut through an existing cam and rotate one half backwards in relation to the other by the desired amount, perhaps 8°, then sweat or dowel the halves together with a thin piece of steel between them. This filler piece is then filed to make the contour and to provide a smooth radius at the nose of the cam and the resulting article makes a very satisfactory master for use in a conventional cam-grinder or in the converted tap-grinder just described. It is possible to make up a whole family of cams in this way without much trouble, and the scheme eliminates all calculation or guesswork in determining the correct lift curves.

The majority of cams are hardened to a depth exceeding .040 in. As there is practically no load on the base circle (unless the tappets are wrongly adjusted, or heavy push-rod return springs are fitted) it is feasible to grind off as much as .025 in. and still retain sufficient hardness to give satisfactory running, if not for an indefinite period at least for long enough to prove the success, or otherwise, of the experiment.

Unless the new contour blends correctly into the base circle, valve clatter may be caused and, worse still, surprisingly heavy loads may be generated. The final shape should be checked with a dial-gauge and a degree-plate attached to the cam-spindle, and supposing .020 in. has been ground off and it is desired to increase the total angle of the cam by 20° (10° on each flank), quiet operation will be obtained if the .020-in. rise is split up in the manner suggested on the following page.

Measuring the lift directly off the cam with a dial-gauge does not give necessarily the actual lift which will be imparted to the valve, so this should finally be determined by assembling the valve gear and measuring the lift curve off the valve itself. In passing, a good idea of how much flexure exists in the system can be obtained by first plotting the lift curve with a very light temporary spring, and then with the correct springs; the result is sometimes rather surprising! When running at high speed the difference will be greater still, particularly at the start of lift, because of the valve inertia, which is, roughly speaking, about equal at peak revs. to the spring strength.

| DEGREES FROM START OF LIFT | RISE OF CAM IN INCHES | DEGREES FROM START OF LIFT | RISE OF CAM IN INCHES |
|---|---|---|---|
| 1 | .001 | 6 | .009 |
| 2 | .002 | 7 | .011 |
| 3 | .0035 | 8 | .014 |
| 4 | .005 | 9 | .017 |
| 5 | .007 | 10 | .020 |

*For quiet operation, the cam-lift modification described above should be graduated.*

If this modification is correctly performed, a greater lift will have been achieved without the necessity for an increase in spring-strength. Should the period already be of satisfactorily long duration but the lift somewhat inadequate, the latter can be increased by itself if the base circle is ground off right up to the marks denoting the original start and finish of the flanks, after which a lot of stoning will be necessary to avoid a sudden and undesirably rapid rate of rise at the junction of flank and base circle. The final effect will be to reduce the case-depth over the heavily loaded flanks and as, in general, stronger springs will be required, subsequently the running life will probably be short. In some designs it is possible to overcome this defect by re-hardening the cams, but this may bring about difficulties through destroying the accuracy of other dimensions, although the latter might be restored by grinding after being built up with hard chrome plating by the " Fescol " process or kindred methods.

It has already been mentioned that altering the cam-follower radius affects the acceleration rate but *not* the timing, and this offers a method of varying the opening diagram without altering the timing or the lift. A curved follower foot, even though it is non-rotating, is moved by the cam exactly as if it were a portion of a roller which *does* rotate. The lift imparted to the follower is determined by plotting out the path of the centre of curvature of the foot or axis of the roller, as the case may be.

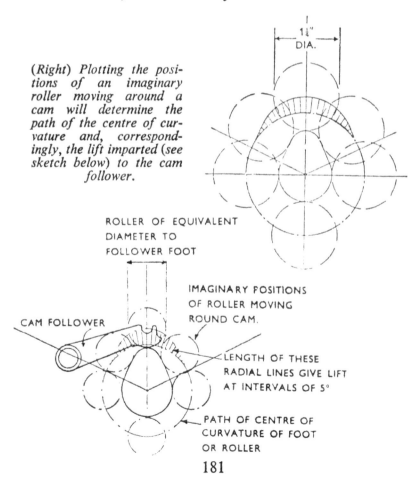

*(Right) Plotting the positions of an imaginary roller moving around a cam will determine the path of the centre of curvature and, correspondingly, the lift imparted (see sketch below) to the cam follower.*

ROLLER OF EQUIVALENT
DIAMETER TO
FOLLOWER FOOT

CAM FOLLOWER

IMAGINARY POSITIONS
OF ROLLER MOVING
ROUND CAM.

LENGTH OF THESE
RADIAL LINES GIVE LIFT
AT INTERVALS OF 5°

PATH OF CENTRE OF
CURVATURE OF FOOT
OR ROLLER

181

Even if the follower is flat, the same statement applies, as a flat surface can be considered as part of a cylinder with an infinitely large radius. The lift curve can be depicted, first by plotting out the rise of the follower-centre as it traverses the cam, and then, in effect, straightening out the curved line so obtained; this has been done in the accompanying graphs (*see page* 183), which show the effect of different follower radii. While the rate of rise or fall is greater with the larger follower at the start of lift and finish of the drop (which increases the stresses in the gear at those times), the accelerations and decelerations near the crest of the cam are less and higher revs. can be attained with the same strength of spring. The main gain, however, is to be expected from the increased valve-lift at the vital period extending for a few degrees before and after t.d.c.

Followers can be ground to shape by hand on an emery-wheel, using a sheet-steel template previously made to the desired curvature as a gauge, but care must be taken to see that the surface is at all points parallel to the axis of the follower-pivot, otherwise highly concentrated loads and rapid wear will ensue. A good method is to make up a simple swivelling jig, which can be clamped to the machine-table and fed in to the required depth. If more than .020 in. is taken off, the follower will definitely require to be re-casehardened.

A factor which must be allowed for when lever followers are used is the effect of their angular swing; if the cam is symmetrical, the effect of the swing will be to make the lift-curve unsymmetrical and the flatter the follower the greater

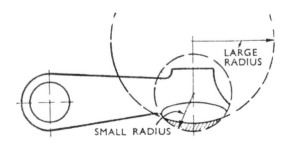

*Varying the radius of a cam-follower base circle serves to alter the acceleration rate but not the overall valve timing.*

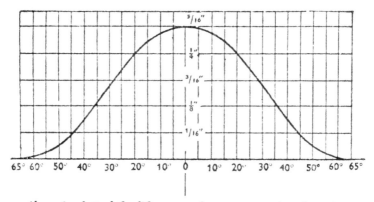

*Above is plotted the lift curve of a cam operating the valve via a follower with a ⅜-in. radius foot. Below is the lift curve provided by the same cam operating via a follower with a ⅝-in. radius foot, the shaded area representing the increase in valve opening.*

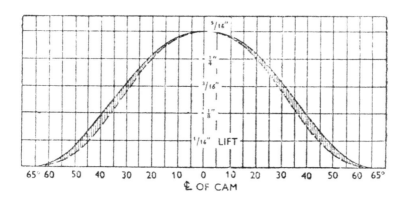

this effect will be. The distortion of the lift curve varies according to whether the follower is leading or trailing the cam, and occasionally the effect is turned to good use to obtain a rapid lift and slow drop (or *vice-versa*) with a symmetrical cam contour.

In this volume it is possible to touch on the fringe of the subject only. It cannot be emphasized too strongly that cam modification is a thing not lightly to be undertaken, and is likely to do more harm than good unless carried out with extreme care and with the aid of good equipment.

# CHAPTER XIV

## IGNITION TOPICS

IF there is any doubt about its internal condition, the best plan is to get the magneto overhauled by the makers or a reputable specialist in the art. Symptoms such as heavy sparking at the points, a noticeable grey deposit in the region of the points which this malady causes, or slackness or tightness of the armature spindle would justify such a course of action, since they are indicative of actual or impending troubles which are beyond the ability of most amateurs to rectify. When having a magneto tested, particularly if it appears to be correct but the engine misfires or just refuses to run up to speed after a period of running, get the test conducted after the instrument has been heated up to around 100°C. in a stove. This sometimes shows up a fault which was not obvious before.

Dead-certain starting, even with fully retarded ignition, is absolutely essential. The magneto must, therefore, give a good spark even when just flicked over with the fingers. If it does not do so, although otherwise in good condition as regards the points, brushes and slip ring, observe whether there is an appreciable magnetic resistance to rotation just prior to the points opening. If this " armature pull " is weak, it indicates, in conjunction with the poor spark, that re-magnetizing is necessary. This is not a usual malady with modern instruments having cast-in magnets of the "Alnico" type, but it does occur in older patterns and also in flywheel magnetos.

While not wishing in the slightest degree to cast any aspersions on them, combined magneto-dynamo instruments are intended primarily for touring purposes. For racing it is best to discard these devices and obtain one of the several types of magneto which have been built for the job. The ideal is, of course, a modern B.T.-H. or Lucas instrument, but failing these one of the old M.L. models will give excellent results if properly reconditioned.

Given everything in order in the sparks department, the magneto can be attached to the motor and, if driven by chain, adjusted so that the chain has $\frac{1}{4}$ in. up-and-down play in the middle of its run. Turn the engine over several times, feeling the chain meanwhile to check if its tension varies. This will be the case if the chain is worn unevenly, or the sprockets are eccentric, or one or both shafts are not dead true. Uneven tension in the magneto drive means that the ignition timing will be perpetually varied over a small range; thus the cause should be discovered and eradicated.

If the magneto holding-down bolts pass through slots, adjustment is effected quite easily, but in other cases (mainly on o.h.c. engines) where there is no such provision the base will have to be packed up on steel or brass shims of the same area as the base and suitably drilled. Owing to the high expansion of aluminium, the chain will usually tighten a little as the engine warms up, and some allowance must be made for this; besides wasting power, an overtight chain will ruin the armature bearing in a very short time.

Frequently there is little or no provision for preventing grit entering the slot provided in the chain case to allow for adjustment. This omission should be rectified by cutting out a piece of felt large enough to cover the slot and a little thicker than the gap between the case and magneto. The felt is slipped over the shaft before assembling the magneto and is of particular value if racing on sand or dirt is contemplated.

Gear-drive magnetos invariably have some form of oil-retaining device fitted behind the pinion. This should be examined and, if necessary, components such as felt washers, which have a limited life, should be renewed. There is a number of 100% efficient proprietary oil-seals on the market to-day. They cause only a negligible amount of friction, and in obstate cases of oil leakage it may be worth while looking into the matter of fitting one, although this

185

will, in all probability, entail some additional machining operations. If a gear-driven magneto is found to be full of oil, probably the seal surrounding the mainshaft has become ineffective, so that cleaning out will be merely a temporary measure. The seal should be renewed; this can be done externally in B.T.-H. magnetos, but Lucas instruments must be first dismantled. In this event, make sure that the new seal is of the type which has a garter spring to contract it on the shaft, and not one of the early pattern which does not possess this feature.

There is little else to check in a gear drive unless the wheel is made of some non-metallic material such as " Tufnol " or " Fabroil." In such a case, if any teeth appear to be damaged it is advisable to obtain a new wheel, as if one tooth fails completely the rest will follow suit very shortly. Owing to the high expansion rate of these materials the teeth should have a perceptible amount of backlash, even when new; also the tips of the teeth must be well clear of the roots in the other gear, otherwise an annoying whine, which will *not* cure itself as time goes on, will be set up when running.

Racing magnetos are commonly equipped with manual advance mechanism, but on many sports machines fixed magnetos are used in conjunction with a centrifugal A.T.D. These are quite satisfactory, but for racing the scheme has two disadvantages: one is that the accuracy of the timing cannot be checked when running; the other is that it is not possible to drive a rev-counter direct from the magneto nut, which is one of the accepted methods, because the power absorbed by the drive, though slight, might prevent full advance being obtained. There are methods by which the drive can be taken off the fixed stops on the pinion, allowing the advance mechanism to work freely, but this is rather a matter for personal ingenuity. Some riders prefer to lock-up the device by welding together the fixed and moving stops after taking out the bob-weights, and either convert the magneto to hand advance, or use fixed ignition.

Engines running on alcohol, and not requiring more than

35° advance, will usually start quite well with no method of retarding but, if petrol is used, or much more than 35° is required, the engine may be prone to kick back, and so some form of retard control may be essential.

With the adjustment of the drive correct, and the contact-breaker points set to the correct gap (.012 in. in the case of racing instruments), the ignition can be timed in the usual manner, making sure that the cam-ring is in the fully advanced position and that the points are just breaking, with all the slack taken up in the drive. With automatic advance, it is also necessary to wedge the device into the fully-advanced position, as this is more accurate than setting at full retard and trusting that the extra advance will be as stated by the maker.

The method of using a flashlamp battery and bulb to determine the exact point of breaking is very good, but the time-honoured scheme of inserting a cigarette paper between the points and noting when this just comes free has the advantage of being available in almost any circumstances. Whichever method is used should be adhered to regularly — mixing up two schemes is bound to bring in discrepancies.

When one finally tightens the magneto drive nut, the spindle frequently creeps on a little way and thus retards the timing a degree or so; it is therefore essential to check the timing, and, if necessary, to reset it, if some particular "spot on" advance is being aimed at. The vernier device used on A.J.S.

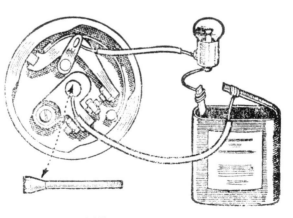

*The flashlamp method of checking ignition-timing referred to. Note that the centre screw must either be removed or insulated from the block holding the fixed point.*

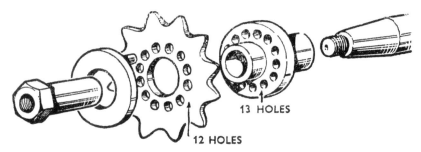

13 HOLES

12 HOLES

*A great aid towards obtaining optimum timing of ignition and valves is provided by a vernier adjustment. Here is the simple but excellent system applied to the magneto sprockets of certain early A.J.S. models, also to the camshaft drive.*

machines does not suffer from this trouble and provides a very simple method of setting or altering the timing.

On twin-cylinder engines the timing after being set on one cylinder must be checked on the other one. It will very likely be found to be a degree or two different owing to small variations or errors in the contact breaker or cam. If the error is only slight, the easiest way is to split the difference between the two cylinders; if more serious, careful grinding or oil-stoning of the cam ring will effect a cure. On single-carburetter V-twins the rear cylinder filling is rarely so good as that of the front one; consequently it will stand a little more advance and thus a difference between the two timings, provided it is not more than a degree or so, will not be a disadvantage. This does not apply to V-twins with two carburetters, which should take the same advance on both "lungs." Vincents, prepared for fast road work, run rather more sweetly low down if any difference is arranged to give the front cylinder less advance than the rear, rather than *vice-versa*.

In Chapter XII various makers' timings are quoted. These should provide a useful guide so long as it is appreciated that in many cases they are intended for use with comparatively slow engines. Broadly speaking, racing engines require less, not *more*, advance than their touring counterparts for the following reasons.

Rapid combustion is aided by high compression-pressure, a clean mixture (the result of good scavenging) and a high rate of turbulence within the cylinder. All these factors are present to a greater extent in racing power units than in touring engines. Matters of detail design, such as the shape of the combustion chamber, the location of the plug and the angle of inclination of the inlet port, exert an effect and account for the big differences in timing found in engines which, to a casual glance, appear to be fairly similar.

As a general rule, if an engine has had its compression raised from, say, 6 to 8 to 1 and has been otherwise attended to as regards its ports and exhaust system, the ignition point will need to be brought back by about 5°, and possibly more. The spark advance also varies according to the fuel or more accurately according to the flame-rate or speed of combustion of the mixture. The rate of burning of methanol is slow compared to petrol and for this reason requires nearly as much advance at 14 to 1 compression as petrol-benzole does at its maximum permissible compression ratio in the same engine. But with blended fuels such as Shell 811 or Shell M, which contain a proportion of petrol and benzole yet can be run at over 12 to 1 C.R., the ignition point may be perhaps 4° later. Some representative examples may be seen in the table overleaf. The only way to discover the best setting—and even an error of 1° in either direction will make quite a big difference in a highly tuned engine—is by test under power, preferably on a brake, a method of which few amateurs can avail themselves.

Failing that, the best method is by road test using a rev. counter, the ignition being first set a little on the early side. When the engine is at its maximum revs. in top gear, retard the ignition very slightly. If the revs. increase, retard a little more until the needle begins to fall back again. Then leave the control in its last position, check the timing, and reset the magneto to give the same timing, but with the lever at full advance. For this test it is best to select a road which is slightly uphill, so that the engine is definitely pulling hard. Another method is to leave the ignition at full advance and

| MODEL | FUEL | COMP. RATIO | IGNITION ADVANCE |
|---|---|---|---|
| B.S.A., B 32 | Petrol-benzole | 9 | $38\frac{1}{2}°$ |
| | Methanol | 13 | $34\frac{1}{2}°$ |
| B.S.A., B 34 | Petrol-benzole | 9 | $40\frac{1}{2}°$ |
| | Methanol | 11 | $38\frac{1}{2}°$ |
| NORTON 30 M | Petrol 80 Octane | 7.5 | $37\frac{1}{2}°$ |
| (79.6 × 100 mm.) | Petrol-benzole | 7.5 to 10 | 36° |
| | Methanol | $12\frac{1}{2}$ | 34° |
| NORTON 40 M | Petrol 80 Octane | 7.5 | $37\frac{1}{2}°$ |
| (71 × 88 mm.) | Petrol-benzole | 7.5 to 10 | 36° |
| | Methanol | $13\frac{1}{2}$ | 34° |
| NORTON 30 M | Petrol 80 Octane | 9.5 | 34° |
| (86 × 85.6 mm.) | 100 Octane | | |
| NORTON 40 M | Petrol 80 Octane | 9.7 | 39° |
| (76 × 76.7 mm.) | 100 Octane | | |
| VINCENT | Petrol 80 Octane | 9 | 38° |
| | 100 Octane | | |
| | Methanol | $12\frac{1}{2}$ | 34° |

make several runs, altering the contact-breaker gap in stages by one-sixth of a turn on the points. A good magneto will fire perfectly between the limits of .010 in. and .014 in. gap measurement. If a notable increase is gained by, say, the wider gap, check the actual timing, then reset the gap to the correct figure of .012 in. and re-time the magneto to the same figure. This is about the only satisfactory method with a fixed magneto or when using an A.T.D.

Unfortunately, though the correct advance can be determined very accurately by either of these methods, they cannot be applied until the whole machine is ready for the road. In the meantime a fairly accurate estimate can be made from the maker's figures, taking into account the effects of any modifications which have been made to the engine internally.

CHAPTER XV

TWIN-CYLINDER ENGINES

So far as the cylinder head and valve gear are concerned there is no fundamental difference between the
work to be done on a single-, a twin- or even a four-cylinder
engine, provided that they all have individual inlet and
exhaust ports and pipes of equal length. Multi-cylinder
engines built in that way act simply as a collection of
singles and will give off power proportionate to the number
of cylinders. However, when a single carburetter feeds more
than one cylinder, the inlet passages are necessarily less
direct and, therefore, offer more restriction to flow, whilst
slight differences in the manifold shape frequently cause the
mixture supplied to one cylinder to be richer than the other.

If for reasons of cost, or because the race regulations
demand it, a single carburetter has to be retained, there is
the choice of running one cylinder at correct mixture
strength and the other too lean, or of increasing the jet size
to make the weak cylinder correct and possibly dropping
speed by reason of the other being over-rich. If the difference
is slight, the last-mentioned expedient is the best alternative
as there is less risk of damage to the engine, but it is
usually possible to eliminate the trouble by inclining the
carburetter towards the weak side. For initial experiments, a
thick gasket of medium-hardness rubber can be fitted and
the inclination can be adjusted by tightening the flange bolts
more on one side than the other. This enables rapid
comparisons to be made in a short period but, when the
angle has been established, a solid gasket should be made up
for permanent use.

Most parallel twins have a manifold with fairly sharp
bends, forcing the mixture to turn two right-angled corners,
this arrangement having been found to give better all-round

191

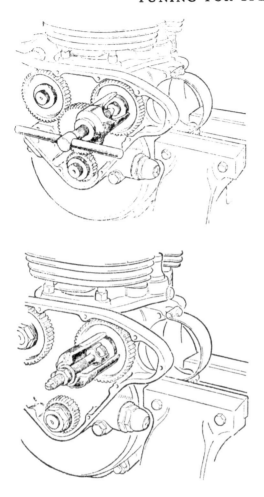

*Special tools are necessary to remove or replace (see sketches above and below respectively) the cam wheels of Triumph twin-cylinder models. Similar tools are available from other manufacturers.*

results than one in which the two ports blend together at a narrow angle close to the carburetter flange. For maximum power, it is of course best to fit two carburetters mounted on spacers of the same thickness as the manifold, or possibly a little greater. If the head studs and the carburetter bolt holes do not coincide, a little ingenuity is required in making up the spacers if it is not possible to buy them as spares.

Owners of speed-twin Triumphs are fortunate in that they can purchase a racing kit containing all the necessary bits and pieces. This is intended for engines supplied as standard with aluminium heads and "Grand Prix" type con-rods, but can be for earlier engines with iron heads which are quite satisfactory on alcohol fuel. The rods in these engines were of a lighter pattern than those fitted to the genuine "Grand Prix" engine and it is best to obtain a pair of the latter type if possible. The change of rods **and** pistons will call for some re-balancing and, though the factory balance factor is 62%, some riders find that 70% gives better results.

Triumph camshafts are driven by wheels which are a tight fit on the shafts and have three keyways for accurate adjustment of timing. When fitting racing camshafts, the wheels are pulled off with a special remover (part number D178) and forced on again with a replacer (part number D182), and it is wise to obtain these tools before commencing the change-over. The sequence of re-assembly is to fit the crankshaft and camshafts into the drive side, not forgetting to place the rotary breather-valve disc and spring in the inlet cam-bush, then the timing-side case with the usual precautions for making an oil-tight joint and again not forgetting the two internal bolts just inside the crankcase mouth. Assemble the pistons, cylinder block and head in the normal manner, but fit only the exhaust rocker-box and pushrods with the clearance adjusted to zero so that the rockers are just free enough to slide sideways.

Replace the key and half-time pinion, fit a timing disc and pointer, accurately adjusted to t.d.c.; set the crankshaft at 70° before b.d.c. and rotate the exhaust camshaft *forwards* until one rocker is just tight enough to resist side movement. Without allowing anything to move, offer up the camshaft wheel so that one of the three keyways is in line with the key at the same time that the teeth line up with those on the intermediate wheel. Pull the wheel into place, and rotate the crankshaft backwards until the rocker again becomes tight. This is the closing point and should be 52° before t.d.c. is reached.

Check the figures on the other cylinder and if the discrepancy between the two is greater than 4° it should be equalized by re-positioning the wheel. It is unlikely that the exact figures quoted will be realised at all four points on both cylinders, but aim to obtain the nearest approach, remembering that the exhaust opening point is the least critical and a degree or two early will make little difference. Before worrying too much about minor differences, check again with the clearances set to, say, .005 in. The figures will, of course, then be different, but may be more consistent between the two cylinders, in which event the difference between the figures at zero clearance is not unduly serious.

Procedure for timing the inlet valves is exactly the same as for the exhaust, after which the rocker-boxes are fitted permanently and the clearances set to .002 in. inlet and .004 in. exhaust. The ignition timing varies according to fuel and is 42° for petrol or petrol-benzole, or 38° for methanol, or alcohol-rich fuels with the appropriate high-compression pistons. If alcohol is used with low-compression pistons just for the sake of cooler running then an advance of up to 45° may be necessary (*see* page 206 for later engines).

Triumph crankshaft assemblies are built up with the fly-wheel sandwiched between flanges. This is a very rigid construction but, with the main bearings spaced very widely apart, flexure is bound to occur to some extent and it is prudent to avoid exceeding the maker's recommended limit of 7,500 r.p.m. When working on an engine of unknown history, get the crankshaft tested for cracks in the region of the junction of crankpin and web and, if any defect is found, replace the component. The halves are accurately spigotted and dowelled to the flywheel and alignment will be accurate provided cleanliness is observed during the change-over. This precaution should be taken with any make of two-bearing shaft after a considerable period of use.

The Norton "Dominator" shaft is of similar three-piece construction and it is wise, when tuning an example which has done much road work to dismantle the shaft and clean out the large cavity which forms a sludge-trap in the centre of the flywheel assembly. Mark all three components before-hand so that they can be refitted exactly as they were so as to preserve original accuracy of alignment and balance.

194

As a rule parallel twins utilize forged aluminium rods, and though those in up-to-1955 Triumphs run direct on the shaft with white-metalled caps to provide a measure of safety in the event of lubrication failure, it is usual to employ precision-type thin-wall renewable steel big-end shells, such as are commonly used on cars. These components must be handled with care and, in particular, must not be assembled unless the locating nibs are snug in their recesses in rod and cap. If the clearance with the bearing dry exceeds .003 in. the shells should be renewed; the temptation to file the faces of the rod and shells must be firmly resisted, as the amount of "nip" or pinch on the shells has been very carefully determined and it is extremely difficult to maintain the same fit exactly. In addition, once a rod or cap has been filed, replacement shells cannot be fitted correctly unless they also are filed, and, thus, the valuable feature of interchangeability is lost.

Plain bearings must be given a greater quantity of oil at a higher pressure than roller-bearings; they are more easily damaged by fine abrasive which embeds itself in the white metal and acts as a lapping compound. The greatest care, therefore, must be taken to see that every vestige of dirt is removed from oilways and filters; moreover, the efficiency of the oil-feed mechanism to the crankshaft must be checked. The "Dominator," for instance, has a rubber oil-seal installed in the timing cover; it fits over an extension of the crankshaft. This cannot be removed without it being destroyed completely, but it is a simple matter to fit a new one, which is pressed into place with the metal-covered face visible.

Matchless and A.J.S. twins employ a three-bearing shaft, which imparts extra rigidity and permits oil to be supplied through the centre main bearing, and with little likelihood of over-supply to one big-end at the expense of the other. When working on an early A.M.C. model it is worth considering changing the original head with small fins to the later large-finned pattern, which affords considerably greater cooling area. Similarly several pounds of weight

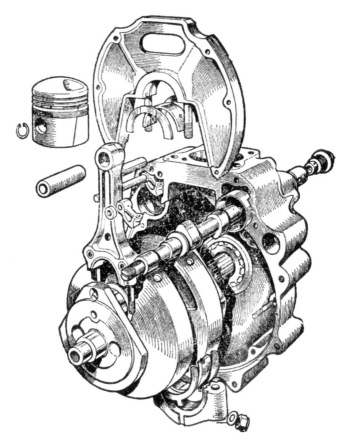

*An extended impression of the A.J.S./Matchless crankshaft layout showing the camshaft and centre bearing support. A.M.C. Ltd. are unique in providing this design feature.*

can be saved by fitting the late-pattern aluminium head to an early Norton "Dominator" with a cast-iron head.

There are three examples of V-twins in current use, namely the 1,100 c.c. and 1,000 c.c. J.A.P. engines, built expressly for racing, mainly in sprint events, and the 1,000 c.c. Vincent in its various guises, "Rapide," "Black Shadow" and "Black Lightning." Additionally, there must still be in existence a number of obsolete makes, of design which could be well worth working on in the light of present-day knowledge. There are of course also the American Harley-

196

Davidsons and Indians from which formidable power can be wrung.

Dealing first with current J.A.P. engines, the 1,000 c.c. model, known as the "8.80," is virtually two speedway singles on a common crankcase, and has cast-iron heads and barrels with shallow finning and therefore can only be run on pure methanol, Shell "A" or J.A.P. fuel consisting of $97\frac{1}{2}\%$ methanol, $2\%$ acetone and $\frac{1}{2}\%$ Castrol "R." Lubrication is either on the total-loss system with sight-feed pump, or on the dry-sump system, according to model; the former is usually used for pure sprint work and sidecar racing on speedways, the latter is superior for longer distances, as some measure of internal cooling is obtained from the oil circulation. Being designed expressly for speed, this engine does not call for much work apart from the routine assembly procedure described in previous chapters.

One major constructional feature is the con-rod arrangement, the rear being forked and the front one plain and running on needle roller bearings on the outside of the sleeve which forms the outer race of the main big-end. The two rods cannot be separated unless the sleeve is pressed out, and as it has three diameters, it can only be pressed out in one direction. This scheme is adopted mainly to simplify assembly as the sleeve can be pushed in by hand for two-thirds of the full distance.

When reassembling, locate the needle rollers in the plain rod with thick grease or with a dummy disc which can slide out ahead of the sleeve as the latter is pressed home.

The 1,100 c.c. version was designed for use in cars and has aluminium heads with inserted seats, and aluminium-jacketed barrels; though usually used with alcohol fuel at around 14 to 1 C.R. it can also be run on petrol merely by changing to 7.5 to 1 pistons and tuning the carburetters to suit. The crankpin has parallel ends and shoulders, instead of the usual J.A.P. tapers, and floating thrust washers, which must not be omitted, are used to locate the rod assembly. Similar washers are also used on each side of the flywheel assembly and their thickness can be varied if necessary to adjust the end-float to the design figure of .010 in.

The overhead rockers and also the valve guides are lubricated by a suction system common to o.h.v. engines of this make; oil-mist, escaping past the rotary release valve which ventilates the crankcase, condenses in a box below the timing-case and is drawn thence up small-bore pipes to the rocker-boxes by virtue of the depression which exists within the engine. This system only functions if the rocker-covers are in place and are reasonably air-tight, so that it is not possible to check the flow of oil to the rockers by inspection with the covers off. The rotary release valve is driven by the rear camshaft at engine speed and must be replaced with the timing marks in line. In the unlikely event of having to renew the bronze bush, this must be fitted with the slot vertically downwards so that the valve actually closes when the crankpin is a few degrees past its lowest position in the crankcase, or about 30° after rear cylinder b.d.c. The timing can be verified by inserting a piece of wire into the outlet pipe after removing the screwed plug in the bottom of the oil-box. The two rocker-oil pipes projecting into this compartment clear the floor by $\frac{1}{32}$ in.; this dimension is important and must not be altered.

The duplex pump controls both the pressure and scavenge oil supplies, the latter being drawn from the sump by an external pipe. The slightest air-leak in this suction line will impair the scavenging much more than one would think, and it is vital to make sure that the unions are seating properly and that the nuts are undamaged, otherwise the engine will be sluggish and prone to oil the rear plug.

As two magnetos are fitted, each cylinder can be timed individually. The recommended figure is 36° for the 1,100 c.c. engine and 34° for the smaller one both at a 14 to 1 C.R.

The three versions of the Vincent unit are basically the same; crankcase, flywheels, barrels and timing gear are identical, except for the cams, and so are the heads and valve gear, except for the port shapes and polishing of the rockers.

"Black Shadows" have the same cams as "Rapides," except that they are selected to give "long" timings within the limits of manufacturing tolerances, and con-rods are selected for 65-tons minimum tensile strength and polished. "Black Lightnings" have different cams, 85-ton "Vibrac" con-rods, and a steel idler wheel is used in some early examples; larger inlet ports, and of course racing carburetters and a special racing Lucas magneto are used, with fixed timing pinion instead of the A.T.D. used on the two touring engines. It will be seen therefore that either of these can be "Lightningized" so far as performance goes, without too much expenditure of time or money, and without fear of overtaxing the "downstairs" section.

Standard heads have $1\frac{1}{8}$ in. inlet ports which can be opened out to any size up to $1\frac{5}{16}$ in. according to the size of carburetters to be used—$1\frac{3}{16}$ in. T.T.10 Amals are the usual choice, for which a pair of flanged adaptors, part Nos. ET32/6 and ET 32/7, are required. The ports can be enlarged on the lines described previously, taking care not to go through into the rocker box. As the guide is very short, it is not advisable to cut it off, and a streamlined boss leading to the guide must be left to avoid cutting through into the recess in which the guide lock-ring is screwed. When ultimate in power output is desired, obtain another front head and a pair of $1\frac{3}{8}$ in. 5GP carburetters, mounted on adaptors 3 in. long, though very good results can be achieved with 32 mm. carburetters. The reason for using a front head on the rear cylinder is that as the port is not positioned on the same side as the rocker box, it can be opened up to $1\frac{1}{2}$ in. diameter.

These engines are very suitable for short sprint work such as speedway sidecar racing, and quite good results can be obtained by retaining the standard port size and using ordinary $1\frac{1}{8}$ type 29 carburetters as fitted to the "Black Shadow," but suitably modified for alcohol fuel. "Black Shadow" adaptors, which are bronze, are also required, as the standard aluminium ones are rather too thin for safety when opened up to suit the larger carburetters. Inlet valves with the heads $\frac{1}{16}$ in. larger than the standard 1.800 in. diameter can safely be installed and the seat-ring tapered to suit; it is, in fact, preferable to do this rather than to fit new seat-rings if the latter are badly worn.

The inner valve guides are normally of aluminium bronze and held in place with lock-rings. When alcohol fuel and castor-base oil are used, guide-wear may be excessive due to lubricant being washed out by the fuel and cast-iron guides may be a better proposition. Their reduced heat conductivity is not a detriment owing to the cool running nature of the fuel. A special tool is required to remove the lock-rings, which only need firm pressure when being replaced, but must be retained by punch-dots at two points other than opposite the slots. "Black Lightning" cams have about .040 in. more lift than standard cams and, unless the seats have sunk considerably, the guides must be shortened by .050 in. to avoid any chance of the collar contacting the guide. This job can be done *in situ* with a spot-facing tool cutting the guides back until there is $\frac{7}{16}$ in. space between the guide and the step on the valve stem. Do not use an ordinary drill for the work, as the countersink which it will form in the bore acts as an oil-collector and plug-oiling may result.

Six types of piston are available, giving ratios between 6.8 and $12\frac{1}{2}$ to 1. The latter ratio can be used with Shell "M," but Shell 811 gives slightly more power. Although the difference in weight between the extremes in the range is over 3 ounces the change-over causes no perceptible roughness up to 6,800 r.p.m., and, therefore, the motor can be changed from petrol to alcohol without being re-balanced.

Although the ring equipment is apparently the same, the compression rings in pistons E 7/9, 10 and 11, which are the three highest, are of thicker radial depth than those in E 7/6, 7 and 8, and, while it is possible but not advisable to use standard rings in the racing pistons, it is fatal to use thick rings in standard pistons as they project above the ring lands. The oil ring, however, is identical.

For adjusting the compression ratio, base washers up to

.062 in. thick may be used, or a small amount—not more than .030 in.—may be turned off the jacket, though, generally speaking, this should be avoided. There is not much free length on the rocker adjusters, neither is there much room between the head of the adjuster and the inside of the rocker inspection cap at full lift, and damage to the valve gear will result if the adjuster cannot lift freely, which will be the case if the barrels are shortened excessively. However, the pushrods are easily shortened by grinding up to .030 in. off either, or both, ends, and, if necessary, new ones can be made from $\frac{9}{32}$ in. silver steel, with the ball-ends hardened simply by heating them to redness and plunging into water. Apart from polishing, do not endeavour to lighten the rockers; more will be lost in flexure than will be gained by the reduction in weight.

The rocker spindles are .497 in. in diameter and, if one loosens in the rocker, it is often possible to fit a .500 in. gudgeon pin shortened to suit, or else use a piece of hardened silver steel which is simply driven into place, though, naturally, the rocker-bearing bore must be reamed

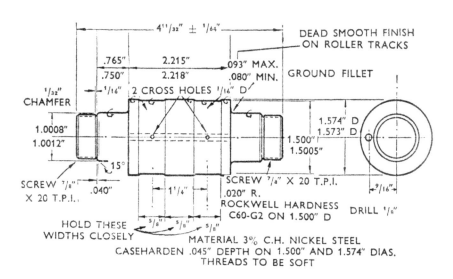

*Details of a modified crankpin suitable for use in a 1,000 c.c. Vincent engine.*

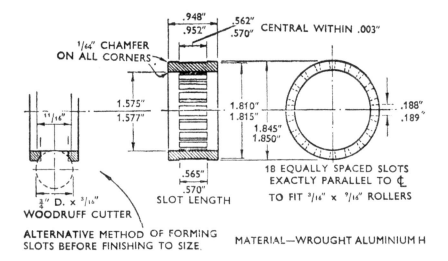

.948"
.952"

.562"
.570"  CENTRAL WITHIN .003"

¹⁄₆₄" CHAMFER
ON ALL CORNERS

1.575"
1.577"

1.810"
1.815"

1.845"
1.850"

.188"
.189"

¹¹⁄₁₆"

.565"
.570"
SLOT LENGTH

¾" D. × ³⁄₁₆"
WOODRUFF CUTTER

18 EQUALLY SPACED SLOTS
EXACTLY PARALLEL TO ℄
TO FIT ³⁄₁₆" × ⁹⁄₁₆" ROLLERS

ALTERNATIVE METHOD OF FORMING
SLOTS BEFORE FINISHING TO SIZE.

MATERIAL—WROUGHT ALUMINIUM H

*Dimensions of the MSS-type bearing cage, two of which are used
in conjunction with the modified crankpin illustrated earlier.*

out to suit beforehand. Looseness of the rocker-bearing in
the head is of no consequence so far as speed is concerned.

In the crankcase section, the standard big-end bearing with
three rows of 3 mm. by 5 mm. rollers works satisfactorily
for a long period if revs are kept below 5,800, but prolonged
work above that speed shortens its life, so also does racing
the engine from cold before the oil has a chance to warm up
and circulate freely. If genuine spares cannot be obtained, a
very satisfactory big-end can be made by making a new pin
as per the diagram, using two MSS Velocette cages with
18 $\frac{3}{16}$ in. by $\frac{9}{16}$ in. rollers in each. Four of the original
roller spacers must be ground down to .078 in. thickness and
placed one each side of the cages to centralize them, while
the original sleeves which are hard all through can be ground
out without moving them from the rods to 1.875 in. The
MSS cages must be bored out to slip neatly over the shoulders
of the pins but, if these components are not available, cages
may be made up. Their width should be .950 in. so that the
steel spacers can be omitted altogether, although, of course,
the central distance-piece must be retained.

As the big-end oil is fed into an annular space, the oil supply cannot be cut off by incorrect assembly, but the two oil holes leading to the rollers should be placed at a three o'clock position looking towards the drive side. If placed at 12 o'clock, the additional oil pressure created by centrifugal force causes almost all the oil to pass out through the first hole, thus starving the drive-side big-end.

In the timing-gear department, the front exhaust cam-spindle should be locked, after fully tightening, by angle-drilling a small hole from the end of the slot in the head back towards the camshaft and fitting therein a split-pin. Worn cam followers can be trued by grinding or oil stoning, but the face must be kept parallel with the hole. Care must be taken to note the positions of all the thin hardened washers behind the steady-plate and to replace them in exactly the same order. The lowest hole in the plate is purposely made a loose fit on the idler wheel spindle to allow for adjustment, but it is best to cut a strip of soft aluminium as wide as the plate thickness and $\frac{1}{32}$ in. thick, wrap it into a circle round a $\frac{5}{16}$ in. bar and pull it into position in the steady plate with the idler-spindle nut. This holds the outer end of the spindle positively in position, the soft bush being able to flow somewhat to accommodate itself to any slight eccentricity of the hole and spindle.

Better crankcase ventilation is obtained by filing straight across the breather-valve sleeve until the slot is fully $\frac{3}{8}$ in. wide, then rounding the outer edges of the flat so that the outgoing air has a clearer passage; the edges of the slot should be left sharp to act as oil scrapers. Replacing the external banjo and pipe with a straight union and a large-bore pipe running upwards and rearwards also helps ventilation.

Cams and camwheels are press-fitted together and are regarded by the factory as inseparable units. Consequently, "Black Lightning" cams are only supplied with the wheels attached, but it is possible to change cams and wheels provided that the interference fit is between .001 in. and .002 in., otherwise either the wheel may slip or it may crack through overtightness. All cams are ground in relation to the slot in the end-face, which must be placed in correct relationship to the marked teeth. This can be accomplished by scribing lines on both the faces of each gear, and accurately lining up the new cams with the lines before pressing them home level with the face of the gear. There are timing dots on both gear-wheel faces, so be careful to place each gear on the same way as it was originally; the timing should then be correct when all the gears are again assembled to the marks.

A rev. counter cannot be driven from the magneto-pinion nut satisfactorily, partly because it is a clockwise magneto and the nut would tend to unscrew, and partly because the automatic advance would not operate correctly. It is possible to devise a component which fits loosely over the A.T.D. and is driven from the fixed stops on the fibre pinion, but the better scheme is to obtain a fixed pinion as used on the "Black Lightning," together with the driving dog and special magneto pinion cover.

Strictly speaking, the magneto should be converted to manual advance, but with high-alcohol fuel the engine will start at the full advance of 34° at a 12½ to 1 C.R.

As there is no provision for measuring tappet clearance the method adopted for checking valve timing is to attach a dial indicator to one head stud and screw the tappet adjusters down until the valve is just lifted from its seat by .002 in. to .003 in., the exact amount being immaterial as it merely serves to take up all backlash. Re-set the dial gauge to zero and turn the engine until the valve is lifted a further .005 in.—this is important. The point at which this lift occurs is taken as the opening or closing point of the valve according to whether the valve is lifting or dropping, and all the points so obtained should agree with those quoted in the Table in Chapter XII. If there is an average discrepancy of more than 4° between the two cylinders and there is still a discrepancy when re-checked at .010 in. lift, it may be necessary to re-fit one of the two camwheels; the timing as a whole can of course be set by re-positioning the half-time pinion on any one of its five keyways.

Before replacing the timing cover, see that all four of the synthetic rubber seals are in place in the recesses provided, and in no circumstances omit to fill the filter chamber with the correct oil before fitting the banjo plug in the cover. Failure to observe this precaution may lead to damage occurring in the time lag before the pump fills the chamber.

In final assembly, verify that all shock-absorber springs are nestled in the recesses in the spring plate and then get the mainshaft nut really tight. The hexagon size is $\frac{3}{4}$-in. Whitworth (the same as the crankpin nuts), and an S.A.E. spanner $1\frac{5}{16}$ in. across flats also fits. The tube spanner in the kit is inadequate for the job, which requires a solid steel box or ring spanner.

The best scheme is to hold the crank assembly with a $\frac{7}{8}$-in. bar through one small-end eye; in any case it is always advisable to tighten up the shock-absorber assembly before reassembling the cylinders, so being able to verify that all is correct down below, and to measure the centrality of the small-ends in the crankcase bores. The Series "C" Lightnings were fitted with caged big-ends; each cage has 12 slots containing three $\frac{1}{4} \times \frac{1}{4}$ in. rollers. The $1\frac{5}{16}$ in. diameter crankpin, instead of being shouldered down where it abuts against the hardened side-plates is deeply recessed into the flywheels, which are pulled up by the usual nuts against the ends of the pin. Because of this, this design of big-end cannot be fitted directly to standard wheels, but these can be re-machined to suit by very accurately boring and facing the required recess. New side-plates and spacer are also required, though the big-end sleeves remain as before. "Picador" engines (the version developed for small pilotless target aircraft) utilized a similar big-end, but with a parallel crank pin, without nuts, which has a .006 in. interference fit in the flywheels and needs special equipment for assembly or dismantling. The main-shafts are larger than standard, so the "Picador" assembly cannot be used as a direct substitute for the standard assembly.

Series "D" engines were fitted with a much improved shock-absorber with a greater number of springs and pro-

205

vision for positively locking the mainshaft rut. No additional machining is required to make the conversion, which is well worth doing.

The foregoing notes are in the nature of underlining some features of this power unit which are a little unusual to those not familiar with its construction, and must be read in the light of what has been said elsewhere in this volume.

Earlier in this chapter the Triumph GP conversion kit was described. For T100, TR5, T110 and TR6 engines a set of components is available, including a cylinder head with splayed ports which besides affecting gas-turbulence provides plenty of room for two carburetters. The new camshafts supplied must be used in conjunction with the new followers to obtain the correct valve-opening diagram, and the method of timing them is substantially as previously outlined, but instead of setting the tappets to zero clearance, they must be set to .020 in. and the camwheels positioned to obtain the nearest approach, on all four valves, to the figures shown on page 165. For running, of course, they must be re-set to the correct clearances, and as an illustration of the effect which the amount of clearance makes, the actual timing then alters from 35°, 56° to 59°, 80°, an increase in valve-open period of 48°. Ignition point is 42° for the 500 c.c. engines, but only 39° for the 650 editions.

The splay-port head will not fit directly on early cast-iron or aluminium barrels, because of an alteration in spigot height from .187 in. to .124 in. When using alcohol with a compression-ratio of 12 to 1, an iron barrel should be used, partly because of the thermal requirements of this fuel and partly because of the added strength in the base flange. However, irrespective of which type of barrel is used the spigot height must be checked and reduced if necessary to .124 in. if a splay-port head is being fitted; alternatively, iron barrels with the low spigot height are obtainable as spares.

## Twin-cylinder Carburation

Mention has been made already of the advisability of using separate carburetters on a vertical twin, and the need is even greater on a V-twin since it is virtually impossible to obtain equality of mixture with a single carburetter owing to the unequal periods between induction strokes.

The usual method of operating two carburetters is by means of a single wire from the twist-grip to a junction box, from which separate wires run to each throttle. This system sometimes causes the grip operation to be rather heavy and some riders are persuaded to shorten the throttle springs as the easiest way out. This is a bad idea because, if the slides do not close properly, erratic tick-over results. Pay attention to the run of the wires, leaving off all clips so that the wires can adopt their natural position. This usually effects a cure, but the best method is to obtain a dual-cable twist-grip or modify the existing one to take two wires.

It is essential to adjust each control so that both cylinders accelerate absolutely in unison. The best method with standard Amals is first to slacken both cables and set the tick-over on each cylinder by means of the throttle stops and pilot screws until even running is obtained. Next set the cable adjusters so that the slightest grip movement causes a rise in engine speed with each cylinder firing equally.

If with both slides apparently moving simultaneously, firing is still uneven, try the effect of closing each air lever in turn. If, say, one cylinder is missing or does not fire at all yet cuts in when its air control is closed, less cutaway is required on the throttle slide. In border-line cases, an enriching of the pilot mixture may help the offending cylinder to come off the pilot at the expense of slightly erratic slow-running. It is, of course, essential to have an individual air control to each cylinder; by intelligent use of that control equal carburation can be obtained throughout the entire range.

As there are no throttle-stops on racing-type carburetters, this system cannot be used; the idling speed can only be adjusted by varying the cable lengths but, if cut-aways on both slides are equal it is essential to verify that they both disappear simultaneously at the tops of the choke as the grip is opened, otherwise acceleration will not be good. If there is a big difference it will be necessary to check for air leaks or fuel blockage which may have affected the idling speed. Incidentally, it is quite useless to attempt to adjust the idling setting on one cylinder only with the other cut out by shorting the plug. The amount of throttle required to pull the engine round with only one lung operating is so much greater than with both in action that the scheme gets you nowhere.

Accuracy of the main jet settings must be verified finally by the appearance of the plugs, in exactly the same way as for a single-cylinder machine. Even if both carburetters are of exactly the same type and size, there is no certainty that the main jets, throttle cutaways and needle settings will all be exactly the same, because these are likely to be affected to varying extents by the air-pressures existing at the intakes and which are almost bound to be different in each case according to the local air-flow or the localities in which the intakes are placed. The position of the float-chambers in relation to the jets has a marked effect on mixture-strength during acceleration as described in Chapter XVIII, and this may be another cause of a difference in setting between the two instruments for optimum results.

CHAPTER XVI

TWO-STROKE ENGINES

TWO-STROKE engines differ fundamentally from four-strokes insofar as the charge is not induced directly into the cylinder, but is transferred to it from the crankcase, or from a separate pump which may be either a rotary blower or a cylinder-and-piston mechanism. Either of the two last-mentioned devices are permissible for record-breaking but, under the rule that prohibits the use of super-chargers in road-racing, an auxiliary pump which has a greater swept volume than that of the cylinder is definitely "out" and so are additional pumping pistons which act to increase the volume drawn into the crankcase.

Of recent years, therefore, the tendency has been to dis-card supercharged, or augmented-induction, designs which were in vogue before 1939 and to concentrate on the much simpler forms, relying solely upon straightforward crank-case compression such as are commonly used for touring work. Some really amazing results have been achieved by working upon these engines, speeds of 85 m.p.h. and over being obtained by private owners from 125 c.c. B.S.A. "Bantams" without recourse to fuels such as nitromethane and good results can also be obtained from Villiers engines, which are used in many current machines, and the more complex but still relatively simple split-single E.M.C. and Puch designs.

The basic line of development remains the same as for the four-stroke, namely to get the maximum quantity of fresh charge into the cylinder at the highest possible r.p.m., but it is more difficult to carry out because there are two sources of loss in volumetric efficiency—one in getting the fresh mixture into the crankcase and the other in transferring it to the cylinder. Consequently every endeavour must be made to reduce any losses in breathing ability to a minimum.

Dealing with the crankcase first, the initial step is to reduce the clearance space within it as much as possible by using disc flywheels or by building up existing flywheels or crankwebs until they almost fill the surrounding space and only just clear the connecting rod. This procedure may introduce some problems of balancing which may have to be solved later, but, at the outset, filling must be done in the lightest fashion either by using magnesium blocks or by sheet metal work, though in the latter case all joints communicating with cavities must be air-tight, otherwise the value of the scheme is largely lost. There must however be some clearance between moving and stationary surfaces. A certain amount of gas movement takes place therein, so it is advisable to polish both the flywheel assembly and the whole interior of the crankcase to assist this movement.

When, as is usual, the inlet port is controlled by the piston skirt, the time available for induction is extremely short, less than 1/300 sec. at 6,000 r.p.m., which can be considered a comparatively low speed for this type of engine in highly-tuned form. The ability of the port to pass gas depends upon its "time-area integral"; that is the combination of the area open at any given instant and the total amount of time elapsing between opening and closing points. Widening the port around the circumference gives a greater area, without altering the timing; deepening the port increases both the area and the time of opening, but must be done with great care, because the effective compression stroke of the piston in relation to the crankcase does not commence until the inlet port closes, unless the induction tract is of such a length that an appreciable ramming effect is generated by the fast-moving column of gas. To some extent, this ramming action is always present, but unless it comes at the right time, which is just towards the latter end of the closing period, it will be of little assistance. Actually, the combination of the crankcase and induction pipe (including the carburetter) constitutes a resonant system equivalent to a closed vessel with extension pipe and has a natural vibration frequency which can be used over a limited speed range to augment the ramming effect very considerably. Whether the problem is amenable to calculation with any accuracy is rather doubtful because of the number of variables involved, so the solution is best arrived at by trial and error.

Widening the port around the circumference is quite permissible and has little adverse effect because the piston-rings do not usually traverse this port, and naturally all the interior surfaces must blend well into each other and be polished. Provided that one is prepared to sacrifice low-speed torque, relatively enormous carburetters can be used; $1\frac{1}{8}$ in. or $1\frac{3}{16}$ in. type 29 Amals give very good results, and are less expensive than the R.N. or T.T. patterns.

From the crankcase, the gas, after compression, enters the cylinder through the transfer ports, and the angle of entry of these into the cylinder is of great importance in all flat-top piston designs. The early versions used two opposed exhaust ports and four transfer ports, the latter being so arranged that the streams of gas from each impinged at the centre-line and deflected each other up towards the top of the cylinder whence they curled downwards towards the exhaust ports. In later versions with only a single exhaust port there are only two transfer ports, which direct the fresh gas across the piston crown almost in the opposite direction to the outgoing exhaust gas. The streams then combine, travel upwards towards the head and then downwards towards the exhaust ports, the principle being referred to as loop-scavenging.

The angles of the entering gas streams are most important to obtain best scavenging with least loss of fresh charge out through the exhaust port and, though the ports can with advantage be enlarged a little, this process is best done in stages. In some designs, small cover-plates are provided through which access to the ports can be obtained but in others the casting is solid. In the case of the latter it is possible to build up around the elbow of the transfer passage with bronze, then machine the surface off level and break into the passage. The holes can finally be closed by fitting screwed-on cover-plates with internal extensions shaped to conform exactly to the interior contour. Any obstruction to gas-flow in this region is extremely detrimental, so that the whole of the transfer passages must be smoothed off and particular care taken to improve the entry into them from the crankcase by rounding off all sharp corners.

Exhaust ports in touring engines are usually made with the top edge inclined or angular; this gives a gradual opening and, by taking some of the "crack" out of the exhaust noise, simplifies the silencing problem to some extent. The inclined edge gives the rings an easier passage as they pass over it on the upward stroke. For racing, it is desirable to obtain the quickest possible rate of opening in order to make use of what is termed the "Kadenacy effect." Kadenacy discovered that, if the ports are large enough and are opened with sufficient rapidity, escaping gas rushes out with such vim that the cylinder pressure drops several pounds below that of atmosphere, and, by adding an exhaust pipe of the appropriate length, fresh gas is drawn into the cylinder through inlet ports even without the aid of crankcase compression or an external blower. In fact, one industrial engine, the Petter "Harmonic," after being started on crankcase compression, is run thereafter purely on air induced through the agency of tuned exhaust and intake pipes. This engine, being a diesel, operates all the time with a full air supply to the cylinder and is thus not directly comparable with the carburetter-type engines under discussion, but it is mentioned to indicate the great influence and importance of the exhaust system.

During the period of port-opening we have a cylinder, with its capacity continually varying as the piston moves towards b.d.c., connected by an orifice (the exhaust port), also of varying area, to an exhaust pipe, which is the only non-variable item in the system. As a further complication, the natural frequency of any system depends upon the speed of sound in the gas contained in it, and though it is usual to take 1,500 ft. per sec. as being a reasonably close figure for a normal four-stroke engine, sound-wave velocities of up to 4,000 ft. per sec. may be attained in a short exhaust system with a rapid discharge of high-pressure gas through piston-controlled ports. This factor alone would make calculation of suitable exhaust-pipe length difficult, to say the least, and may, in conjunction with the other variables, account for the wide diversity of systems in use. The Lambretta, for instance, had, in effect, a curved megaphone which starts right at the port and widens to about 4 in. diameter in 16 in. length, whereas the Eysink Villiers had two pipes, of more normal length, exhausting into fishtailed expansion boxes. B.S.A. "Bantams" operate well with a $1\frac{3}{4}$ in. pipe about 20 in. long, but for r.p.m. in excess of 8,000 the pipe can be shortened to about 10 in. if the regulations will permit a system of that length.

The functioning of a two-stroke exhaust is more complex than that of a four-stroke; it must first assist in evacuating the cylinder rapidly and in so doing is almost bound to draw a certain amount of fresh charge out through the port. By correctly proportioning the exhaust system, this charge can not only be retained in the pipe but can be rammed back into the cylinder by a wave of positive pressure arriving at the port towards the end of its closing period. Conversely, if the system is incorrect or the relationship of the transfer and exhaust closing points is wrong, a considerable portion of the charge may be lost irretrievably. Poor power development with a high fuel consumption and the strong smell of unburnt fuel in the exhaust are all signs that serious charge-loss is taking place. If the work is being conducted under laboratory conditions, an Orsatt gas analyser is an invaluable instrument for determining charge-loss as, by its use, an accurate measurement of the amount of free oxygen in the exhaust is obtained. There is bound to be some free oxygen, up to perhaps 2%, due to combustion not being absolutely complete, but anything above this figure (provided the mixture is correct) represents an actual charge-loss of *five times* the amount of excess, because, of course, only $\frac{1}{5}$ of the atmosphere is oxygen. With the aid of the Orsatt device, therefore, the effect of port- or exhaust-pipe modifications can be determined quickly, but without it, recourse must be had to the time-honoured "cut-and-try" method which, fortunately, is not too difficult or costly with a small single-cylinder engine.

A general scheme which has possibilities is to raise the upper edge of the inlet port until it is $\frac{1}{8}$ in. or so higher than the edge of the piston crown at b.d.c., so placing the carburetter in direct communication with the cylinder for a few degrees of crank-travel when the exhaust port is almost fully open. The reduction of cylinder pressure which comes about by the Kadenacy effect then causes fresh mixture to be induced through the inlet port at the same time that the normal supply is being fed into the cylinder via the transfer ports. There will be no supercharging created thereby, but a gain in power will result because of improved scavenging of the residual exhaust products. This device is essentially one which will work well only over a limited speed range and may result in very poor power output at other speeds.

When modifying port heights, the simplest method for trial purposes is to alter the cut-off edges of the piston instead of altering the barrel. The effect is not exactly similar because whilst the port timing is altered the actual area is not, but it will at least give an indication, and if a mistake is made, it is cheaper to replace a piston than to start all over again with another barrel. One of the most exasperating things about two-strokes is the difficulty of duplicating results; two barrels with ports which appear to be identical will rarely give equal power, possibly because small differences in port contour, which are difficult to measure, create differences in the direction of gas-flow and modify the degree of scavenging to a much greater extent than might be expected. The moral of this is that if you do get a good barrel, look after it; do not think that all you have to do when the experimental one is worn out is make another which looks the same.

One of the difficulties with a two-stroke is cooling; the cylinder does not have the benefit of the idle inlet stroke, nor is the fuel vaporized actually in the cylinder as in a four-stroke. Consequently the heat-loss to the walls is high, yet a large part of their area is occupied with ports which cause unequal temperatures and local distortion. Some riders go to the trouble of turning off the fins above the ports and shrinking on a finned aluminium jacket, but this does not really get down to the root of the matter and it is doubtful if it is worth doing on an engine used on road circuits where the greater cooling required by the increase in power is automatically supplied by the increase in air-speed.

Cylinder-heads with larger fins and a smaller combustion space giving compression ratios of about 12 to 1 have become commercially available for B.S.A. "Bantams"; as the pattern-work is relatively easy these are not difficult to make, though trouble with cracking round the plug-boss may be experienced unless the material is good. Heat-treated Y-alloy or R.R.53 will be perfectly satisfactory. In designing such a head it is easy to obtain an impressive appearance without much gain in cooling; to be of real value, fins must spring directly from the actual metal around the combustion space, there being little or no virtue in putting a fin on a fin. The old Villiers system of radially-disposed fins is excellent as the positioning of the fins is good and the air-stream has a clear path past each one, which is not always the case with deep parallel fins.

Flywheel magnetos appear to be able to run satisfactorily at any speed which can be got out of the engine but some experimenters prefer to utilize a 180° twin-cylinder magneto, running at half-engine speed with both leads going to one plug, which was standard practice on the E.M.C.-Puch, or with each lead going to its own plug in a special two-plug head, a scheme which gives the plugs an easier life. The reason for using a half-speed magneto is simply to reduce stresses in the instrument, as a normal magneto is not ordinarily called on to run at more than 4,000 r.p.m. It is essential, however, to have the magneto checked electrically to verify that the sparks do occur precisely at 180°, otherwise correct ignition cannot be obtained as a one-degree variation on the magneto means 2° variation on the engine.

It is general practice to use uncaged roller big-ends, there being insufficient lubrication to permit the use of cages. In some Villiers engines, the steel rollers are alternated with bronze rollers of slightly smaller diameter, the idea being that the bronze rollers do not carry any load but merely separate the steel rollers and rotate backwards; other models use the conventional crowded-row system. The big-end assembly of the B.S.A. was enlarged in 1954 and the later pattern should be used as a replacement on early models.

Interference-fit crank-pins without retaining nuts are commonly employed and can be assembled either in a press or a stout vice with parallel jaws. As there is some loss of interference-fit caused by removal and refitting, the replacement pins should be .001 in. larger than the originals. Villiers spares are supplied as standard with this amount of oversize. Great care must be taken to start the pin squarely in the hole to avoid any chance of damaging the surface, and a piece of shim steel .010 in. thick should be interposed between the rod and one crank-web to limit the final position of the crank-web and provide the necessary amount of side clearance. For finally truing-up the shafts, the easiest way is to hold the assembly in one hand and knock one crank-web in the required direction with a copper hammer; this is more effective with small assemblies than the "bumping" method employed with much heavier four-stroke flywheels.

Although seemingly simple, the design of a twin two-stroke crankshaft is not easy, because of the necessity to provide a sealed bearing between the crank chambers. On the Excelsior "Talisman" the right-hand assembly is built up and fitted to the case; one-half of the left-hand assembly follows and the central retaining nut fully tightened. Then the con-rod is fitted to this assembly and the last crank-web is placed in position. To facilitate this part of the work, the crank-pin is not a very tight fit in the web, the necessary rigidity being provided by supporting the main-shaft in two relatively widely-spaced bearings.

Crankcase pumping efficiency depends largely upon the seals provided at the main bearings, and which vary from make to make. The system common to all modern Villiers engines consists of flanged bronze bushes which are a sliding fit in the crankcase and have a slight clearance on the shafts. The flanges are pressed lightly against the crankcase by star-washers; none of these parts can be examined unless the case is heated and the bearing tapped out but they give little trouble unless the engine has been run with loose main bearings.

On B.S.A. "Bantam" engines there is a number of shims and one collar on the mainshafts; these must be replaced in exactly the same order, so their initial position should be remembered or noted down.

Mention was made in an earlier chapter of the necessity for accuracy of fit of two-stroke pistons, which have to be reasonably gas-tight on the skirt and must not run with excessive clearance. One line of attack is to fit the piston deliberately a little on the tight side, and give the motor a short burst on full throttle after sufficient running to warm everything up thoroughly. Then strip down and very carefully ease off piston areas on which excessive pressure is evident; a fairly rough file is better than a smooth one for this work, as the file marks act as oil reservoirs and may save a bad seizure. This process should be repeated several times until the motor will hold full throttle for a couple of miles with no sign of tightening.

It is useless attempting to run-in a two-stroke piston by covering a long distance at part-throttle openings; it is almost bound to seize the first time it is given a prolonged burst at full bore, because the temperature

*A step in the crankcase-transfer port joint hinders gas-flow and, therefore, impairs performance.*

STEP

217

distribution and, consequently, the shapes and dimensions of piston and barrel are then quite different from what they were during the light-load running period.

Obviously, the lower the coefficient of expansion of the piston material, the less will be the amount of distortion for the same temperature difference, and this has led to the introduction of pistons made from 16 per cent or 22 per cent silicon alloy, which are much better in this respect than any of the alloys regularly employed in quick four-strokes. The 1959 A.M.C. two-stroke piston is in 22 per cent silicon which enables the skirt clearance to be reduced to $1\frac{1}{2}$ thou. without fear of seizure. This alloy is also said to be less prone to burning of the top land at the danger-zone opposite the exhaust port: in an endeavour to eliminate this trouble completely some designers have experimented with chrome-plating applied to the crown and top land, but this is by no means a general practice and severe trouble would follow if the plating ever decided to flake off.

Another line of attack against the distortion problem pursued on the 125 and 250 twin M.Z. racing engines is to fit a relatively thick austenitic cast-iron liner, in which the ports can be accurately machined, into a very rigid finned sleeve made from high-silicon alloy and therefore closely matching the liner in its rate of expansion. Before fitting the liner, the transfer passages can be fully machined in the sleeve and given a high degree of surface finish; when finally assembled, the liner forms the dividing walls between the transfer passages and the bore. Incidentally, whilst a relatively small crankcase volume is desirable in order to increase pumping efficiency, it appears that there is more to be gained in the long run, by using transfer passages of generous cross-section and reduced resistance to flow, than by restricting their size in order to raise the crankcase compression ratio. Positive pressure existing on the down-stroke and negative pressure on the up-stroke both give rise to internal power loss and should therefore be kept as low as is possible, consistent with maintaining pumping efficiency.

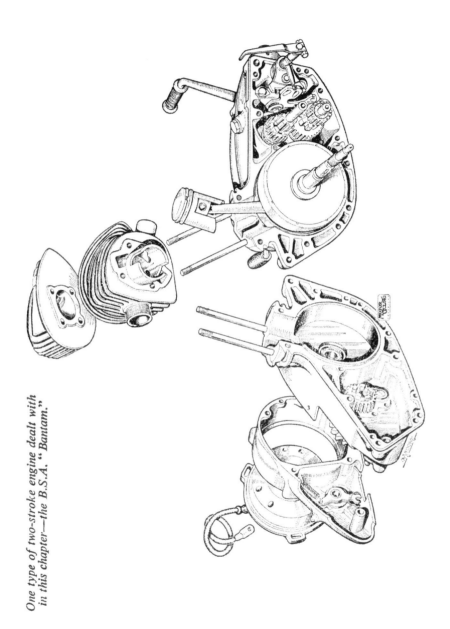

*One type of two-stroke engine dealt with in this chapter—the B.S.A. " Bantam."*

## Mechanical Inlet Valves

Piston-controlled inlet ports are only open for a short while at the top of the stroke, and a negative pressure of five or six pounds per square inch will be present for a considerable portion of each up-stroke; in addition, the very short time of opening must limit the amount of mixture which can be induced, even with the aid of a long induction pipe to give a ramming action, as used on the Adler. Lengthening the port increases the time element, but reduces the effective piston stroke, a condition which can only be eliminated by the use of some sort of valve which may be either automatic or positively operated. In the former class come the "reed" or diaphragm valves, once employed by D.K.W. and used with good effect today on some American outboard engines, and in the latter come the rotary valve built into the centre main bearing of the British-Anzani twin, and the disc valve used in some model aircraft engines and in the M.Z. In this specific instance, the disc is made of sheet steel, only half a millimetre thick, attached to a splined boss which floats on the mainshaft so that the disc is free to centralize itself in a narrow space provided between the crankcase wall, which is ported, and a cover plate which carries the inlet pipe and carburetter. Portion of the periphery of the disc is cut away so that it uncovers the port for a period of about 200°, but in order to maintain crankcase pressure during the transfer period, the inlet port opening does not commence until the transfer ports are nearly closed. One great advantage of this form of valve is that it is quite simple to alter the duration of opening by cutting away more of the disc or to alter the timing by re-positioning the boss on its splines, so it offers a fruitful field for investigation.

In the British-Anzani layout, the ports are formed by holes drilled in the centre journal, but are necessarily limited in size compared to the areas possible with a disc valve. Nevertheless, this engine gives a very good performance, which could perhaps be improved by careful work in the port-drillings to improve their shape and surface finish.

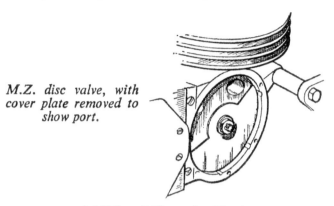

*M.Z. disc valve, with cover plate removed to show port.*

### Additional Transfer Ports

An idea used on D.K.W. and M.Z. engines and on which J. Ehrlich, the designer of the E.M.C. has done a great deal of work culminating in the granting of patents, is to utilize one or more additional transfer ports in the cylinder communicating with passages termed "regenerative" or "booster" chambers though neither term is an exact description. In the M.Z. version, a single chamber is located immediately opposite to the exhaust, and it opens to the cylinder via a port slightly lower than the transfer ports. At the inner end, there is another port in the cylinder-liner which is closed for most of the time by the piston, but is opened to the crankcase by a port cut in the piston wall just below the rings. During this "open" period compressed mixture is forced into the boost-chamber and retained there by the further descent of the piston until the boost-port into the working cylinder is opened by the top edge of the piston. A "puff" of mixture is thus discharged across the crown and clears away any dead gas which has not been scavenged by the streams from the two transfer ports. An additional and very real benefit of the scheme is that the mixture inside the piston does not remain stagnant, but is moved on at each stroke, thereby ventilating and cooling the underside of the crown.

221

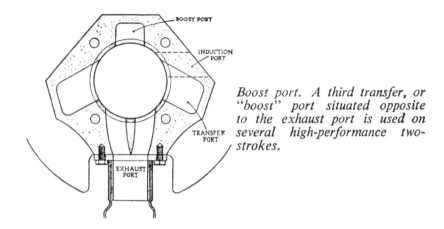

*Boost port. A third transfer, or "boost" port situated opposite to the exhaust port is used on several high-performance two-strokes.*

One Ehrlich design utilized two boost-ports, each located between the exhaust port and the transfer port, but the water-cooled version used on the E.M.C. from 1960 on has only one boost-port located, as in the M.Z., opposite to the exhaust. The Japanese Suzuki also contains this feature which, in conjunction with the rotary disc-valve, produces a power output of over 180 b.h.p. per litre at 11,000 r.p.m. Since reduction of internal friction is most important at these high revs, roller-bearing small-ends and chrome-plated steel rings are used.

In the 54 × 54 mm. 125 c.c. M.Z. the divided exhaust port is 25 mm. high and opens and closes 80° each side of b.d.c. The transfer ports are 15 mm. high, opening and closing at 68°, while the boost-port is 12 mm. high, opening and closing at 64°. The disc-valve opens at 45° after b.d.c. and remains open for 205°.

## Exhaust Systems

Earlier in this chapter, mention was made of the wide diversity of exhaust systems which have been tried, but of recent years the principle of exhausting into an expansion chamber with a very small outlet is universally used on Continental two-strokes. The details differ between make

222

and make and are finally settled by experiment, but the general scheme is to connect an expansion chamber of twelve to fifteen times the cylinder volume to the exhaust port with a very short pipe of large diameter, and to restrict the outlet either by using a very-small-diameter pipe (D.K.W.) or a larger pipe possibly with a variable method of reducing its area. On the 250 c.c. twin racing Adler, for instance, a washer with a hole about 18 mm. diameter is brazed into each tail-pipe, but on the M.Z. the pipe is clear, the whole proportions being approximately as shown in the sketch below. The "washer" method of varying the restriction would enable a series of experiments to be made very quickly and obviously there is much to be gained by arriving at a correctly-proportioned system of this nature.

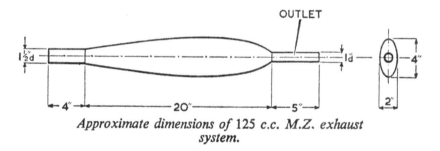

*Approximate dimensions of 125 c.c. M.Z. exhaust system.*

## Combustion-chamber Shape

The latest tendency in combustion-chamber shape is to employ a certain amount of "squish" by machining a portion of the surface so that it conforms to the section of the crown when the piston is at t.d.c. with 30 to 40 thou. clearance; with any amount appreciably less than this, the piston may touch at maximum revs.

The most favoured crown shape is a flattened segment of a sphere which provides the best combination of strength with absence of distortion, and provides good flow-lines for the working gas as it enters or leaves the ports.

The compression ratio can be as high as 14 or 15 to 1, even with petrol if of 100 octane, and the required volume

223

is obtained by machining a depression into the squish area; a position slightly off-centre and towards the front of the engine is used on the M.Z. but the optimum position and also the location of the plug may vary, as both depend on the direction taken by the gas at the end of compression under the influence of the turbulence created during the scavenging period. As the cylinder-bolts are usually disposed in a square formation, it is a simple matter to try the effect of reversing the head to alter the position of the combustion space in relation to the cylinder centre line. Sometimes, it is found that a plug-position which gives the best power is one which is prone to oiling or "drowning" the plug when starting or when opening-out after shutting-off for a corner and in that case a compromise may have to be effected.

The foregoing remarks are mainly of a generalized nature and many apply to engines which are unlikely to come into the hands of private owners, but they do show the lines along which the ultra-high-speed two-stroke is developing and indicate ways in which an earnest seeker after power may attain satisfactory results, if he has the right facilities. Most people will, however, have to be content with extracting more urge from commercially-obtainable motors which usually have piston-controlled inlet ports and are commonly though not quite correctly, referred to as the "flat-top piston" type. Of these, the B.S.A. "Bantam" has often been selected as a basis for the tuner's art, and the following remarks are based on the experience of A. E. Rose, who had a considerable degree of success with this engine. Although dimensional details would naturally differ, the same procedure would apply to other makes such as C.Z. or Jawa which operate on similar design principles.

The standard B.S.A. port timing, according to Rose, is:

Exhaust opens 70° b.b.d.c.
Transfer ports open 60° b.b.d.c.
Exhaust fully open 10° b.b.d.c.

224

Transfer ports fully open 10° b.b.d.c.
Transfer ports close 60° a.b.d.c.
Exhaust closes 70° a.b.d.c.

Opening period slightly later on recent engines.

The carburetter inlet aperture has a V-notch at the bottom, and for this port the timings are:

Closes to bottom of rectangle 50° a.t.d.c. (130° b.b.d.c.)
Closes to bottom of V-notch 60° a.t.d.c. (120° b.b.d.c.)
Opens to bottom of V-notch 60° b.t.d.c. (120° a.b.d.c.)
Opens to bottom of rectangle 50° b.t.d.c. (130° a.b.d.c.)
Fully open but shrouded by $\frac{1}{32}$ in. of piston skirt at t.d.c.

To obtain better breathing it is necessary to extend the ports both in height and width. In order to minimize the amount of grinding work and filing, and to improve access to the port, the inlet stub should be sawn off to within $\frac{3}{16}$ in. of the rear fin tips. Three first-class riffler files, double-ended and of assorted shapes, should be obtained by people not in possession of a grinding shaft. The standard port outline, where it enters the cylinder, is shown overleaf with the new shape superimposed. Gradually open out the port and blend it into a $\frac{7}{8}$ in. diameter orifice at the cut-off stub.

No more than $\frac{1}{32}$ in. should be removed from the top of the inlet port. The sides may be swept out up to $\frac{1}{8}$ in. and the base curved around to about $\frac{1}{64}$ in. below the original "V." Do not exceed a total depth of $\frac{3}{4}$ in. or the width shown, for the piston-ring ends lie comparatively near to this port at the bottom of the stroke. Owing to the size of the "Bantam" cylinder casting at the cut-off stub, it may not be possible to attain a truly circular port of $\frac{7}{8}$ in. diameter but this may be overcome by introducing a slight ovality, blending into the increasing width of the port.

A piece of $1\frac{1}{8}$ in. O.D. $\frac{7}{8}$ in. I.D. tube should be counter-bored at one end to accept the $\frac{3}{16}$ in. stub (here only about $\frac{1}{32}$ in. thick) and bronze-welded (not brazed) to the cylinder

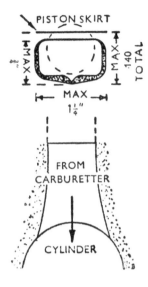

*The original inlet-port profile and (shaded) the area of metal to be removed to procure a modified outline suggested to improve "Bantam" induction.*

barrel. The bore of the tube may then be blended into the port so as to leave no step. A further sketch illustrates this job. Alternatively a flange may be welded on.

The shape and position of their upper orifices at the cylinder bore determine the "opening" and "closing" of the transfer ports, and the behaviour of the jets of mixture issuing from them. In standard form they are not capable of passing the greatly-increased quantities of mixture now induced into the crankcase and it will be necessary to modify

*Details of modifications to the inlet-port stub.*

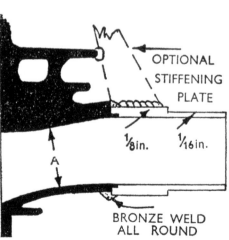

them. This can be affected in two ways, (1) by greatly increasing the width circumferentially, or (2) by moderate increase of the whole cross-section of the ports, very slightly altering the height of the cylinder orifices and reshaping the width to a streamlined form. The latter course is preferable.

Be careful not to leave a lip at the rear of the transfer port exit; this will cause the incoming column of gas to swing to the front of the cylinder, which is undesirable. It should be noted that the orifices are offset to the rear of the bore centre line for a distance of $\frac{1}{16}$ in. This assists the new gas to move toward the rear of the cylinder to displace the residual gases. One further point remains. The cylinder

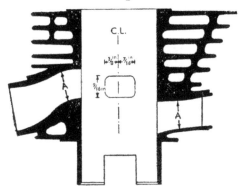

*Modified port dimensions. The reference "A" denotes the point of commencement of swell.*

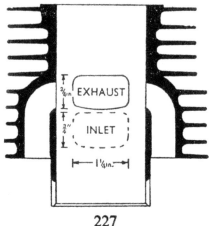

cutaway at the spigot should be streamlined where it is bevelled at the lower entrance to the port. Later "large fin" barrels have transfer ports adequate in size.

The timing of the exhaust port, as determined by its upper boundary, presents a problem. If the port is opened considerably earlier, its closing is similarly delayed, with the result that, when using a highly extractive exhaust system, a proportion of the hard-won fresh mixture may follow the exhaust gases. No doubt this does occur, anyway, at certain engine revolutions, but this is of little moment, provided the effect occurs outside the speed-range which will be employed. It has already been mentioned that in the ideal exhaust system, the rapid drop in pressure which follows the initial discharge is followed by a high-pressure pulse which is able to prevent any further flow through the port and may even reverse the flow, thus returning some of the lost charge to the cylinder. This enables a very early opening of the exhaust to be used, at the cost of reducing power at low speeds, and at the outset it is suggested that the exhaust port be modified only to the extent shown in the sketches by straightening the top edge and radiusing the sides. It is most important not to exceed the widths shown otherwise ring-breakage may follow through the tips being able to spring out into the ports. This is a point which must be watched most carefully in any other engine, with respect to all and not just the exhaust port only.

Attention can now be given to cleaning-up the transfer ports and their junction with the crankcase to remove any steps as indicated on page 217. The simplest method is to deal with each crankcase-half separately, applying a smear

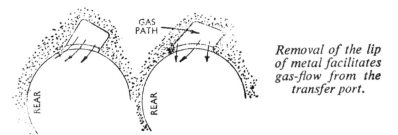

*Removal of the lip of metal facilitates gas-flow from the transfer port.*

of bearing-blue to the flange-faces to show up discontinuities. At the same time, the slots cut in the cylinder skirt should be matched up with the ports and the inner edges of the slots rounded off to assist in smooth gas-flow. A small additional improvement may be made at this stage by opening out the entrance to the main bearing oil-feed holes a trifle.

Where the last ounce of power is desired it is possible to fill up the crankcase a little. Two aluminium discs should be made to fit inside each crankcase half to reduce the volume. These should be a little less than $\frac{1}{16}$ in. in thickness in order to clear the flywheels and they should be cut away in the centres to permit main bearing replacement and also at the top so as to coincide with the "step" in the crankcase.

Fix the plates to the crankcase walls by drilling in suitable positions, tapping and using $\frac{3}{16}$ B.S.F. set-screws. The discs should be drilled and countersunk; screws with countersunk heads should be used. The heads should be filed flat if they protrude in order to clear the flywheels. Coating the threads with jointing compound will eliminate the chances of leakage should the walls be penetrated when drilling, and also help to secure the screws.

It may appear that these discs have little practical value. Calculation of their volume will show that they account for several cubic centimetres and an appreciable percentage of the crankcase and under-piston volume. The general effect will be to maintain higher crankcase pressures, possibly increasing carburetter blowback at low engine speeds, but assisting proper transference of the charge at useful racing speeds.

Piston shape determines, with the port positions, the timing of the engine, and perhaps the most important dimensions are those which operate over the inlet tract. It will be seen that the longer the rear skirt is, the later it will uncover the inlet port when ascending and the sooner it will close it when descending. Provision has already been made for "longer" timings by bringing down the bottom of the inlet port and a further improvement may be made by filing

*Driving out the crank-pin and parting the fly-wheels in order to get access to the big-end bearing is simplified by Service Tool 61–3206.*

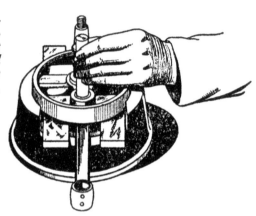

away the bottom of the piston skirt at the rear. It can be seen that, in a standard engine, the skirt does not clear the port when the piston is at t.d.c. This factor, in addition to reducing the effective area of the port, also causes turbulence around the skirt, reducing the port efficiency.

If necessary, therefore, the skirt should be cut away $\frac{1}{8}$ in. at the rear or $\frac{3}{16}$ in. (up to the base ring of aluminium) for racing. This alteration will have the following effects: (1) to open the port earlier and close it later. (2) to eliminate the port obstruction. (3) to allow a "dwell" period of full open-

|  | NEW | OLD | INCREASED PERIOD |
|---|---|---|---|
| Exhaust opens, b.b.d.c. | 75° | 70° | — |
| Exhaust closes, a.b.d.c. | 75° | 70° | 10° |
| Transfer ports open, b.b.d.c. | 65° | 60° | — |
| Transfer ports close, a.b.d.c. | 65° | 60° | 10° |
| Inlet port opens, a.b.d.c. | 115° | 120° | — |
| Inlet port closes, a.t.d.c. | 65° | 60° | 10° |

ing of the port as the crankpin swings across its top arc, the total alterations giving this timing.

The next operation is to build up the flywheel assembly, piston and cylinder on one crankcase half and mark the piston so that it may be radiused at each cut-away to blend with the cylinder and crankcase ports which have already received attention. Repeat on the other side and then bevel the front of the piston skirt slightly and put a $\frac{1}{8}$ in. radius on the base of each cut-away corner. Some authorities prefer to use second-hand pistons, suitably polished; they have settled down and, therefore, have little tendency to seize.

Coming now to compression ratio, this can be increased to about 9 to 1 for fast road work, but for racing on 80 octane petrol, 11 to 1 may be used with confidence and for 100 octane or alcohol fuels up to 13 to 1 is feasible. The volume of the raised crown of the 125 c.c. Bantam is 3 c.c., so the actual volume of the head for any required ratio should be 3 c.c. bigger than that obtained from the graph on page 54. One way of reducing the head volume is by building-up the existing chamber by argon-arc welding and then re-machining the sphere and plug-hole as depicted, as the central position is said to increase maximum speed slightly and the plug does not oil-up. Other workers have also reported good results with squish-type heads, particularly at very high compression ratios.

The improved volumetric efficiency and higher compression pressures call for a reduced ignition advance, though the exact amount depends upon many factors, including the type of fuel; a figure around 20° is a good starting-point with ratios of 11 or 12 to 1. With the B.S.A. flywheel magneto it is necessary to cut away the contact-breaker housing in the region of the three slots and clamp down by means of short distance-pieces and washers and the original screws. Measured on the stroke, the breaker-points should open at .110 in. before t.d.c. for 21° or .096 for 19°, according to the amount of advance required. Some users of two-strokes with flywheel magnetos prefer to substitute a lighter, plain wheel, merely retaining the con-

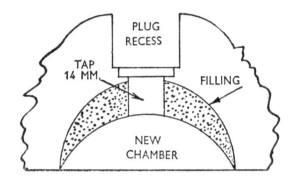

*A sectional impression of a modified high-compression cylinder-head showing filling material machined to the required hemisphere.*

tact-breaker to operate a battery and coil ignition system. One popular arrangement is to use a 6-volt battery, and a 4½-volt coil as fitted to Ford side-valve V-eight engines, the reason being that this combination will deliver the right number of sparks, despite some degree of voltage-loss inseparable from the high speed of operation.

## "Bantam" Carburetter Tuning

Assuming that a T.T. Amal of ⅞-in. bore is used, the setting to start off with, for petrol, is No. 4 slide, needle 2nd groove from top, main jet around 300, but this varies according to the exhaust system used. For alcohol it may have to go up to 650 or 800. Still larger carburetters can be used for fast, open circuits, but whatever the size, the object when tuning is to select a main-jet which will just cause the engine to begin to four-stroke when the air-lever is moved back to three-quarters open from the full-open position; the air-lever should always be mounted where it can be conveniently operated at speed. New checks should always be made whenever the inlet or exhaust lengths are altered, however slightly, and a highly-tuned two-stroke should always be run on a slightly rich mixture rather than a slightly weak one, as the former keeps the engine cooler and an occasional stutter through richness will not reduce speed appreciably. After determining the main jet size, experiments must be made with the throttle valve and needle position in order to get the cleanest acceleration, as outlined in Chapter XVIII. This is especially important when standing-starts have to be made, as otherwise the engine may die immediately the clutch is let in.

When alcohol fuel is used, Castrol "R" or a similar type of oil must be employed, because it is soluble in this fuel whereas mineral oil is not. Castor oil is also able to dissolve in some modern petrols and should be used whenever possible. Some riders prefer to increase the proportion from the normal 16 or 20 to 1, to as much as 10 to 1, in the interests of mechanical reliability, but the presence of oil in the mixture in effect lowers the octane number of the fuel and detonation may rise from this cause. The latest Continental two-strokes appear to function quite well on a proportion of 25 to 1. The amount of oil in the fuel affects the main-jet size appreciably, and once determined the proportion should be adhered to.

Experiments have been carried out with a 12-in.-long megaphone and a 12° pipe divergence, the exhaust pipe being shortened gradually. Sometimes a length which gives good power at high revolutions introduces a "miss", or flat spot, in the carburation at other speeds. A fairly sound scheme is to have an exhaust pipe which terminates at the "Bantam" front chain-cover studs, or up to 3 in. shorter if a megaphone is attached.

If the big-end is in good order, there is not much more to do. An improvement to the lubrication of the "Bantam" big-end is possible, however, by belling out the slots of the connecting-rod eye on the outside. This can be done by

*Belling out the oil slot in the connecting-rod big-end eye of pre-1953 model "Bantams", tends to improve lubrication at this highly stressed point.*

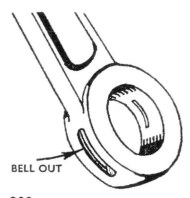

BELL OUT

running the lip of a grinding wheel around the edges. The 1953-type rod is cut away at the big-end faces to achieve the same result. This, with the more liberal oil supply coming from the new, larger jets, results in bearing reliability. Attention is drawn to the fact that the "Bantam" 1953 big-end bearing is ⅛ in. wider than its predecessors and, therefore, has a better load capacity.

An improvement to magneto-side main-bearing lubrication can be carried out by drilling the duralumin distance collar, which fits against the bearing, so that the holes line

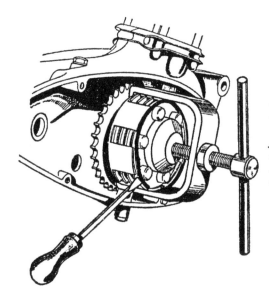

*Special tool No. 61–3191, in conjunction with a screwdriver facilitates the dismantling of the "Bantam" clutch-retaining circlip and main clutch assembly.*

up with the balls in the bearing. Ten ⅛ in. holes will do. If, when reassembling the crankshaft and case, there is a sense of stiffness, or a tight spot, suspect your initial inspection of the bearings. New bearings will be slightly stiffer in rotational movement. Or possibly the shafts are not in line; they should be tested in the usual way between centres. True them by tapping—before the covers are put in position—and re-test.

Obviously, gearbox bearings and bushes should be checked; the splines and dogs should be inspected because the increased power it is hoped to attain may reveal weakness in the transmission component. Irrespective of condition,

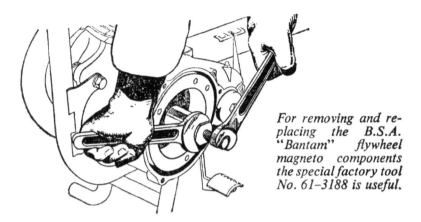

*For removing and replacing the B.S.A. "Bantam" flywheel magneto components the special factory tool No. 61–3188 is useful.*

the following improvement is suggested. The second-gear notch in the selector should be deepened to a $\frac{3}{16}$ in. "V" and the selector spring shimmed to a depth of $\frac{1}{8}$ in. in its housing. The gear selector-arm retaining spring, located by a cup and secured by a split-pin, should be reinforced by adding a short spring inside. This spring should be about $\frac{3}{8}$ in. O.D. and care should be taken that the coils do not bind at normal movement of the selector mechanism.

Alternatively, a heavier main spring may be fitted but this "mod" must not prevent the change mechanism from functioning properly. These improvements to a "Bantam" box are necessary to avoid the tendency for second gear to be forced out of engagement due to the selector mechanism side-thrust under racing loads.

The clutch on the average two-stroke unit is quite up to its job and will perform well under racing conditions without any increase being made in spring pressure. Inspection should be made, of course, to ensure that the friction inserts are not worn. Running under oil-bath conditions, these clutches are most reliable and heat-resistant.

The magneto flywheel is fitted with the engine installed; care should be taken to see that it is well home on its taper and tightly locked up. The Wico-Pacy instrument will give very good service and the engine can be revved to well over 7,000 r.p.m. without misfiring.

## Close-ratio Gears

The inevitable effect of increasing the top-end power and speed is to diminish the engine's ability to pull at low speeds, and consequently five- or six-speed gear boxes are now the accepted thing. These are not normally obtainable on English models, although a five-speed Albion box is now available; four-speed boxes are fitted as standard to many English and continental units, and it is usually possible to obtain special close-ratio sets for racing. In the case of the "Bantam", the parts required for conversion to close-ratio gears are:

(1) Gearbox main shaft and fixed pinion with 19-t. B.S.A. Part No. 90-445.
(2) Layshaft pinion 23-t. meshes with (3). Part No. 90-447.
(3) Mainshaft primary gear (sleeve gear) with 24-t. Part No. 90-474.
(4) Layshaft sliding pinion (C.R.) 25-t. Part No. 90-449.
(5) Layshaft gear—meshes with (1)—28-t. Part No. 90-448.

Use the standard layshaft but remove the 19-t. gear, observing correct way round, and press on the 23-t. gear pinion.

The ratios of the two sets are as below:

STANDARD "BANTAM" RATIOS

| | SLEEVE | SLIDING | INTEGRAL | RATIOS |
|---|---|---|---|---|
| Mainshaft | 28-t | 22-t | 15-t | Top 7:1 |
| Layshaft | 19-t | 25-t | 32-t | 2nd 11.7:1 |
| | | | | 1st 22:1 |

*All ratios with 15-t gearbox sprocket and standard 47-t rear wheel sprocket.*

CLOSE RATIO

| | SLEEVE | SLIDING | INTEGRAL | RATIOS |
|---|---|---|---|---|
| Mainshaft | 24-t | 22-t | 19-t | Top 7:1 |
| Layshaft | 23-t | 25-t | 28-t | 2nd 8.4:1 |
| | | | | 1st 10.78:1 |

# CHAPTER XVII

## ASSEMBLING THE ENGINE IN THE FRAME

ASSUMING that the frame of the machine is not suspected of having been damaged or is not out of line in any way, the next step is to assemble the engine into it; this is usually a fairly straightforward matter calling for little comment in itself.

If the design is such that the unit can be built up as a whole on the bench and then dropped into the frame, that is the best sequence to employ, because it permits the rear engine plates and bolts to be fitted without any juggling or forcing into line. Whatever the method, however, it is important that those bolts and others which connect the plates to the frame lugs really *are* a good fit in their respective holes, and that all mating holes are accurately in line. Slack-fitting bolts are very prone to work loose, however tight the nuts may be, and if the holes are out of line to an extent, calling for a considerable amount of levering (and perhaps a few hammer blows) to work the bolts into position, peculiar internal stresses are created, which accentuate any tendency there may be for vibration to be set up at certain speeds.

Commercial engine bolts are generally made from mild steel, but for serious racing something better is worth while, particularly in view of the fact that the bolts will have to be

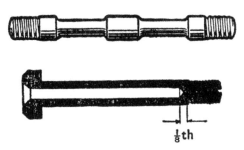

$\frac{1}{8}$th

*Waisting bolts down to a diameter equal to that of the bottom of the threads, leaving a central parallel portion for registering purposes, or, if a bolt has a solid head, drilling down the centre makes for lightness without sacrificing strength.*

taken out and replaced several times in a season. For such bolts, heat-treated K.E. 805 steel cannot be bettered; this material is very strong and tough, and is not liable to strip the threads if tightened by an over-zealous hand. A less expensive grade, such as 3% nickel steel, is a good substitute.

A not inconsiderable saving in weight can be effected by waisting the bolts down to a diameter equal to the bottom diameter of the threads, leaving a short parallel portion at each end to centralize the bolt or act as a register for the engine plates if required; alternatively, if the bolts have

TABLE OF DRILL SIZES

| BOLT SIZE | CORRECT HOLE DIAMETER | DRILL SIZE | NEAREST FRACTIONAL SIZE |
|---|---|---|---|
| 1/4 in. B.S.F. (26 T.P.I.) | 0.151 | No. 25 | 9/64 in. |
| 5/16 in. B.S.F. (22 T.P.I.) | 0.185 | No. 13 | 3/16 in. |
| 5/16 in. × 26 T.P.I. | 0.174 | No. 17 | 11/64 in. |
| 3/8 in. B.S.F. (20 T.P.I.) | 0.208 | No. 4 | 13/64 in. |
| 3/8 in. × 26 T.P.I. | 0.185 | No. 13 | 3/16 in. |
| 7/16 in. B.S.F. (18 T.P.I.) | 0.239 | Size B | 15/64 in. |
| 7/16 in. × 20 T.P.I. | 0.228 | No. 1 | 7/32 in. |
| 7/16 in. × 26 T.P.I. | 0.202 | No. 7 | 13/64 in. |
| 1/2 in. B.S.F. (16 T.P.I.) | 0.271 | Size 1 | 17/64 in. |
| 1/2 in. × 20 T.P.I. | 0.244 | Size C | 1/4 in. |
| 1/2 in. × 26 T.P.I. | 0.217 | 7/32 in. | 7/32 in. |

solid heads they can be drilled down the centre, as shown in the diagram, the hole (which must be accurately concentric with the outside) extending very nearly to the beginning of the thread. Far from weakening the bolts, this treatment actually makes them less prone to fatigue-failure and, if carried out consistently throughout the whole machine, a perceptible mass of excess metal will be eliminated.

The table above gives the right drill sizes to employ for the varying diameters and thread pitches which are commonly used for engine and frame bolts.

When making up those engine-securing bolts which also

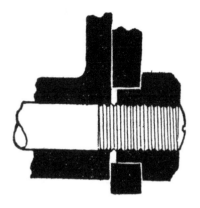

*Spigot nuts made to fit enlarged engine-plate holes cure wear and obviate the risk of vibration.*

pass through the engine plates, the length of the thread should be such that the plates have at least half their thickness bearing on the full bolt diameter and not on the crests of the thread, otherwise the latter will rapidly hammer down and looseness will develop. Occasionally in old machines some of the plate holes will be found to be oval or enlarged, in which event they can either be reamed out to $\frac{1}{8}$-in. oversize, and bushed to bring them back to original size, or else special spigot nuts can be made up to fit the enlarged holes. The latter is a good idea, particularly if the plates are thin, because the bolt threads are then protected from further damage from the action of the plates.

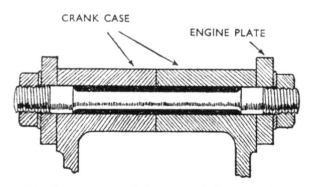

CRANK CASE

ENGINE PLATE

*Whether or not a bolt, or stud, is waisted, be careful to see that at least half the width of the engine plates bear on the full bolt diameter—not wholly on the thread crests which will rapidly wear.*

239

With all engine and gearbox bolts tight, the chain alignment should be carefully checked. Two straight edges should be used in preference to one, since this method shows up any errors more clearly. The most common error is for the sprockets, though parallel, to be displaced sideways relative to each other; in some designs this may be caused by clutch inserts of incorrect thickness, for which the remedy is obvious, but in other patterns (such as the Burman, in which the insert thickness cannot influence the chain-line) the spacer-washers between the clutch body and the shoulder on the gearbox mainshaft may be of incorrect thickness.

Another cause met with when an engine-shaft shock-absorber is fitted, is wear on the inner face of the engine-sprocket, but in any event this form of error is usually not difficult to eliminate. Lack of parallelism is rare, which is fortunate, as it is more difficult both to trace the source and effect a cure.

If the engine plates are interchangeable a quick check can be made by swopping them over, side for side, and if the error has vanished, or is still there but in the opposite direction, obviously the plates are at fault. If this course cannot be adopted, or yields negative results, the faces of the box lugs may not be square to the mainshafts, which can be verified by bolting the box down on to a block on a surface plate and checking the parallelism of the sprocket with the plate. Should an error thereby be brought to light, the lug faces will have to be carefully filed up to eliminate it.

When under load, the pull of the chain has a tendency to deflect the shafts towards each other and, consequently, a slight *outward* divergence of the shafts is not necessarily detrimental. But if the shafts are inclined *towards* each other when at rest, both sprockets will be badly out of line when under load. It is not sufficient merely to check the alignment along the top run of the chain; the bottom run should also be checked, and any noticeable difference between the two is evidence that the box is twisted relative to the engine. This can be caused by lack of flatness of the engine plates, or, in designs where the box is mounted on a bracket separated

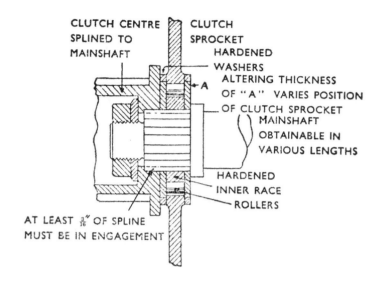

CLUTCH CENTRE
SPLINED TO
MAINSHAFT

CLUTCH
SPROCKET
HARDENED
WASHERS
ALTERING THICKNESS
OF "A" VARIES POSITION
OF CLUTCH SPROCKET
MAINSHAFT
OBTAINABLE IN
VARIOUS LENGTHS

A

HARDENED
INNER RACE
ROLLERS

AT LEAST $\frac{3}{16}''$ OF SPLINE
MUST BE IN ENGAGEMENT

*Self-explanatory methods of (above) adjusting chain line from the clutch end, and (below) making similar alteration to the engine sprocket assembly.*

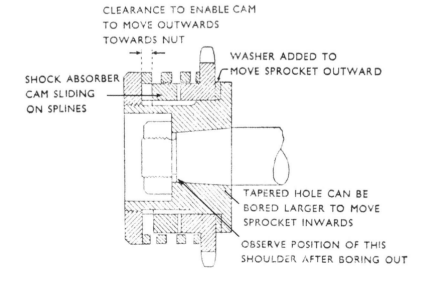

CLEARANCE TO ENABLE CAM
TO MOVE OUTWARDS
TOWARDS NUT

WASHER ADDED TO
MOVE SPROCKET OUTWARD

SHOCK ABSORBER
CAM SLIDING
ON SPLINES

TAPERED HOLE CAN BE
BORED LARGER TO MOVE
SPROCKET INWARDS

OBSERVE POSITION OF THIS
SHOULDER AFTER BORING OUT

from the engine, there is a possibility that the frame itself is twisted.

Accuracy of alignment is particularly important at speeds of 6,000 r.p.m. and over; for instance, on A.J.S. racers of recent manufacture, provision is made to obtain almost dead accuracy by the addition of shims behind the sprocket. It is somewhat confusing, therefore, that speedway J.A.P. engines are fitted with floating sprockets with about $\frac{1}{4}$-in. lateral movement, but this is to allow for the flexure which is inherent in the very light frames employed for this work. So long as the chain does not come off the sprockets, it does not matter much if its life-span is short in this instance.

Chain lubrication is vital for high speed; the best scheme with an open chain is to adopt the Norton practice of feeding mineral oil through a suitable jet to a divided pipe from which the oil drips on to the side-plates just before the chain starts to run on to the clutch sprocket. The aim is to get the lubricant directed into the actual joints, as the rollers themselves need little lubrication externally.

When adjusting a primary chain in a layout employing aluminium engine plates, or in a unit-construction plot, allowance must be made for thermal expansion, by permitting about 1 in. up-and-down play; a little too much slack does not harm a chain nearly so much as too little. The best plan is to adjust a little on the tight side then to operate the adjuster to bring the box slightly forward: the adjuster then holds the box forward against the pull of the rear chain, and there is no possibility of the box being shifted rearwardly.

# CHAPTER XVIII

# MAINTENANCE OF RACING CARBURETTERS

THE standard needle-jet Amal carburetter is a very simple instrument which, owing to its "straight through" construction, gives a higher power output, size for size, than other types which make use of butterfly throttles. From the standard pattern there have been developed a number of special racing editions with the object of obtaining maximum power and acceleration throughout the whole of the speed range. Of these the best known are the T.T. type and the remote-needle or R.N. type. In addition, non-needle models have been produced for track and dirt racing, where engines are operating at full bore most of the time, and in 1952 the GP types appeared.

In the T.T. pattern the needle—which meters the fuel at certain throttle openings—is suspended from the top of the throttle slide, and thus hangs across the centre of the choke. In the R.N. pattern—as its name implies—the needle is suspended from an extension on the throttle slide and is housed within a chamber cast on the side of the carburetter body; thus the needle offers no obstruction to air-flow, and as a result the R.N. type is slightly faster than the T.T. pattern for any given choke size.

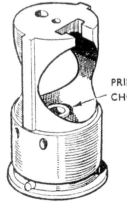

PRIMARY CHOKE

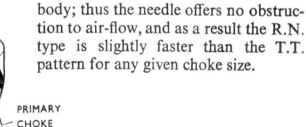

*The main choke, showing the small primary choke protruding into the airstream. The block is of the standard type but T.T. and R.N. types are similar in principle.*

243

The more devious fuel passages in the R.N., however, render it rather more sensitive at low engine revs., which means that the T.T. pattern offers more foolproof carburation and is a little easier to tune than the R.N. The latter also occupies more space (due to the presence of the remote-needle chamber), which sometimes makes it difficult to house.

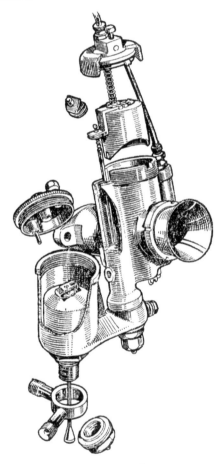

*The position of the taper needle, which is "remote" from the main intake tract, gives the initials R.N. to this type of racing carburetter. Being carried in a separate chamber off-set from the main barrel of the instrument, the needle offers no obstruction to the air-flow.*

In all types the diameter of the main choke, at the point where the small primary choke protrudes upwards into the airstream, is usually bigger than the bore of the instrument immediately on the engine side of the throttle. This latter and smaller diameter is actually the choke size and corresponds to the figure stamped on the outside of the mixing chamber for identification.

The increase in diameter referred to is provided (*a*) to minimize the obstruction to air-flow caused by the uprush of liquid fuel from the primary choke, and (*b*), in the case of the T.T. type, to help overcome the obstruction caused by the needle. Therefore, when discussing choke sizes, it is important to remember that the choke size refers to the diameter of the bore just past the throttle valve, and not to the larger diameter at the point where the throttle-valve works. In $1\frac{3}{16}$ in. and 32 mm. carburetters, however, this reduction in diameter is not present.

The normal R.N. type is essentially a petrol-benzole instrument, and cannot be used with a main jet size larger than 900, whereas simply by fitting a larger size of needle jet, the T.T. type can be used with straight alcohol up to a jet size of around 1500. The needle jet is formed by the hole in the upper end of the brass component into the lower end of which the main jet is screwed, and is varied for different sizes of carburetters.

Up to 1-in. choke diameter, the standard size is .107 in., and over 1-in. diameter it is .109 in. For alcohol fuel the .107-in. jet must be replaced by one of .113-in. diameter, while the .109-in. jet should be replaced by one of either .113 in. or .120 in., according to the size of main jet which the fuel necessitates. Incidentally, alcohol fuels vary considerably in their chemical make-up and some require a much larger jet than others; one characteristic of these fuels is their relative insensitivity to jet size as compared with petrol, and excessively rich mixtures can be handled without the loss of power which would be associated with petrol.

A special type of R.N. carburetter has been evolved for use with alcohol, primarily for use on the dirt; this has a .160-in. needle jet, as opposed to the .109-in. size fitted in the petrol-benzole edition. But other considerations are involved, and if the two sorts of fuel are to be used, then two R.N. carburetters will be required, whereas a single

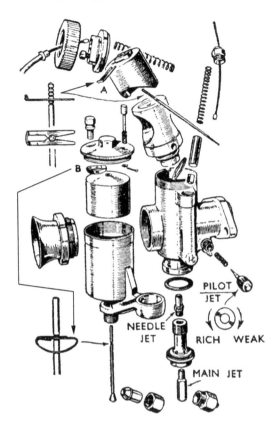

*On the T.T. pattern carburetter it is the air slide only which operates in a separate chamber; the taper needle is centrally disposed as in the standard instrument.*

T.T. type will suffice for both fuels with the requisite change in needle and main jets.

To obviate this situation, and also to incorporate some design features which render the carburetter less sensitive to "megaphoning" and yet retain an unobstructed choke, the GP type has been evolved. The salient feature of this type is that the needle is suspended from the throttle-valve so that it is just to one side of the choke, and the fuel enters the choke through a spray-tube inclined at an angle instead of directly underneath as in the R.N. and T.T. types. The passage from the needle jet to the end of the spray tube is, therefore, quite short and direct, a most desirable feature. To furnish a more precise tuning control, the metering jets are supplied in two tapers but there are only five adjusting grooves in each, instead of seven, and there is an additional mixture control provided by an air jet, situated between the air control slide and the needle-jet passage. This jet, which can be unscrewed after removing the hexagon plug at the base of the air slide, is made in two sizes, .100 in. and .125 in. bore, and the appropriate size is fitted to each carburetter by the manufacturers. Normally no alteration is necessary, but if difficulty is found in obtaining absolutely precise mixture control, it may be advantageous to alter the size from that already fitted. Increasing the size weakens, and decreasing it enriches the mixture (see page 260).

The main jets are interchangeable with those used in R.N. and T.T. carburetters, but the needle jets, throttle valves and needles are different. There are three basic models in the GP series, the 15 GP in choke sizes from $\frac{7}{8}$ in. to $1\frac{1}{16}$ in., 10 GP from $1\frac{1}{16}$ in. to $1\frac{7}{32}$ in. and 5 GP from $1\frac{7}{32}$ in. to $1\frac{3}{8}$ in., which is considerably larger than that of any R.N. or T.T. previously obtainable commercially. The two smaller groups utilize similar needles, designated and marked GP (standard) and GP6 (weak) and are flange-mounted with bolts at the regular 2 in. centre distance, but the 5 GP range uses its own needles, marked 5 GP (standard) and 5 GP6 (weak) and has flange bolts spaced at 65 mm. or 2.56 in. Hence, while all the other types are interchangeable, so far as the flanges are concerned, the 5 GP cannot be fitted directly unless the head has been drilled especially for it, as in the case of the short-stroke "Manx" Nortons. GP instruments are fitted with long air-intakes and although less bulky laterally than the R.N. types, may be difficult to instal on account of extra length. In this connection it is essential to place the mouth of the intake in a position where carburation cannot be upset by stray air currents blowing across or into it. Some odd effects can be created by, for instance, the flat surface of an oil tank within an inch or so of the intake; carburation trouble was prevalent on the early A.J.S. "Porcupine" owing to the air whistling at high velocity through the tunnel in the saddle tank in which the carburetters were placed. (See pages 260 and 276 for more notes on GP, GP2 and Monobloc carburetters.)

## Float Chambers and Location

Both T.T. and R.N. carburetters use orthodox single float chambers, with enlarged passages capable of passing as great a flow of fuel as the double float chambers which were popular some years ago, and which are still used at times with alcohol fuel.

With twin floats, the fuel lines also can be duplicated and there is less risk of complete fuel supply failure. But it must be remembered that, if one side blocks, the other cannot pass enough methanol to supply the engine and a hole may be burnt in the piston crown very rapidly, this being the inevitable outcome of running with a weak mixture at ratios of more than 12 to 1.

*Variation in fuel level, caused, for example, by cornering with a sidecar, gives this effect, and causes "cutting-out."*

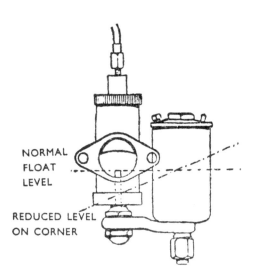

NORMAL
FLOAT
LEVEL

REDUCED LEVEL
ON CORNER

Amal top-feed float chambers, type 302 or 504, fitted to all GP carburetters can handle all the fuel required for the largest jets ever used, and are also equipped with an anti-frothing baffle. Frothing can be a puzzling reason for loss of revs., owing to the rich mixture which it causes, and to minimize this possibility, it is advisable to mount the float chamber on an adjacent part of the frame connecting it to the jet block by a flexible petrol-proof hose, or a piece of

P.V.C. plastic tubing, making sure that it is not bent so sharply that it may kink and shut off the flow. A bronze spring pushed inside the tube will obviate kinking.

It is preferable to place the float chamber fairly close to the carburetter, but the hose must be long enough to absorb engine vibration without undue flexing and possible damage

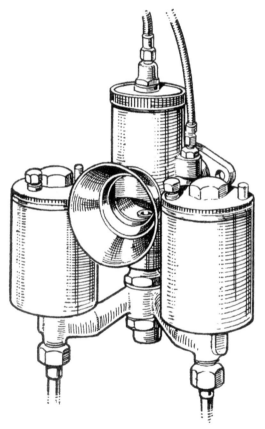

*Twin-float carburetters offer advantages where alcohol fuel is used.*

to the lining; the relative movement which occurs between the cylinder head and frame on some machines is much larger than might be imagined.

One method of remote mounting is to clamp the bowl bodily to an object such as the tank; another, and very neat system is to screw a rod into the chamber top or union nut and hang the chamber from a flexible rubber mount bolted to some convenient spot such as a tank bracket.

The float should not be placed appreciably to the rear of the jet, as the fuel will tend to lag behind during violent acceleration, and this may cause the engine to hesitate when opened up on the road. Somewhat the same effect occurs when cornering sharply on a sidecar outfit, and can be entirely eliminated only by using a double float chamber, or by the addition of a " swill pot " (which resembles a small float chamber, minus the float, needle valve and petrol union) placed at the side of the mixing chamber farthest from the main float chamber, the latter being remotely mounted in the approved fashion. Under the action of centrifugal force the fuel level drops in one chamber and rises in the other; thus the level of fuel at the jet remains approximately constant.

### Carburetter Tuning

On page 276 is given a range of carburetters and approximate main-jet sizes which have been found suitable on various machines, but it must be understood that any such list can form only a very rough guide. So many varying characteristics are involved that hard-and-fast rules cannot be laid down, and every racing engine must be treated as an individual unit when final tuning is being performed. Note that the main jet sizes for GP carburetters are very much smaller than for any of the other types.

The fuel used, the nature of the course and its geographical position, all have their effects, which can be allowed for only by experience coupled with trial-and-error methods of obtaining the optimum settings. The exhaust system in use also exercises a profound effect on carburation; as will be seen later, a larger jet is required with a megaphone than with a straight-through pipe, whilst a smaller jet is required if any form of silencer is fitted.

The best method of determining the correct main jet is to drive the engine (after it is fully warmed up) " flat out " over a distance of at least a quarter-mile, and at the finish to slam the throttle shut, cut the engine dead and immediately lift the clutch, thus avoiding any alteration to the sparking-

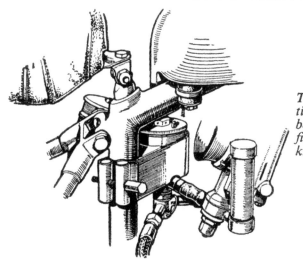

*The tendency mentioned above may be corrected by fitting what is known as a "swill pot."*

plug condition caused by the slow-running mixture or excess oil. The sparking plug is then removed and examined. If the end of the body is of a grey or lightish colour, then the mixture is weak and a larger jet is required. If it is heavily coated with soot, the jet is too big and a smaller one is required. With a correct mixture, the end of the plug should have the appearance of polished ebony; but, of course, this condition will be achieved only if the plug was clean (and preferably lightly polished) on the face before fitting. "Reading" a plug is quite an art which takes a little experience to acquire. Also, modern plugs with ceramic insulators are less easy to read than the now almost obsolete mica patterns. The former exhibit a rather harsher-looking brown colour with a correct mixture instead of the ebony of the mica type, but, in either case, any suspicion of greyness on the electrodes or body is a sign of weak mixture and the jet size must be increased. Some people prefer to go up one size further as a safety precaution if the race is on a course with long sections calling for full-throttle work unless they are able to check the plug reading on the actual circuit during practice.

On T.T., R.N. and GP types the air-lever — or, more accurately, the mixture control — operates an air-valve on the side of the carburetter, and so controls the depression on the main jet via the primary choke tube; consequently, this control can be used as a mixture-correcter without reducing the effective bore of the carburetter. The effect on mixture-strength between the fully open and fully shut positions is approximately equal to three or four jet sizes. It can therefore be used as a rough indication of correctness of jet size; if the engine runs happily with the control shut, the jet is too small, whereas if it sounds woolly or misfires with the control fully open, or nearly so, the jet is too large.

This, however, is not in any sense a true test of mixture correctness, for which the sparking-plug test is the only safe method. The real value of the air control is in its use as a correcter for temporary conditions. In the Isle of Man, for instance, it can be used for the first mile or so on the first lap, when both the motor and air temperature are definitely cold. To permit of such use the main jet should be of a size which provides a correct mixture with the air control fully open when the engine is hot.

Having satisfied oneself that the main jet is correct, attention must next be given to obtaining clean running and acceleration throughout the entire throttle range. The three factors which affect this are: (1) the pilot adjusting screw, situated on the side of the mixing chamber; (2) the cut-away of the throttle valve; (3) the adjustable taper needle.

The pilot adjuster screw on the T.T., R.N. and GP instruments controls the amount of *fuel* supplied to the engine for slow running; screwing the pilot adjuster clockwise weakens the mixture, and, conversely, screwing it out enriches it. This is the opposite way to the adjustment of the pilot screw on standard, Monobloc and GP2 carburetters, which controls the amount of *air* to the jet. The adjuster should be set as rich as possible consistent with a good tick-over; the *rate* at which the engine turns is controlled by adjusting the throttle-cable stop to give the necessary small opening of the throttle valve when the twist-grip is shut, but as the position of the valve also affects the slow-running mixture strength, the cable adjustment and the pilot adjuster position are to some extent inter-related.

252

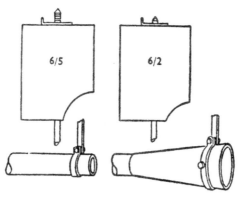

*A diagrammatic explanation of the tuning rule referred to in the text. With (left) a straight-through exhaust pipe, the jet needle is fitted higher and the throttle-slide cut-away is greater than when (right) a megaphone exhaust is employed.*

Eventually, a setting for both can be arrived at which gives a reasonably good tick-over, erring, if anything, on the fast side, and with the mixture strength slightly rich. If pains are taken to obtain a really super tick-over, it is sometimes found that snap acceleration suffers; clearly, it is essential that the engine should never fail to respond instantly if the throttle is slammed open.

The throttle valve cut-away (i.e., the bevel milled on the slide on the side farthest from the engine) controls the mixture strength from low openings up to about half-throttle. The cut-aways vary in steps of $\frac{1}{16}$ in. in height; the No. 5, for instance, has $\frac{5}{16}$-in. cut-away, and consequently allows more air to enter than a No. 3, which, as its number indicates, has a $\frac{3}{16}$-in. cut-away. Generally speaking, the lower the cut-away can be kept, consistent with clean running, the better will be the snap acceleration, and this should be borne in mind when tuning. It is advisable, therefore, to have on hand a range of slides varying from, say, No. 2 to No. 6, and to select from them the one which is the most suitable.

These racing slides are very delicate, and a close fit in the body; if they are handled roughly or assembled in a dirty condition, binding may occur, and it may be impossible to get even running at small throttle openings.

## Position of the Jet Needle

The taper needle is adjustable to five or seven positions in the valve by a spring clip; the lower the needle the weaker the mixture, and the higher the richer, for any particular throttle position. Any flatness or tendency for the engine to eight-stroke at over half-throttle can always be eliminated by needle adjustment. A very common position on both T.T. and R.N. types is 4: that is, the fourth groove down from the top; the final setting should, if anything, be on the rich side.

By systematic attention to the adjustments described, a setting can be obtained which furnishes clean and lively running from tick-over right up to full-throttle, particularly when the engine is being used with a straight-through exhaust system.

As is well known, the fitting of a megaphone exhaust affects the running of the engine adversely at low and medium speeds, a disinclination to run at anything below 3,000 r.p.m. and a tendency to cut right out when the throttle is opened rapidly from low speed being typical symptoms. Almost invariably the carburetter is blamed unfairly for these troubles—a change-over to a straight-through pipe will prove otherwise—but it is necessary to alter the carburetter tuning in order to minimize the ill-effects as much as possible.

A megaphone exhaust system usually requires a main jet about 40 c.c. larger than that used with a straight pipe—incidentally, Amal jets are calibrated in c.c.'s., the numbers stamped on them indicating how much fuel the jets will pass under a given standard set of conditions, although not necessarily in the carburetter. To counteract the tendency to cut out, it is necessary to fit a throttle-valve with greatly reduced cut-away. Very often a No. 2 slide has to be used, but whilst this helps appreciably in getting the engine to open up from low r.p.m., it may introduce a rich spot at small throttle openings. To attempt to balance out this excessively rich setting it is usually necessary to employ a very weak needle setting; for instance, in conjunction with a No. 2 slide one may have to lower the needle to position 1, i.e. with the clip in the topmost groove.

Unless the increase in lap speed gained by fitting a megaphone really warrants its use, the carburetter people advocate straight-through pipes every time; but if a megaphone has to be used the foregoing instructions should be followed, otherwise a chaotic setting will result.

Racing carburetters are made in brass or light-metal, the latter being most usual. When used with alcohol, a precipitate in the form of white powder gradually accumulates; thus it is very necessary frequently to dismantle and clean the whole instrument, paying particular attention to the small fuel passages and preferably blowing them clear with compressed air.

Alcohol fuel is prone to leave a deposit of jelly which can block the fuel flow completely, and it should be a firm rule to drain the carburetter by loosening the jet-plug after every race meeting.

Throttle slides in light-alloy carburetters are very sensitive to grit and before a slide is pulled right out, the interior of the mixing chamber must be cleaned, for if a grain of sand does get in and jam the slide, the only safe course will be to dismantle the whole thing, including removing the jet-block from the body, in order to remove the offending particle from the narrow annular gap in which the throttle valve works. For very dusty conditions brass bodies are superior to those made of light alloy, but, in either case, efficient air filters should be made up, not only to prevent premature wear, but as a safety precaution to obviate a jammed throttle. To be fully effective, this filter or a small auxiliary one, must also cover the slot in the side air-control.

On light metal carburetters the threads of screwed parts tend to seize rather easily, and any brute force exerted will result in a scrapped component. The correct treatment, when partial seizure is detected, is to dose the thread with penetrating oil, leave it for a few minutes and then carefully

255

ease the component out in a series of quarter-turns. Before replacement, the threads should be smeared lightly with graphite grease. To conclude these remarks on racing carburetters, it cannot be emphasized too strongly that they are precision instruments which will not perform properly unless well cleaned and nicely adjusted; it is, unfortunately, a common sight at race meetings to see riders putting jets, throttle slides, etc., down on a dusty road, forgetful of the fact that any dirt or grit picked up may, a few minutes later, be the cause of trouble in the race.

## Tuning a Standard Carburetter

In the absence of one of the racing carburetters described, a standard model can be made to perform quite well if it is sufficiently large in the bore. Most sports engines will accept a choke size slightly larger than that normally fitted for touring use, particularly if a lot of work has been done to improve the breathing ability of the engine. (An indication of the sizes which can be employed was given in Chapter II of this book.) On the other hand, it is easy to make the mistake of fitting too large a carburetter; this will result in an engine which can only scream around at high revs., lacking bottom-end power and acceleration.

A small amount of hand-work in smoothing and polishing the bore and carefully blending-in the junction of the air-intake with the carburetter body will improve the air-flow, but care must be taken to see that the tiny slow-running mixture hole (drilled at an angle into the bore immediately on the engine side of the throttle) is not blocked in the process. As with the racing instruments, it also pays to dismantle the mixing and float chambers completely to make sure that the small fuel and air passages which control the idling mixture are free from dirt or sediment.

Basically, the principles of operation and tuning are similar for racing and touring models, thus the tuning sequence already described holds good for the latter. It is important to remember, however, that the pilot adjuster on

256

the standard models is screwed *in*, not out, to enrich the mixture; as a general rule a setting of one to one and a half turns " out " is about right. The tick-over speed is first set by means of the throttle-stop on the side of the mixing chamber, after which the throttle cable is adjusted so that the engine responds immediately to grip-movement. It is surprising how much a well-adjusted and smooth-acting throttle control helps in improving the general " feel " of the carburation.

The standard air control differs from the racing type in that, except when fully open, the air slide obstructs the air-flow, and thus simultaneously enriches the mixture and throttles the engine. It is, therefore, not of the same value as a mixture-corrector, but it can be used as a guide to jet-size when tuning. If the speed increases when the lever is closed slightly, the jet is too small; if the speed falls off, the jet is either correct or too large.

Here, again, the appearance of the sparking plug is the only reliable guide to correct jet size, but when conducting plug tests it is essential (unless a magneto cut-out is fitted) to have the carburetter so adjusted that the engine stops *instantly* when the throttle is snapped shut; even a few explosions with the engine idling are sufficient to mask the true appearance of the plug.

Plug tests *must* be conducted with whatever exhaust system is to be used when racing; the removal of even an efficient silencer usually necessitates an increase in jet size, a point which is sometimes overlooked to the great detriment of the engine.

### Tuning for Alcohol Blends

Standard touring Amals are not suitable as they stand for use with alcohol blends, for none of the passages is large enough to cope with the increased fuel flow, but it is quite simple to modify them to use any blend containing up to 60% alcohol such as Shell "X", "Y", or "M". Fuels such as 811 or "A", containing much methanol, are rather beyond the capacity of these instruments.

The first step in conversion is to enlarge the area of every fuel passage from the connection to the float-bowl right up to the jet. Double the number of drilled holes in the banjo connection and remove all sharp corners of the holes. Bottom-feed float chambers need the float-needle hole enlarged to a size only .030 in. smaller than the head of the float needle; drill out the hole in which the head is housed about .030 in. larger. Careful lapping-in of the head and seat may be necessary after this operation.

Enlarge the holes leading from the needle valve seating into the float chamber, being very careful not to damage the seat, as there is not much room in this region. Remove the small hexagon screw in the banjo end of the float bowl and open out the hole right through about .005 in. larger, which will still leave enough thread for the screw, and double-up the number of holes in the jet-plug. A good check on the efficacy of the work can be made by rigging up a pint tin with a piece of hose to couple up to the float bowl, and timing the interval required to pass a pint of fuel: it should eventually be reduced to less than 40 seconds.

With top-feed bowls, the rate of flow is limited by the feed hole which obviously must be smaller than the needle. It can be enlarged a little, but the best scheme is to make up a large head for the needle and drill the needle seating to suit.

The next step is to remove the needle jet and jet block from the mixing chamber. Enlarge the idling jet, which is the tiny hole at the bottom of a larger hole in the engine side of the jet block, to about twice its present diameter and drill out the needle-jet to .113 in. for "X" or "Y" fuels and .118 in. or .120 in. for "M"; it may be necessary to experiment later on with these sizes if tuning proves difficult.

Main jets of the size required are not very readily obtainable and, although the makers hate the idea, the only scheme is to drill out some standard jets, the size for "M" being in the region of .068 in. (No. 51). For this work, a set of number size drills (ranging from No. 48 to No. 55) is necessary, and a set of jet reamers (which can be obtained from suppliers of tools to the watchmaking trade) is also advisable. The trouble with drilling is that jets opened out with the same drill do not necessarily pass the same quantity of fuel owing to variation in the diameter, length, and roughness of the hole and the only course open is to make up a number of jets and go through the tuning sequence previously described, starting first with the largest sizes to avoid premature damage to the engine.

Other factors, however, may be limiting the flow of fuel, and the precautions to be observed if the engine does not respond to variation in jet size are dealt with in the chapter on Testing the Finished Work (page 267).

### Additional Notes on GP Carburetters

To fill a demand for chokes larger than $1\frac{3}{8}$ in., the 3 GP type was introduced, ranging from that size up to $1\frac{1}{2}$ in. The tuning sequence is exactly as for other GP's; main and needle jets are interchangeable, but the needles are different and stamped 3 GP (standard) and 3 GP6 (weak). In all sizes, a small circle is engraved on the air-jet plug adjacent to the air-slide; the *bottom* of this circle indicates the correct fuel level, and the right height of the float-chamber if this is remotely mounted is best checked by means of a transparent flexible stand-pipe showing the height of the fuel. The maximum allowable down-draught is 20°.

Although the largest air-jet supplied is .125 in., better results are sometimes obtained by drilling out to a larger size and increasing the main jet to suit. On the 7R A.J.S., for instance, the most suitable air-jet is .136 in. The air coming through the jet compensates the mixture-strength for the varying air-speed through the choke if the engine-speed rises or falls on open throttle, and difficulty in tuning GP instruments may be due to an incorrect relationship between the sizes of the air and main jets. As the air-slide overrides the action of the air-jet, intelligent use of the air control will indicate whether the air jet is too large or too small, but once established, there should be no need to alter this jet again.

## Type GP2 and Monobloc Carburetters

To obviate pilot-jet weep at steep down-draught angles type GP2 was introduced in 1961. The pilot jet and adjusting screw are located on the atmosphere side of the mixing chamber and the latter is locked by a nut instead of being spring-loaded. Tuning is exactly the same as for the GP, except that the pilot adjustment screws *in* to richen and *out* to weaken the mixture. Also, the pilot jet is removable from the side away from the adjuster and is made in sizes from 20 to 35 c.c. flow-rate, so that it can be varied if the adjuster-screw alone cannot obtain the correct mixture-strength. These pilot jets are identical with those used in the Monobloc. Main jets, needle jets and needles are as for the corresponding sizes of GP instruments.

A flat float chamber, type 510, was also introduced. This takes up less space than the round types and can conveniently be mounted between a pair of carburetters on a parallel twin.

The Monobloc design, which has replaced most other types on standard models, has an integral float chamber with pivoted float, a variable pilot jet, and it can be mounted at up to 15° down-draught. Tuning for petrol follows normal lines as described on pages 253 and 257, but for use with alcohol a larger float needle (part 376/161) and seat (376/118) are essential, also a needle jet of .120 or .125 in. diameter. Also, fit a larger pilot jet and if necessary slightly enlarge the small hole leading from the pilot jet to the cross-bore, just inside the throttle. When mounted in pairs when space is restricted, one float chamber can be milled off and the lid refitted. The two mixing chambers can then be connected with flexible tubing, joining two banjoes fitted under special long main-jet holders (376/140).

# CHAPTER XIX

# "HARD" AND "SOFT" TYPES OF SPARKING PLUG

THE correct selection of sparking plugs is of the utmost importance in high-speed work; the time has long passed when one could stop for a plug change and still have a sporting chance of winning. Prior to 1939, special racing plugs were produced which were able to stand up to continuous full throttle with unfailing regularity, and in most cases they were of the non-detachable type, with mica insulation. Then " hardness," or ability to withstand heat, was conferred by the use of heavy, high-conductivity, central electrodes, by reducing the internal area of the plug body and by minimizing the amount of insulation exposed to flame round the central electrode. The insulation was also protected to some extent by almost closing the end of the plug body, and the path by which heat could escape from the central electrode to the plug boss was kept as small as possible.

Unfortunately, all such measures designed to keep the plug cool also have an adverse effect in that they make the plug much more sensitive to oil, which may either lodge between the points, and so prevent the passage of a spark, or may give rise to a conducting coating on the insulation, through which the current may leak in preference to jumping the gap.

Speaking very broadly, a hot-running engine is not usually oily, but there are always occasions, such as when starting or at the end of a long downhill stretch, when the engine is not really hot, and it is at these times that the susceptibility of the plug to oil is an important factor.

Each plug maker produces a range of plugs which can cover almost all known engine types and, in addition, supplies what are known as warming-up plugs, for use when riding to and from the start or when not actually racing. These types are usually detachable, and so can be taken apart for cleaning, whilst the non-detachable racing versions can only be properly cleaned by the makers.

Just prior to 1939 plugs with sintered aluminium-oxide insulators, known under various trade names, made their appearance and have since completely supplanted the older types. These usually had their insulation made of mica, a material which, besides being more expensive and liable to unpredictable electrical breakdown under stress, cannot be used for any length of time with fuels containing much tetra-ethyl lead; the lead salts formed during combustion react with the mica to form a conducting coating which it is almost impossible to remove. Apart from this, it may be taken that, provided the selection of type is correct, any of the known makes of plug will function satisfactorily. However, although various grades are supplied in each make none are directly comparable with each other in their characteristics, and it may be found that a change of make is beneficial (or otherwise) merely because the heat value of one type is intermediate between two types of another make.

There may be a few engines still using 18 mm. plugs, but the 14 mm. size is at the moment almost universal; a description of the method of conversion from 18 to 14 mm. was given in Chapter I. In addition, 14 mm. plugs are available with two lengths of thread, known as " short-reach " and " long-reach," the latter being generally employed in engines having aluminium heads. Short-reach plugs should not on any account be used in long-reach heads, except as a purely temporary measure, otherwise the exposed threads in the hole become filled with carbon. When next the plug is changed there is every chance, then, of the threads becoming seized, and it may be very difficult to extract the plug without ruining the thread in the hole.

Conversely, long-reach plugs should never be used in short reach heads; even the expedient of using several plug-washers to shorten the effective length is bad, because they are seldom gas-tight and, besides causing loss of power, gas-leakage heats the plug excessively.

The accompanying tables give various types made by Lodge, Champion, and K.L.G., arranged in order of hardness—i.e., those at the lower ends of the tables will stand the most heat and the least oil; the grades of different makes are, however, not necessarily equivalent and when

### RACING SPARKING PLUGS

The plugs shown below are graded, in each size group, according to their resistance to heat and oil. Those at the top of each group are the "softest" and withstand least heat and most oil, those at the bottom are the "hardest" and withstand most heat and least oil.

The comparisons between the products of the various makers are intended merely as a guide, and may not be strictly accurate for all engines and conditions.

| Thread Diameter | Thread Length (reach) | Lodge | K.L.G. | Champion | Bosch |
|---|---|---|---|---|---|
| 10 mm. | 12 mm. | 10R47 | T240 | | |
| 10 mm. | 12 mm. | | T260 | | |
| 10 mm. | 12 mm. | 10R49 | T280 | | |
| 10 mm. | 12 mm. | 10R51 | T300 | | |
| 10 mm. | 12 mm. | 10R53 | T320 | | |
| 10 mm. | 18 mm. | 10RL47 | TE240 | | |
| 10 mm. | 18 mm. | | TE260 | | |
| 10 mm. | 18 mm. | 10RL49 | TE280 | | |
| 10 mm. | 18 mm. | 10RL50 | | | |
| 10 mm. | 18 mm. | 10RL51 | TE300 | | |
| 10 mm. | 18 mm. | 10RL52 | | | |
| 10 mm. | 18 mm. | 10RL53 | TE320 | | |
| 14 mm. | 12 mm. | R47 | F250 | LA10, L-58R | W260T1 |
| 14 mm. | 12 mm. | | F260 | | |
| 14 mm. | 12 mm. | R49 | F280 | LA11, L-55R | W 275/300 T2 |
| 14 mm. | 12 mm. | R50 | F290 | | |
| 14 mm. | 12 mm. | R51 | F300 | LA14 | W380/400 T2 |
| 14 mm. | 12 mm. | | F310 | LA15, L-53T | |
| 14 mm. | 12 mm. | R53 | F320 | | |
| 14 mm. | 18 mm. | RL47 | FE250 | | W 260 T2 |
| 14 mm. | 18 mm. | | FE260 | | |
| 14 mm. | 18 mm. | RL49 | FE280 | NA12, N-58R | W 275/200 T2 |
| 14 mm. | 18 mm. | RL50 | FE290 | | |
| 14 mm. | 18 mm. | RL51 | FE300 | NA14 | |
| 14 mm. | 18 mm. | RL52 | FE310 | NA18, N-55R | |
| 14 mm. | 18 mm. | | E258/2 | | |
| 14 mm. | 18 mm. | RL53 | FE320 | NA19, N-53T | W 440/480 T2 |

a specific type is claimed by the engine maker to give the best power, that recommendation should be adhered to.

The symbol denoting the plug-type indicates whether it is of short or long reach, but when ordering it is essential to quote the full symbol or to mention which length is required.

For warming-up, any of the softest plugs in the ranges quoted, i.e., those at the upper end of each group, are very suitable, but one of the "hard" varieties of sports plugs, such as the Lodge HN or HHN, can be used quite satisfactorily. For actual racing, the correct plug is that which will stand up to the engine under the conditions prevailing, which in this sense embraces the length of race and severity of the course, and the fuel in use. There is nothing to be gained by using a harder plug than is necessary, and by so doing one runs the risk of the plug failing through oiling-up halfway through a race, when, perhaps, the piston rings are not as good as they were when they started.

Courses where full throttle is held for long stretches will call for harder plugs than short courses with many slow corners; but the most careful choice has to be made for long-distance races, such as the T.T., where it is not unusual to hear engines missing or cutting-out entirely after shutting off for Creg-ny-Baa corner. This happens less often to top-flight riders who come down the mountain really hard than to those who start to ease back a trifle up near Kate's Cottage. As an initial choice, a plug near the middle of the range should be selected, such as K.L.G. 250 or 280, or Lodge R49. It has been found, however, that, owing to their construction, the latest Lodge plugs with Sintox insulators have a very wide heat range, and even the hardest, R51 or RL51, will deal with a range of conditions which once had to be covered by four types, BR48 to 54, in the old mica series. On the other hand, when conducting mixture tests, as described in the part dealing with carburation, these plugs will appear, even with a correct mixture, to be running much hotter than would be considered advisable with the mica variety. This point must be borne in mind when tuning, otherwise too large a jet may be fitted in an attempt to attain the correct appearance of the plug.

A few engines are fitted with 10 mm. plugs, usually because there is insufficient room for a larger one, and not from reasons of superiority of the smaller type. In some cases when two plugs have been fitted in one combustion chamber, one may be a 14 mm. and the other one 10 mm., purely because of this difficulty of fitting the second one into the space available. Two-plug heads were tried around 1937 in large single-cylinder engines and the general experience was that little extra power resulted except at moderate speeds when gas-turbulence is too low to afford rapid combustion, and the scheme lost favour, not being considered worth the extra complication.

Lately, however, it is coming back into use, especially on very high-revving Continental engines possibly because the time-element involved in lighting up the charge is so incredibly small at around 12,000 r.p.m. The position of the plug relative to the inlet port also has a bearing on power output, and it may well be that the second plug is simply in a more advantageous locality. Firing both plugs simultaneously can be achieved either by using a specially-wound magneto with two high-tension leads, or by employing two coils with their primary circuits connected in series and opened and closed by a single contact breaker.

Having settled by experiment on the most suitable plug, it is not a bad scheme to carry, as the spare, another which is one grade softer, for obviously if the hard one oils up, another of similar grade is likely to do the same thing. Spare plugs should be looked after very carefully both when in store and when being carried, and always kept with their threads and open ends protected, to prevent damage to the threads or the ingress of dirt or fluff, which may get up inside the plug and cause an internal short. Spare plugs should always have fresh washers in place, the best form of washer being the solid copper type, as this provides the best heat conductivity, and does not pack down and allow the plug to loosen, as either the copper-and-asbestos or rolled-copper varieties can do; a loose plug will overheat very rapidly.

Racing plugs are invariably supplied with the correct gap, and in many instances the gap cannot be altered; in others this is not the case, but if the gap has to be set, it must be done by bending only the *earth* electrode, for attempting to bend the *central* electrode is almost certain to damage the insulation. Non-detachable racing plugs are not easy to clean: the best method, if convenient, is to return them to the factory for reconditioning, which is done for a moderate fee. They can also be cleaned by sand-blasting in an ordinary garage plug cleaner, using a low air pressure to avoid damage to the surface of the insulator and subsequently taking particular care to see that every vestige of sand is removed from the thread and from the small annulus between insulator and body.

For most work, there is nothing to beat the K.L.G. spring-wire clip for retaining the high-tension lead, but when excessively wet conditions are the rule it is better to use one of the proprietary types of umbrella terminal which protect the plug from water or mud.

Another point is the plug spanner; it pays to obtain a really good example, which fits the hexagons properly and with the shank bent to the minimum amount necessary to clear the adjacent head fins. A badly fitting spanner can easily cant over in use, until it bears on the upper end of the plug, and may then either bend or crack the insulated core

# CHAPTER XX

## TESTING THE FINISHED WORK

THE ideal method of testing an engine is, of course, on a brake. With just a small Heenan and Froude brake, type DPX1 for preference, an accurate rev.-counter and an Amal flowmeter, much information can be collected, and the effects of varying induction and exhaust pipe lengths, ignition and valve timing and compression ratios can be studied and tabulated. Naturally, to do this sort of job thoroughly takes a fair amount of time, and is rather beyond the scope of this book, but apart from such development work, a brake is invaluable simply for determining whether an engine is, or is not, developing its correct horse-power, and for finding out its peak r.p.m.—that is to say, the speed at which it gives off its maximum power, not necessarily maximum speed at which it will turn over.

Very briefly, the method is to run the engine against a light brake load until it is thoroughly warmed up, and during this period the lubrication system can be checked to ensure that oil is reaching everywhere it should. Then the throttle is opened up and the load on the brake increased until the engine is pulling the maximum load it can at a medium speed of, say, 3,000 r.p.m. (most racing engines do not like full-throttle at anything below this speed).

Readings are then taken of the r.p.m., brake load, and fuel consumption, and by means of the air control an indication can be obtained as to the correctness of the jet size. Obviously, if closing the air-control causes the speed to rise, the jet is too small and should be increased before proceeding further, as much damage can be done by running for long on a lean mixture.

Likewise, the ignition setting can be checked by operating the ignition control: if the speed rises as the spark is retarded the advance is too great, but if it falls there is insufficient advance. The ideal setting for bench-testing is one which gives maximum power when the lever is pulled back just a trifle, as then you can always check the effect of giving a little extra advance at any time. It is, however, not a good plan to run continuously with the magneto considerably retarded, as the spark then being delivered is not of maximum intensity; it is wiser to stop the engine and re-set the timing to the correct figure. Incidentally, when observing the effects of adjustments to ignition or mixture, it is better to watch the pointer on the load dial of the brake rather than the tachometer, because the former is far more sensitive to a slight variation in speed than the latter.

The brake does not give a direct reading of the horsepower; this has to be calculated, but the arithmetic involved is very simple. All one has to do is multiply the load in pounds shown on the dial by the r.p.m., and divide by a fixed figure, called the "constant," which depends upon the type of brake in use; on modern DPX1 brakes the constant is 4,500. Put into the shape of a formula:

$$\text{B.H.P.} = \frac{\text{R.P.M.} \times \text{load}}{4,500}$$

As an example, if the engine is pulling 28 lb. at 5,000 r.p.m., it is then developing $\frac{5,000 \times 28}{4,500} = 31.1$ b.h.p.

It will be seen that the accuracy of the b.h.p. figure depends upon the accuracy of the rev. counter; should this be at fault, the whole business is worse than useless, it is most misleading, and it is easy enough to delude oneself into believing an optimistic result without the added complication of inaccurate instruments. Consequently it is best always to have at least two separately driven rev-counters, one which, preferably, will be used on the motorcycle itself. This serves as a check on the proceedings and avoids subsequent discrepancies in readings when the model is tested on the road. A simple method of checking the speed indication stroboscopically consists of painting a white mark on the drive coupling, and observing this solely by the light from a neon lamp. In England and all countries using 50-cycle mains frequency, the mark will appear stationary at 3,000 and 6,000 r.p.m., while in the U.S.A., Canada and all countries with 60-cycle current, the stationary speeds will be 3,600 and 7,200 r.p.m. There are, of course, more accurate methods of checking such as by Strobotac or the Ashdown Rotoscope, and these devices can also be used for observing the behaviour of valve springs, etc.

By manipulation of the brake, the horse-power developed at various speeds at intervals of, say, 500 r.p.m. can be determined, and from the figures so obtained the power curve can be plotted on graph paper. Readings should always be taken after the engine has settled down to a steady speed; "snap" readings can be deceptive and are usually optimistic. It may be found that the ignition timing and jet size which are correct at low speeds are not necessarily correct at high r.p.m., and if so, it is best to re-set them to suit the latter condition. The effect of varying the induction and exhaust pipe lengths can be determined very easily, and sometimes quite surprising results can be achieved by obtaining just the right combination. Sometimes, of course, such a combination cannot be used on the eventual installation, either for structural reasons or because of regulations which restrict or define the layout of the exhaust system, in which case the next best combination which does comply with the rules must be sought. In this connection, builders of 500 c.c. racing cars are somewhat better off than motor-cyclists, because they have room to use almost any conceivable arrangements, and are not restricted by regulations regarding pipe lengths.

Usually a gain in power at the upper end of the speed range, where it is mostly required, is accompanied by a drop in power somewhere lower down, although this is not of much consequence on a racing motorcycle, where the revs. are always kept up by use of a close-ratio gearbox. There are, however, conditions where it may be better to sacrifice a little at the top end in order to get more power low down, or

269

to eliminate a flat spot in the power curve; for instance, on dirt-track machines, which are single-geared, it is essential to have plenty of power available to give traction and keep the rear wheel spinning when coming out of the corners, and, therefore, good pulling power at around 3,000 r.p.m. is a vital necessity. Then, again, the comparatively great weight of a 500 c.c. motor car demands wider gear ratios, particularly for standing-start hill climbs, and if the engine torque is inclined to fall off rather badly with a diminution in speed, the acceleration following a change to a higher ratio may suffer.

Mention was made earlier of taking fuel consumption readings on a flowmeter, of which the Amal pattern is the one most frequently used. This instrument indicates the rate, in pints per hour, at which the engine is consuming fuel and from this the " specific consumption " can be found by dividing the consumption by the power being developed. For short-distance racing, a lavish consumption does not matter greatly, but if the specific consumption, when using petrol, works out at much more than .8 pint per b.h.p. per hour, there is something wrong somewhere. Probably the jet is too large; but if reducing the jet also reduces the power or causes overheating of the plug, then either the valve timing is not correct, the exhaust system is of the wrong length, or the compression ratio is too high necessitating a large flow of fuel to keep the internal temperature down.

The flowmeter may show also that an increase in power gained by some alteration has been accompanied by a disproportionately great increase in consumption, this being particularly liable to happen with two-strokes. That may be a serious matter for long-distance work, as the increase in performance may, or may not, be nullified by the necessity for carrying more fuel, or perhaps making an extra pit stop. In such cases the alternative settings should be carefully noted, so that subsequent experiments can be conducted in practice on the course, to determine which is the better of the two over the distance of the race.

Arguments frequently arise as to the power which various

engines can or have developed. Few motorcycle engines are subjected to officially observed tests as aero engines are, and such arguments are likely to continue. It may be said, however, that anything over 50 b.h.p. for a 500 c.c. engine and proportionately less for other capacities, is very good indeed. Atmospheric conditions exert quite a large effect on power, which increases when the barometer reading is high, or when the air temperature is low, and vice versa. For that reason, it is always advisable, particularly in a changeable climate, to correct all power readings to N.T.P. —i.e. normal temperature and pressure, which are respectively internationally fixed at 15° C. and 29.92 in. mercury. Correction is made by the following formula:

Corrected B.H.P.=

$$\frac{\text{Observed B.H.P.} \times 29.92}{\text{barometer reading}} \times \frac{400 + \text{air temp. (degrees C.)}}{415}$$

From this it will be seen that a drop of 1 in. in the barometer reading lowers the horsepower by approximately 3%, and although the effect of temperature change is less important over the ranges normally met with in an enclosed room with the engine running, it is certainly advisable to correct the readings fully to avoid subsequent confusion.

Other figures, such as the torque of the engine and its B.M.E.P. can also be obtained from the brake test, and for those who are interested the relevant formulae are included in the Appendix.[1]

## Power Requirements

The power required to propel a vehicle depends upon two main factors—rolling resistance and air resistance. The former depends upon the gross vehicle weight, the state of the road surface and the size and inflation pressure of the tyres, but it remains substantially constant over a wide range

[1] For those who are really interested in this work, A. W. Judge's book *The Testing of High-speed Internal-combustion Engines* (Chapman and Hall Ltd.) provides a wealth of information.

of speed provided the factors stated do not vary. Air resistance depends upon the frontal area and the aerodynamic shape, and increases as the square of the speed, and, therefore, the power absorbed in overcoming it increases as the *cube* of the speed, whereas that required to overcome rolling resistance increases only directly as the speed. In consequence, on a good surface, the power absorbed by wind pressure at speeds in the region of 100 m.p.h. is nearly 10 times that absorbed by rolling resistance, hence the necessity for adopting the most compact riding position possible. The air resistance can be found from the formula:

$$\text{Resistance (pounds)} = A.V^2.C$$

where A = the frontal area in square feet.

V = velocity in feet per second.

C = a constant called the " drag coefficient."

A, the frontal area, is difficult to determine accurately for such an irregular shape as a motorcycle and rider, but it can be taken as being about 5 sq. ft. for a rider of the average physique, lying down on a Senior T.T. machine; it would obviously be less, perhaps $4\frac{1}{2}$ sq. ft. for a small man on a 125 c.c. model. For the factor C, a figure of .0008 has been found by experiment to give results which tally reasonably well with known performance figures, though it may be slightly less for a clean design of machine with the rider exceptionally well tucked in.

Using these figures, the air resistance of a Senior T.T. model, without fairing, at 124 m.p.h. (182 ft. per sec.) is

$$5 \times 182^2 \times .0008 = 132 \text{ lb.}$$

Taking the total all-up weight as 520 lb. and rolling resistance at 2 per cent, which is a good average figure to employ, then the rolling resistance is approximately 10 lb., a very small figure compared to the air resistance. The total resistance is therefore 132 plus 10=142 lb.

The horsepower required to overcome a known resistance at a known speed is found from the expression

$$H.P. = \frac{\text{resistance} \times \text{feet per second}}{550}$$

therefore, in this instance, $H.P. = \dfrac{142 \times 182}{550} = 47.$

This is the power required at the rear tyre; assuming 96 per cent transmission efficiency, 49 B.H.P. would have to be developed by the engine to achieve the quoted speed of 124 m.p.h. This result agrees very closely with the power development and maximum speed of known racing machines, particularly the 1938 Senior Norton, but there is always bound to be a certain amount of guesswork in estimating the factors involved. The drag coefficient " C " for instance can be brought down to .0003 by full stream-lining and though this usually results in a simultaneous increase in frontal area, the net gain is very considerable. To avoid much laborious calculation, the accompanying graph has been compiled from a number of known per-formance figures and gives a fairly accurate guide to power requirements; the lower curve is for light, small-capacity machines in track condition, the middle curve being for heavier machines in road-racing trim, and the upper curve is for large, heavy mounts in the big-twin class. These curves do not appear to rise so rapidly as might be expected with increase of speed, but this is because in the examples chosen greater efforts had been put into reducing wind resistance by streamlining, and rolling resistance, partly by reducing weight, and partly by using special tyres. With the aid of this graph and the performance figures of the engine an estimate of the speed attainable and of the gear-ratio to employ can be obtained which will be sufficiently close to serve as a " jumping-off place " pending final settlement on the course.

Most amateurs will, of course, have to do what they can without the advantage of knowing the actual developed horsepower, unless they can get their engines tested for them. In any case, even if the figures are available, final tuning has eventually to be done under race conditions, as

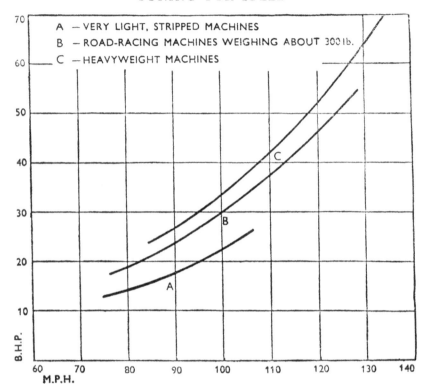

*In graph form this approximate guide to the tie-up between b.h.p. and m.p.h. gives the tuner an idea of the results his efforts should produce—always bearing in mind wind and other resistance factors.*

it is almost impossible to duplicate them on the bench. For this work a correctly geared *front-wheel-driven* speedometer is a great help, although so far as the indirect gears are concerned it is not so useful as a rev. counter, because it is difficult at racing speeds to convert m.p.h. into r.p.m. The rev. counter is also considerably more sensitive to small variations in speed.

Runs can be made over a stretch of the course, or a similar piece of road, using the correct exhaust system and the " official " fuel, if any is stipulated. First of all, the correct jet size should be determined by the method described in Chapter XVIII and experiments made, when the jet is approximately correct, to check the accuracy, or otherwise, of the ignition timing.

This is done when running on full throttle by moving the

lever back a very small amount in progressive stages, and noting the rise or fall of the r.p.m. Alternatively, the timing can be altered very easily over a range of about 4 degrees by opening or closing the contact-breaker points, remembering that one-sixth of a turn on the adjustment is roughly equivalent to two degrees. Care must be taken to see that the effect of one adjustment does not mask the effect of the other; for instance, if the advance is too great, the plug tends to run hot and an over-large jet will have to be fitted in an attempt to obtain the right appearance of the plug-face; speed will suffer, both on account of the excessive advance and the over-rich mixture.

When using alcohol fuels, it is not uncommon to find that an increase in jet size has no effect on the mixture strength. This is a sure sign that the fuel flow is being restricted elsewhere; possibly the needle-jet is not large enough, or else the float chamber or fuel pipes cannot deliver a sufficient quantity to keep the jet supplied. If this symptom is noted it is useless to continue going up in jet sizes. The real cause of the trouble must be found and cured, because, although an engine runs very cool in a correct alcohol mixture, piston failure will take place with great rapidity if the mixture becomes weak through any cause, and there may be no premonitory symptoms of engine distress to warn the rider of the impending trouble.

Modern testing plant and the wealth of technical data now available do much to obviate trial-and-error methods of eliminating the minor snags enumerated in this concluding chapter. Such facilities, however, must be regarded as going hand in hand with the skill of the man doing the job, and in putting finishing touches to work assembled carefully down to the finest detail, it is patience and perseverance which ultimately produce the desired result.

## REPRESENTATIVE CARBURETTER TYPES AND SETTINGS

*(Petrol unless otherwise specified)*

| MODEL | CARBURETTER | | JETS | | REMARKS |
|---|---|---|---|---|---|
| | TYPE | BORE | MAIN | NEEDLE | |
| A.J.S. 498 c.c. o.h.v. | T10TT9 | $1\frac{3}{16}$ in. | 1250 | .120 | Alcohol |
| A.J.S. 7R, pre 1955 | 10RN | $1\frac{1}{16}$ in. | 320 | .109 | |
| A.J.S. 7R, 1955–59 | T10GP | $1\frac{5}{32}$ in. | 270 | .109 | GPG needle |
| A.J.S. 7R, 1959–62 | T5GP | $1\frac{3}{16}$ in. | 310 | .109 | 5 GP6 needle .136 Air jet |
| Ariel 350 c.c. "Red Hunter" | 15TT38 | 1 in. | 260 | .107 | |
| Ariel 500 c.c. "Red Hunter" | 10TT38 | $1\frac{1}{8}$ in. | 320 | .109 | |
| B.S.A. 350 c.c. "Gold Star" | T10TT9 | $1\frac{5}{32}$ in. | 360 | .109 | |
| B.S.A. 350 c.c. "Gold Star" | T10TT9 | $1\frac{3}{32}$ in. | 1200 | .120 | Alcohol |
| B.S.A. 350 c.c. "Gold Star" | T10GP | $1\frac{3}{8}$ in. | 280 | .109 | .125 Air jet |
| B.S.A. 500 c.c. "Gold Star" | RN | $1\frac{1}{16}$ in. | 520 | .109 | |
| B.S.A. 500 c.c. "Gold Star" | T10TT9 | $1\frac{1}{8}$ in. | 360 | .109 | |
| B.S.A. 500 c.c. "Gold Star" | T10TT9 | $1\frac{3}{16}$ in. | 1700 | .120 | Alcohol |
| B.S.A. 500 c.c. "Gold Star" | T5GP | $1\frac{1}{8}$ in. | 330 | .109 | .125 Air jet |
| B.S.A. 500 c.c. "Gold Star" | T3GP | $1\frac{1}{4}$ in. | 350 | .109 | |
| B.S.A. 500 c.c. Scrambler | T10GP | $1\frac{5}{32}$ in. | 240 | .109 | .100 Air jet GP6 needle |
| B.S.A. 650 Road Rocket | T10TT9 | $1\frac{1}{16}$ in. | 340 | .109 | |
| B.S.A. 650 Super Rocket | T10TT9 | $1\frac{1}{16}$ in. | 410 | .109 | |
| Indian, 700 c.c. Apache | T10TT9 | $1\frac{3}{16}$ in. | 480 | .109 | |
| J.A.P. Speedway; 8–80 twin | 27/013 | $1\frac{1}{8}$ in. | 960 | NIL | Alcohol |
| Matchless 500 c.c. G45 | 10GP | $1\frac{5}{32}$ in. | 240 | .109 | .125 Air jet |
| Matchless 500 c.c. G80R | T3GP | $1\frac{1}{4}$ in. | 450 | .109 | 3GP6 needle |
| Matchless OHC G50 | T3GP | $1\frac{1}{4}$ in. | 450 | .109 | 3GP6 needle |
| Norton 350 c.c. "Manx" | 10TT38 | $1\frac{3}{32}$ in. | 350 | .109 | |
| Norton 350 c.c. "Manx" | 10TTRNI | $1\frac{3}{32}$ in. | 500 | .109 | |
| Norton 350 c.c. "Manx" 1946 | T10TT | $1\frac{3}{32}$ in. | 350 | .109 | |
| Norton 350 c.c. "Manx" 1946 | T10RN | $1\frac{3}{32}$ in. | 500 | .109 | |
| Norton 350 c.c. "Manx" | T10GP | $1\frac{1}{8}$ in. | 230 | .109 | |
| Norton 350 c.c. Short stroke | T10GP | $1\frac{5}{32}$ in. | 350 | .109 | |
| Norton 490 c.c. "Manx" | 10TT38 | $1\frac{5}{32}$ in. | 460 | .109 | |
| Norton 490 c.c. "Manx" | 10TTZN1 | $1\frac{5}{32}$ in. | 600 | .109 | |
| Norton 499 c.c. "Manx" | T10RN | $1\frac{3}{16}$ in. | 560 | .109 | |
| Norton 499 c.c. "Manx" | 10RN9 | $1\frac{3}{16}$ in. | 560 | .109 | |
| Norton 499 c.c. "Manx" | T10GP | $1\frac{5}{32}$ in. | 260 | .109 | |
| Norton 499 c.c. Short stroke | T5GP | $1\frac{5}{16}$ in. | 310 | .109 | |
| Norton 499 c.c. Short stroke | T5GP | $1\frac{5}{16}$ in. | 390 | .109 | 5GP6 needle |
| Norton 500 c.c. Dominator | T15GP | 1 in. | 190 | .107 | |
| Royal Enfield Constellation | T10TT9 | $1\frac{1}{16}$ in. | 480 | .109 | |
| Triumph "Cub" Racing | 376 | $\frac{15}{16}$ in. | 140 | .106 | |
| Triumph T100 *straight* | 376 | 1 in. | 210 | .1065 | |
| Triumph T100 *megaphone* | 376 | 1 in. | 540 | .120 | Alcohol |
| Triumph T100 *megaphone* | 15GP | 1 in. | 220 | .107 | GP6 needle |
| Triumph T110 *straight* | 376 | $1\frac{1}{16}$ in. | 250 | .106 | |
| Triumph T110 *megaphone* | 376 | $1\frac{1}{16}$ in. | 340 | .106 | |
| Triumph T100 | 76 | $1\frac{1}{16}$ in. | 190 | .109 | |
| Velocette KTT | T10tt | $1\frac{3}{32}$ in. | 400 | .109 | |
| Velocette Viper | 376/61 | $1\frac{1}{16}$ in. | 270 | .1065 | |
| Velocette Viper *straight* | TT9 | $1\frac{1}{16}$ in. | 360 | .109 | |
| Velocette Venom *silencer* | 389/15 | $1\frac{1}{16}$ in. | 330 | .1065 | |
| Velocette Venom *straight* or *megaphone* | 389/15 | $1\frac{3}{16}$ in. | 370 | .1065 | |
| Velocette Venom *straight* or megaphone | 10TT9 | $1\frac{3}{16}$ in. | 390 | .109 | GP6 needle |
| Vincent Black Lightning | T10TT9 | $1\frac{3}{16}$ in. | 360 | .109 | |
| Vincent Black Lightning | T10TT9 | $1\frac{3}{16}$ in. | 1400 | .120 | Alcohol |
| Vincent Black Lightning | T10TT | 32 mm. | 1400 | .120 | Alcohol |
| Vincent Black Lightning | T5GP | $1\frac{3}{8}$ in. | 800 | .120 | Alcohol .150 Air jet |

For an increase in altitude the percentage *decrease* in jet size required is approximately $1\frac{1}{2}\%$ per **1,000** feet above sea level.

# APPENDIX

## Power Calculations

$$\text{B.M.E.P.} = \frac{\text{B.H.P.} \times \text{C}}{\text{R.P.M.}}$$

C depends upon size and type of engine, though not upon the number of cylinders, and is as follows:

| | | |
|---|---|---|
| For 250 c.c. 4-strokes | .. .. | 52460 |
| 350 c.c. 4-strokes | .. .. | 37480 |
| 500 c.c. 4-strokes ⎫<br>250 c.c. 2-strokes ⎭ .. .. | | 26230 |
| 350 c.c. 2-strokes | .. .. | 18740 |
| 1,000 c.c. 4-strokes ⎫<br>500 c.c. 2-strokes ⎭ .. .. | | 13125 |

For other capacities the value of C can be obtained by direct proportion.

$$\text{B.H.P.} = \frac{\text{PLAN}}{33,000}$$

where P = Brake Mean Effective Pressure (B.M.E.P.).
    L = Stroke in feet.
    A = Area of one piston in square inches.
    N = Number of explosions per minute.

$$\text{Torque} = \frac{\text{B.H.P.} \times 5,250}{\text{R.P.M.}}$$

Therefore at 5,250 r.p.m. the torque in lb. per ft. is numerically equal to the b.h.p.

## Froude Brake Calculations

$$\text{B.H.P.} = \frac{\text{P} \times \text{R.P.M.}}{\text{C}}$$

where P = Pull in pounds shown on dial.

    C = A constant, usually either 4,500 or 5,500, depending on type of brake.

To find Torque or B.M.E.P. directly from the " pounds-pull " reading, multiply by the following factors, irrespective of the number of cylinders in the engine:

| | ENGINE SIZE | BRAKE CONSTANT | |
|---|---|---|---|
| | | 4,500 | 5,500 |
| TORQUE | ALL CAPACITIES | 1.167 | .965 |
| B.M.E.P. | 250 c.c. 4-str. | 11.56 | 9.46 |
| | 350 c.c. 4-str. | 8.26 | 6.76 |
| | 500 c.c. 4-str. ⎱ 250 c.c. 2-str. ⎰ | 5.78 | 4.73 |
| | 350 c.c. 2-str. | 4.13 | 3.38 |
| | 1,000 c.c. 4-str. ⎱ 500 c.c. 2-str. ⎰ | 2.89 | 2.36 |

*Example:* If a 500 c.c. four-stroke engine is pulling 30 lb. at 5,000 r.p.m. on a 4,500 constant brake, it is developing

$$\frac{30 \times 5,000}{4,500} = 33.3 \text{ b.h.p.}$$

Its torque is 30 × 1.167 = 35 pounds-feet.
Its B.M.E.P is 30 × 5.78 = 174 pounds per sq. in,

### Engine Calculations

$$\frac{\text{Mean Piston Speed}}{\text{(ft. per min.)}} = \frac{\text{R.P.M.} \times \text{stroke in inches}}{6}$$

$$\text{or } \frac{\text{R.P.M.} \times \text{stroke in mm.}}{152.4}$$

$$\frac{\text{Mean Gas Velocity Through Port}}{\text{(ft. per sec.)}} = \frac{\text{Piston speed}}{60} \times \frac{D^2}{d^2}$$

$$\frac{\text{Mean Gas Velocity Through}}{\text{Valve Seat (ft. per sec.)}} = \frac{\text{Piston speed}}{60} \times \frac{D^2 \times 22}{d_v \times L \times 7}$$

where
D = Diameter of piston.  $d_v$ = Diameter at throat of valve.
d = Diameter of port.    L = Lift of valve.

(Either in. or mm. can be used on the right-hand side of these equations, provided the same scale is used for each of the dimensions used.)

278

## Inertia Load of Reciprocating Parts

Load at T.D.C. (in pounds) $= .0000142 \text{WN}^2\text{S} \left(1 + \dfrac{\text{S}}{2\text{L}}\right)$

Load at B.D.C. $= .0000142 \text{ WN}^2\text{S} \left(1 - \dfrac{\text{S}}{2\text{L}}\right)$

where W = Weight of components in pounds.
N = R.P.M.
S = Stroke in inches.
L = Length of connecting-rod in inches.

## Centrifugal Load on Crankpin

Load $= .0000142 \text{WN}^2\text{S}$

where W = Weight of big-end and rollers.
N = R.P.M.
S = Stroke in inches.

To calculate speed in m.p.h. when time and distance factors are known:

$$\frac{\text{Distance (in miles)}}{\text{Time (in seconds)}} \times 3{,}600$$

For speed over quarter mile, divide 900 by the time in seconds.

## Conversion Factors

| To convert— | | | | | Multiply by— |
|---|---|---|---|---|---|
| Miles to kilometres | .. | .. | .. | 1.609 | (or 8/5 approx.) |
| M.p.h. to k.p.h. | .. | .. | .. | 1.609 | (or 8/5 approx.) |
| Kilometres to miles.. | .. | .. | .. | .621 | (or 5/8 approx.) |
| K.p.h. to m.p.h. | .. | .. | .. | .621 | (or 5/8 approx.) |
| Gallons to litres | .. | .. | .. | 4.536 | (or 4½ approx.) |
| Litres to gallons | .. | .. | .. | .2205 | (or 2/9 approx.) |
| Pounds to kilograms | .. | .. | .. | .4536 | (or 9/20 approx.) |
| Kilograms to pounds | .. | .. | .. | 2.205 | (or 11/5 approx.) |
| Cubic centimetres to cubic inches.. | | .. | .. | .061 | (or 1/16 approx.) |
| Cubic inches to cubic centimetres.. | | | .. | 16.39 | (or 33/2 approx.) |
| M.p.h. to feet per second .. | | .. | .. | 88/60 | (or 1½ approx.) |

## TIME — SPEED TABLE — OVER ONE MILE

| Time per Mile m. s. | Speed m.p.h. | Speed k.p.h. | Time per Mile m. s. | Speed m.p.h. | Speed k.p.h. | Time per Mile m. s. | Speed m.p.h. | Speed k.p.h. |
|---|---|---|---|---|---|---|---|---|
| 0 24 | 150.00 | 241.40 | 1 6 | 54.54 | 87.77 | 1 46 | 33.96 | 54.65 |
| 0 26 | 138.46 | 222.82 | 1 8 | 52.94 | 85.20 | 1 48 | 33.33 | 53.64 |
| 0 28 | 128.57 | 206.91 | 1 10 | 51.43 | 82.77 | 1 50 | 32.72 | 42.65 |
| 0 30 | 120.00 | 193.12 | 1 12 | 50.00 | 80.46 | 1 52 | 32.14 | 41.72 |
| 0 32 | 112.50 | 181.05 | 1 14 | 48.65 | 78.29 | 1 54 | 31.58 | 50.82 |
| 0 34 | 105.88 | 170.39 | 1 16 | 47.37 | 76.23 | 1 56 | 31.03 | 49.93 |
| 0 36 | 100.00 | 160.93 | 1 18 | 46.15 | 74.27 | 1 58 | 30.50 | 49.08 |
| 0 38 | 94.74 | 152.45 | 1 20 | 45.00 | 72.42 | 2 0 | 30.00 | 48.28 |
| 0 40 | 90.00 | 144.84 | 1 22 | 43.90 | 70.65 | 2 5 | 28.80 | 46.35 |
| 0 42 | 85.71 | 137.93 | 1 24 | 42.86 | 68.96 | 2 10 | 27.69 | 44.56 |
| 0 44 | 81.81 | 131.66 | 1 26 | 41.86 | 67.36 | 2 15 | 26.66 | 42.90 |
| 0 46 | 78.26 | 125.94 | 1 28 | 40.91 | 65.84 | 2 20 | 25.71 | 41 37 |
| 0 48 | 75.00 | 120.70 | 1 30 | 40.00 | 64.37 | 2 25 | 24.83 | 39.96 |
| 0 50 | 72.00 | 115.87 | 1 32 | 39.13 | 62.97 | 2 30 | 24.00 | 38.62 |
| 0 52 | 69.23 | 111.41 | 1 34 | 38.29 | 61.62 | 2 35 | 23.32 | 37.37 |
| 0 54 | 66.66 | 107.28 | 1 36 | 37.54 | 60.35 | 2 40 | 22.50 | 36.21 |
| 0 56 | 64.28 | 103.45 | 1 38 | 36.73 | 59.11 | 2 45 | 21.81 | 35.10 |
| 0 58 | 62.07 | 99.89 | 1 40 | 36.00 | 57.93 | 2 50 | 21.17 | 34.07 |
| 1 0 | 60.00 | 96.56 | 1 42 | 35.29 | 56.79 | 2 55 | 20.57 | 33.10 |
| 1 2 | 58.06 | 93.44 | 1 44 | 34.61 | 55.70 | 3 0 | 20.00 | 32.18 |
| 1 4 | 56.25 | 90.52 | | | | | | |

*Note.*—Comparative Distances in Miles and Kilometres may also be found by this table, *e.g.* 60.00 miles equal 96.56 kilometres.

## SPEED — TIME TABLE — OVER TENTHS of a MILE

| Tenths of a Mile | 20 m.p.h. | 21 m.p.h. | 22 m.p.h. | 23 m.p.h. | 24 m.p.h. | 25 m.p.h. | 26 m.p.h. | 27 m.p.h. | 28 m.p.h. | 29 m.p.h. | 30 m.p.h. |
|---|---|---|---|---|---|---|---|---|---|---|---|
| | | | | | Time in Seconds. | | | | | | |
| .1 | 18 | 17.1 | 16.4 | 15.7 | 15 | 14.4 | 13.9 | 13.3 | 12.9 | 12.4 | 12 |
| .2 | 36 | 34.2 | 32.7 | 31.3 | 30 | 28.8 | 27.7 | 26.7 | 25.7 | 24.8 | 24 |
| .3 | 54 | 51.4 | 49.1 | 47.0 | 45 | 43.2 | 41.6 | 40.0 | 38.6 | 37.2 | 36 |
| .4 | 72 | 68.6 | 65.4 | 62.6 | 60 | 57.6 | 55.4 | 53.3 | 51.4 | 49.6 | 48 |
| .5 | 90 | 85.7 | 81.8 | 78.3 | 75 | 72.0 | 69.3 | 66.6 | 64.3 | 62.1 | 60 |
| .6 | 108 | 102.8 | 98.2 | 93.9 | 90 | 86.4 | 83.1 | 80.0 | 77.2 | 74.5 | 72 |
| .7 | 126 | 119.9 | 114.5 | 109.6 | 105 | 100.8 | 97.0 | 93.3 | 90.0 | 86.9 | 84 |
| .8 | 144 | 137.1 | 130.9 | 125.2 | 120 | 115.2 | 110.8 | 106.6 | 102.9 | 99.3 | 96 |
| .9 | 162 | 154.3 | 147 2 | 140 9 | 135 | 129.6 | 124.7 | 120.0 | 115.7 | 111.7 | 108 |
| .0 | 180 | 171.4 | 163.6 | 156.5 | 150 | 144.0 | 138.5 | 133.3 | 128.6 | 124.1 | 120 |

*Note.*—This table will be found useful both in checking speedometer readings and in those trials where a secret check necessitates an exact average speed.

## TIME — SPEED TABLE — OVER QUARTER MILE

| Sec. | M.p.h. | Sec. | M.p.h. | Sec. | M.p.h. | Sec. | M.p.h. | Sec. | M.p.h. | Sec. | M.p.h. |
|---|---|---|---|---|---|---|---|---|---|---|---|
| 15 | 60.00 | 13 4/5 | 65.22 | 12 3/5 | 71.43 | 11 2/5 | 78.95 | 10 1/5 | 88.24 | 9 | 100.00 |
| 14 4/5 | 60.81 | 13 3/5 | 66.18 | 12 2/5 | 72.58 | 11 1/5 | 80.36 | 10 | 90.00 | 8 4/5 | 102.47 |
| 14 3/5 | 61.64 | 13 2/5 | 67.16 | 12 1/5 | 73.77 | 11 | 81.82 | 9 4/5 | 91.84 | 8 3/5 | 104.65 |
| 14 2/5 | 62.50 | 13 1/5 | 68.18 | 12 | 75.00 | 10 4/5 | 83.33 | 9 3/5 | 93.75 | 8 2/5 | 107.14 |
| 14 1/5 | 63.38 | 13 | 69.23 | 11 4/5 | 76.27 | 10 3/5 | 84.91 | 9 2/5 | 95.74 | 8 1/5 | 109.76 |
| 14 | 64.28 | 12 4/5 | 70.31 | 11 3/5 | 77.59 | 10 2/5 | 86.54 | 9 1/5 | 97.83 | 8 | 112.50 |

# SPEED AND R.P.M. FOR 3.25-IN. AND 3.50-IN. × 19-IN. RACING TYRES

| m.p.h. Gear ratio | \ R.P.M. 30 | 40 | 50 | 60 | 70 | 80 | 90 | 100 | 110 | 120 | 130 | 140 | Difference Table 1 | 2 | 3 | 4 | 5 | 6 | 7 | 8 | 9 |
|---|---|---|---|---|---|---|---|---|---|---|---|---|---|---|---|---|---|---|---|---|---|
| 3.5 | 1,382 | 1,844 | 2,304 | 2,765 | 3,226 | 3,688 | 4,146 | 4,608 | 5,068 | 5,530 | 5,990 | 6,452 | 46 | 92 | 138 | 184 | 230 | 277 | 323 | 367 | 415 |
| 3.6 | 1,422 | 1,895 | 2,370 | 2,843 | 3,316 | 3,790 | 4,264 | 4,740 | 5,210 | 5,686 | 6,160 | 6,632 | 47 | 95 | 142 | 190 | 237 | 284 | 332 | 379 | 426 |
| 3.7 | 1,462 | 1,948 | 2,436 | 2,930 | 3,410 | 3,896 | 4,386 | 4,872 | 5,360 | 5,846 | 6,334 | 6,820 | 49 | 97 | 146 | 195 | 244 | 293 | 341 | 390 | 439 |
| 3.8 | 1,500 | 2,000 | 2,500 | 3,002 | 3,502 | 4,002 | 4,503 | 5,003 | 5,503 | 6,004 | 6,504 | 7,004 | 50 | 100 | 150 | 200 | 250 | 300 | 350 | 400 | 450 |
| 3.9 | 1,540 | 2,054 | 2,566 | 3,080 | 3,593 | 4,108 | 4,620 | 5,134 | 5,646 | 6,160 | 6,673 | 7,186 | 51 | 103 | 154 | 205 | 257 | 308 | 359 | 411 | 463 |
| 4.0 | 1,580 | 2,106 | 2,634 | 3,160 | 3,687 | 4,212 | 4,740 | 5,266 | 5,794 | 6,320 | 6,847 | 7,374 | 53 | 105 | 158 | 211 | 263 | 316 | 367 | 421 | 474 |
| 4.1 | 1,620 | 2,160 | 2,700 | 3,240 | 3,780 | 4,320 | 4,860 | 5,400 | 5,940 | 6,480 | 7,020 | 7,560 | 54 | 108 | 162 | 216 | 270 | 324 | 378 | 432 | 486 |
| 4.2 | 1,660 | 2,212 | 2,764 | 3,318 | 3,870 | 4,424 | 4,978 | 5,530 | 6,082 | 6,638 | 7,188 | — | 55 | 111 | 166 | 221 | 276 | 332 | 387 | 442 | 498 |
| 4.3 | 1,698 | 2,264 | 2,830 | 3,397 | 3,963 | 4,528 | 5,096 | 5,660 | 6,227 | 6,794 | 7,360 | — | 57 | 113 | 170 | 226 | 283 | 340 | 396 | 453 | 510 |
| 4.4 | 1,738 | 2,318 | 2,896 | 3,476 | 4,055 | 4,636 | 5,214 | 5,792 | 6,372 | 6,952 | 7,530 | — | 58 | 116 | 174 | 232 | 290 | 348 | 405 | 464 | 521 |
| 4.5 | 1,777 | 2,370 | 2,964 | 3,555 | 4,148 | 4,740 | 5,332 | 5,925 | 6,520 | 7,110 | — | — | 59 | 118 | 178 | 237 | 296 | 355 | 415 | 474 | 533 |
| 4.6 | 1,817 | 2,422 | 3,030 | 3,634 | 4,240 | 4,846 | 5,450 | 6,057 | 6,664 | 7,268 | — | — | 61 | 121 | 182 | 242 | 303 | 363 | 424 | 485 | 545 |
| 4.7 | 1,856 | 2,476 | 3,094 | 3,713 | 4,332 | 4,952 | 5,570 | 6,188 | 6,807 | 7,426 | — | — | 62 | 124 | 186 | 248 | 309 | 371 | 433 | 495 | 557 |
| 4.8 | 1,896 | 2,528 | 3,160 | 3,792 | 4,424 | 5,056 | 5,688 | 6,320 | 6,952 | 7,584 | — | — | 63 | 126 | 190 | 253 | 316 | 379 | 442 | 506 | 569 |
| 4.9 | 1,935 | 2,580 | 3,226 | 3,871 | 4,515 | 5,161 | 5,805 | 6,452 | 7,096 | 7,742 | — | — | 65 | 129 | 193 | 258 | 323 | 387 | 452 | 516 | 580 |
| 5.0 | 1,975 | 2,634 | 3,292 | 3,950 | 4,608 | 5,267 | 5,925 | 6,584 | 7,242 | — | — | — | 66 | 132 | 197 | 263 | 329 | 395 | 461 | 527 | 592 |
| 5.1 | 2,015 | 2,686 | 3,360 | 4,030 | 4,702 | 5,372 | 6,045 | 6,716 | 7,388 | — | — | — | 67 | 134 | 201 | 269 | 336 | 403 | 470 | 537 | 604 |
| 5.2 | 2,054 | 2,738 | 3,424 | 4,108 | 4,793 | 5,476 | 6,162 | 6,847 | 7,532 | — | — | — | 68 | 137 | 205 | 274 | 342 | 411 | 479 | 548 | 616 |
| 5.3 | 2,093 | 2,792 | 3,490 | 4,187 | 4,885 | 5,584 | 6,280 | 6,979 | 7,677 | — | — | — | 70 | 140 | 209 | 279 | 349 | 419 | 488 | 558 | 628 |
| 5.4 | 2,133 | 2,844 | 3,556 | 4,266 | 4,977 | 5,688 | 6,400 | 7,110 | 7,822 | — | — | — | 71 | 142 | 213 | 284 | 356 | 427 | 498 | 567 | 640 |
| 5.5 | 2,172 | 2,896 | 3,620 | 4,345 | 5,070 | 5,792 | 6,517 | 7,241 | — | — | — | — | 72 | 145 | 217 | 290 | 362 | 434 | 507 | 579 | 652 |
| 5.6 | 2,212 | 2,950 | 3,686 | 4,424 | 5,160 | 5,898 | 6,636 | 7,372 | — | — | — | — | 74 | 148 | 221 | 295 | 369 | 442 | 516 | 590 | 664 |
| 5.7 | 2,251 | 3,002 | 3,752 | 4,503 | 5,253 | 6,004 | 6,754 | 7,504 | — | — | — | — | 75 | 150 | 225 | 300 | 375 | 450 | 525 | 600 | 675 |
| 5.8 | 2,291 | 3,054 | 3,818 | 4,582 | 5,345 | 6,109 | 6,873 | 7,636 | — | — | — | — | 76 | 153 | 229 | 305 | 382 | 458 | 534 | 611 | 687 |
| 5.9 | 2,330 | 3,108 | 3,884 | 4,661 | 5,438 | 6,216 | 6,990 | 7,768 | — | — | — | — | 78 | 155 | 233 | 311 | 388 | 466 | 544 | 622 | 699 |
| 6.0 | 2,370 | 3,160 | 3,950 | 4,740 | 5,530 | 6,320 | 7,110 | 7,900 | — | — | — | — | 79 | 158 | 237 | 316 | 395 | 474 | 553 | 632 | 711 |

Note.—For 3.25-in. and 3.50-in. × 20-in. tyres *subtract* 4% from r.p.m. figures. For speeds intermediate between even tens, *add* r.p.m. from "Difference Table." For ratios lower than six select any sub-multiple and multiply r.p.m. accordingly, i.e. For 12 to 1, select speed for 6 to 1 and multiply by 2.

# APPENDIX

COEFFICIENTS OF THERMAL EXPANSION

*(per ° Centigrade for temperatures between 0 and 200° C.)*

| MATERIAL | COEFFICIENT |
|---|---|
| " Invar " | .0000009 |
| Cast Iron | .000011 |
| Mild Steel | .000011 |
| Hardened Steel | .000012 |
| Phosphor Bronze | .000018 |
| Aluminium Bronze | .000018 |
| Austenitic Valve Steel | |
| (D.T.D. 49b, K.E. 965. Jessops G2) | .000018 |
| Austenitic Cast Iron | .000019 |
| Austenitic Stainless Steel (18/8 grade) | .000020 |
| | |
| " Lo-Ex " Aluminium Alloy | .000019 |
| L 33 High-silicon Alloy | .000019 |
| R.R. 53 B | .000022 |
| Y—alloy | .000022 |
| D.T.D. 424 Aluminium Alloy | .000022 |
| Most Wrought High-strength Aluminium Alloys | .000024 |
| 8% Copper Aluminium Alloy, L8 | .000026 |
| | |
| Heat-treated Cast Magnesium Alloys | .000024/26 |
| Magnesium Alloys as Cast | .000029 |
| Wrought Magnesium Alloys | .000029 |

Multiply coefficient by 5/9 to obtain coefficient per degree F.

Example: To find expansion at 200° C. of a 3 in. bore in a jacket cast in L33 material.

Assuming the bore to be measured at 15° C. (normal atmospheric temperature) the temperature rise is 185° C. Expansion therefore is 3 in. × 185 × .000019 = .0105 in.

# FUEL ANALYSIS TABLE

This table gives the symbols and approximate composition of proprietary racing fuels; their availability may vary from country to country.

The increases in jet-flow are approximate only, and are given merely as an indication.

| FUEL | APPROXIMATE COMPOSITION (PERCENTAGES) | MAXIMUM COMP. RATIO | JET FLOW INCREASE (per cent) |
|---|---|---|---|
| Shell TT | Lead-free petrol 50, benzole 50 | 9.5 | 5 |
| Shell 100 | 100 octane leaded petrol, plus I.C.A. | 9.5 | Nil |
| Shell 115/145 | Aviation petrol with T.E.L. | 12.0 | Nil |
| Shell X | Ethyl alc. 30, petrol 40, benzole 30 | 10.5 | 40 |
| Shell M | Methanol 60, petrol 20, benzole 20 | 12.5 | 75 |
| Shell Y | Ethyl alc. 75, benzole 14, acetone 5, water | 14.5 | 100 |
| Shell 811 | Methanol 80, petrol 10, benzole 10 | 14 | 150 |
| Shell A | Methanol 96, acetone 4, + trace castor oil | 15 | 200 |
| Shell AMI | Methanol 94, acetone 6, + trace castor oil (AMI may be used for blending with petrol or benzole) | 15 | 200 |
| B.P. W | Petrol 50, benzole 50 | 9.5 | 5 |
| B.P. 100 | Aviation petrol, 100/130 octane | 9.5 | 5 |
| B.P. 115/145 | Aviation petrol with T.E.L. | 12.0 | Nil |
| B.P. M | Ethyl alc. 20, petrol 40, benzole 40 | 10 | 25 |
| B.P. K | Methanol 50, petrol 35, benzole 10, acetone 5 | 12 | 60 |
| B.P. JA | Methanol 50, 115/145 petrol, benzole | 12 | 75 |
| B.P. JB | Methanol 60, 115/145 petrol, benzole | 12 | 80 |
| B.P. F | Methanol 80, B.P. Super 10, benzole 10 | 14 | 125 |
| B.P. A | Methanol 95, acetone 4, castor oil 1 | 15 | 200 |
| Vac. 1 | Aviation alkylate (lead-free) | 8.5 | 5 |
| Vac. 2 | Petrol plus alkylate; leaded. 100/130 octane | 10 | 5 |
| Vac. 3 | Petrol plus alkylate; heavily leaded. 115/145 oct. | 12 | 5 |
| Vac. 4 | Methanol 30, ethyl alc. 20, alkylate 5, acetone 5 | 12 | 60 |
| Vac. 5 | Methanol 80, ethyl alc. 10, alkylate 5, acetone 5 | 14 | 125 |
| Vac. 6 | Methanol 100 | 15 | 200 |
| Vac. 7 | Methanol 50, alkylate 10, petrol 25, benzole 10 Acetone 5 (Maserati formula) | 12 | 60 |
| Esso Racing Spirit No. 1 | Aviation alkylate (lead-free) | 8.5 | 5 |
| Special 100 | Avgas+3.5 c.c. T.E.L. per gallon. 100/130 oct. | 10 | 5 |
| 115/145 | Avgas; heavily leaded. 115/145 octane | 10.5 | 6 |
| No. 4 | Methanol 30, ethyl alc. 20, alkylate 40, petrol 10 | 12.5 | 70 |
| Cooper | Methanol 50, benzole 10, acetone 5, 100/130 petrol 35 | 12 | 60 |
| No. 5 | Methanol 80, ethyl alc. 10, acetone 5, petrol 5 | 13.5 | 125 |

The limiting compression ratios quoted apply to well-designed, air-cooled cylinders of 500 c.c capacity. Engines with smaller cylinders may utilize higher ratios; those with larger or less well-cooled cylinders may need up to one ratio lower.

# INDEX

"Lo-Ex", 60, 64, 70

Lubrication, gear-type oil pumps, 120; plunger-type oil pumps, 122; reciprocating plunger-type oil pumps, 122; total-loss type, 120; Velocette double-gear oil pump, 121

Lucas types of magneto, 185

Main bearings, removal and refitting, 99, 100

Mainshaft alignment, method of checking, 103, 104, 105

"Manx" Norton, 18, 91; Vernier settings, 160; valve timing, 164

Matchless, 119, 164; G3L main bearings, 125; G3L main bearings, method of assembly, 125; three-bearing, 195, 196

Mean gas velocity, formula, 278

Mechanical condition, an initial check, 6, 7, 8

Methanol, 51, 200, 286

Monobloc, 260

Monochrome Limited, 59

Morrison, J. G., 173

M.Z., 218, 221, 222, 223

New Imperial, 164

"Ni-Resist" nickel-iron alloy, 10

Nitro-methane, 52, 53

Norton, 164, 165; "Dominator" crankshaft details, 194; 30/40M models, 190; main-bearing details, 126

Octane ratings, 50, 200

Orsatt type of gas analyser, 213

Petroil lubrication, 233

Petrol-benzole, 7, 49, 50, 286

Petter "Harmonic" type of engine, 212

"Picador", 205

"Pickavant" hydraulic extractor, 81

Piston alloys, 69

Piston, alignment, 69, 132; essential clearances, 70, 71; speed formula, 278

Piston crown, detail modifications, 135, 137

Piston ring sizes, 75, 76

Plug readings, 250, 251

Power corrections, 271

Proceedings of the I.A.E., 174, 175

"Progress in Motorcycle Engines", I.A.E. paper by J. Craig, 174, 175

Puch, 209

Push rods, 147, 148

Python engines, 29

Rev.-counter drive, 186

Rocker mechanism, Rudge type, 144, 147

Rocker modifications, lightening o.h.v. mechanism, 145, 146

Rockwell diamond hardness numbers, 83

Rolling resistance, 272

Rose, A. E., 224

Rowntree, W.B., 53

R.R. light alloy specifications, 11, 12

R.R.50; alloy 60, 64

R.R.56 alloy, 41, 94, 150

R.R.77 type of alloy, 41

Rudge, 144, 165, 166

S.A.E., American steel specifications, 84

Schweitzer, Dr., 173

Seat grinders, Black and Decker, 12

"Seeger" type of piston circlip, 79, 80

Side-valve engines, 16, 19, 25, 166

Sifbronze welding, 13, 225

Silicon piston alloy, 218

# MAINTENANCE LOG

| DATE | TYPE OF SERVICE | COST | REMARKS |
|------|-----------------|------|---------|
| | | | |
| | | | |
| | | | |
| | | | |
| | | | |
| | | | |
| | | | |
| | | | |
| | | | |
| | | | |
| | | | |
| | | | |
| | | | |
| | | | |
| | | | |
| | | | |
| | | | |
| | | | |
| | | | |
| | | | |
| | | | |
| | | | |
| | | | |
| | | | |
| | | | |
| | | | |
| | | | |
| | | | |
| | | | |
| | | | |

# MAINTENANCE LOG

| DATE | TYPE OF SERVICE | COST | REMARKS |
|------|-----------------|------|---------|
|      |                 |      |         |
|      |                 |      |         |
|      |                 |      |         |
|      |                 |      |         |
|      |                 |      |         |
|      |                 |      |         |
|      |                 |      |         |
|      |                 |      |         |
|      |                 |      |         |
|      |                 |      |         |
|      |                 |      |         |
|      |                 |      |         |
|      |                 |      |         |
|      |                 |      |         |
|      |                 |      |         |
|      |                 |      |         |
|      |                 |      |         |
|      |                 |      |         |
|      |                 |      |         |
|      |                 |      |         |
|      |                 |      |         |
|      |                 |      |         |
|      |                 |      |         |
|      |                 |      |         |
|      |                 |      |         |
|      |                 |      |         |
|      |                 |      |         |
|      |                 |      |         |

# NOTES

# NOTES

## AUTOBOOKS WORKSHOP MANUALS

ALFA ROMEO GIULIA 1300, 1600, 1750, 2000 1962-1978 WSM
BMW 1600 1966-1973 WSM
BMW 2000 & 2002 1966-1976 WSM
BMW 2500, 2800, 3.0 & 3.3 1968-1977 WSM
BMW 316, 320, 320i 1975-1977 WSM
BMW 518, 520, 520i 1973-1981 WSM
FIAT 1100, 1100D, 1100R & 1200 1957-1969 WSM
FIAT 124 1966-1974 WSM
FIAT 124 SPORT 1966-1975 WSM
FIAT 125 & 125 SPECIAL 1967-1973 WSM
FIAT 126, 126L, 126 DV, 126/650 & 126/650 DV 1972-1982 WSM
FIAT 127 SALOON, SPECIAL & SPORT, 900, 1050 1971-1981 WSM
FIAT 128 1969-1982 WSM
FIAT 131 MIRAFIORI 1975-1982 WSM
FIAT 1300, 1500 1961-1967 WSM
FIAT 132 1972-1982 WSM
FIAT 500 1957-1973 WSM
FIAT 600, 600D & MULTIPLA 1955-1969 WSM
FIAT 850 1964-1972 WSM
JAGUAR E-TYPE 1961-1972 WSM
JAGUAR MK 1, 2 1955-1969 WSM
JAGUAR S TYPE, 420 1963-1968 WSM
JAGUAR XK 120, 140, 150 MK 7, 8, 9 1948-1961 WSM
LAND ROVER 1, 2 1948-1961 WSM
MERCEDES-BENZ 190 1959-1968 WSM
MERCEDES-BENZ 220 1968-1972 WSM
MERCEDES-BENZ 220B 1959-1965 WSM
MERCEDES-BENZ 230 1963-1968 WSM
MERCEDES-BENZ 250 1968-1972 WSM
MERCEDES-BENZ 280 1968-1972 WSM
MG MIDGET TA-TF 1936-1955 WSM
MINI 1959-1980 WSM
MORRIS MINOR 1952-1971 WSM
PEUGEOT 404 1960-1975 WSM
PORSCHE 911 1964-1973 WSM
PORSCHE 911 1970-1977 WSM
RENAULT 16 1965-1979 WSM
RENAULT 8, 10, 1100 1962-1971 WSM
ROVER 3500, 3500S 1968-1976 WSM
SUNBEAM RAPIER, ALPINE 1955-1965 WSM
TRIUMPH SPITFIRE, GT6, VITESSE 1962-1968 WSM
TRIUMPH TR2, TR3, TR3A 1952-1962 WSM
TRIUMPH TR4, TR4A 1961-1967 WSM
VOLKSWAGEN BEETLE 1968-1977 WSM

## VELOCEPRESS AUTOMOBILE BOOKS & MANUALS

ABARTH BUYERS GUIDE
AUSTIN-HEALEY 6-CYLINDER WSM
AUSTIN-HEALEY SPRITE & MG MIDGET 1958-1971 WSM
BMW 600 LIMOUSINE FACTORY WSM
BMW 600 LIMOUSINE OWNERS HAND BOOK & SERVICE MANUAL
BMW ISETTA FACTORY WSM
BOOK OF THE CARRERA PANAMERICANA - MEXICAN ROAD RACE
COMPLETE CATALOG OF JAPANESE MOTOR VEHICLES
DIALED IN - THE JAN OPPERMAN STORY
FERRARI 250/GT SERVICE AND MAINTENANCE
FERRARI 308 SERIES BUYER'S AND OWNER'S GUIDE
FERRARI BERLINETTA LUSSO
FERRARI BROCHURES AND SALES LITERATURE 1946-1967
FERRARI BROCHURES AND SALES LITERATURE 1968-1989
FERRARI GUIDE TO PERFORMANCE
FERRARI OPP, MAINTENANCE & SERVICE H/BOOKS 1948-1963
FERRARI OWNER'S HANDBOOK
FERRARI SERIAL NUMBERS PART I - ODD NUMBERS TO 21399
FERRARI SERIAL NUMBERS PART II - EVEN NUMBERS TO 1050
FERRARI SPYDER CALIFORNIA
FERRARI TUNING TIPS & MAINTENANCE TECHNIQUES
HENRY'S FABULOUS MODEL "A" FORD
HOW TO BUILD A FIBERGLASS CAR
HOW TO BUILD A RACING CAR
HOW TO RESTORE THE MODEL 'A' FORD
IF HEMINGWAY HAD WRITTEN A RACING NOVEL
JAGUAR E-TYPE 3.8 & 4.2 WSM
LE MANS 24 (THE BOOK THAT THE FILM WAS BASED ON)
MASERATI BROCHURES AND SALES LITERATURE
MASERATI OWNER'S HANDBOOK
METROPOLITAN FACTORY WSM
MGA & MGB OWNERS HANDBOOK & WSM
OBERT'S FIAT GUIDE
PERFORMANCE TUNING THE SUNBEAM TIGER
PORSCHE 356 1948-1965 WSM
PORSCHE 912 WSM
SOUPING THE VOLKSWAGEN
TRIUMPH TR2, TR3, TR4 1953-1965 WSM
TUNING FOR SPEED (P.E. IRVING)
VEDA ORR'S NEW REVISED HOT ROD PICTORIAL
VOLKSWAGEN TRANSPORTER, TRUCKS, STATION WAGONS WSM
VOLVO 1944-1968 ALL MODELS WSM

## BROOKLANDS BOOKS & ROAD TEST PORTFOLIOS (RTP)

AC CARS 1904-2009
ALFA ROMEO 1920-1933 ROAD TEST PORTFOLIO
ALFA ROMEO 1934-1940 ROAD TEST PORTFOLIO
BRABHAM RALT HONDA THE RON TAURANAC STORY
BUGATTI TYPE 10 TO TYPE 40 ROAD TEST PORTFOLIO
BUGATTI TYPE 10 TO TYPE 251 ROAD TEST PORTFOLIO
BUGATTI TYPE 41 TO TYPE 55 ROAD TEST PORTFOLIO
BUGATTI TYPE 57 TO TYPE 251 ROAD TEST PORTFOLIO
DELAHAYE ROAD TEST PORTFOLIO
FERRARI ROAD CARS 1946-1956 ROAD TEST PORTFOLIO
FIAT 500 1936-1972 ROAD TEST PORTFOLIO
FIAT DINO ROAD TEST PORTFOLIO
HISPANO SUIZA ROAD TEST PORTFOLIO
HONDA ST1100/ST1300 PAN EUROPEAN 1990-2002 RTP
JAGUAR MK1 & MK2 ROAD TEST PORTFOLIO
LOTUS CORTINA ROAD TEST PORTFOLIO
MV AGUSTA F4 750 & 1000 1997-2007 ROAD TEST PORTFOLIO
TATRA CARS ROAD TEST PORTFOLIO

## VELOCEPRESS MOTORCYCLE BOOKS & MANUALS

AJS SINGLES & TWINS 250cc THRU 1000cc 1932-1948 (BOOK OF)
AJS SINGLES 1955-65 350cc & 500cc (BOOK OF)
AJS SINGLES 1945-60 350cc & 500cc MODELS 16 & 18 (BOOK OF)
ARIEL 1939-1960 4 STROKE SINGLES (BOOK OF)
ARIEL LEADER & ARROW 1958-1964 (BOOK OF)
ARIEL MOTORCYCLES 1933-1951 WSM
ARIEL PREWAR MODELS 1932-1939 (BOOK OF)
BMW M/CYCLES R26 R27 (1956-1967) FACTORY WSM
BMW M/CYCLES R50 R50S R60 R69S (1955-1969) FACTORY WSM
BSA BANTAM (BOOK OF)
BSA ALL FOUR-STROKE SINGLES & V-TWINS 1936-1952 (BOOK OF)
BSA OHV & SV SINGLES - 250cc 1954-1970 (BOOK OF)
BSA OHV & SV SINGLES 1945-54 250-600cc (BOOK OF)
BSA OHV SINGLES 350 & 500cc 1955-1967 (BOOK OF)
BSA PRE-WAR MODELS TO 1939 (BOOK OF)
BSA TWINS 1948-1962 (BOOK OF)
BSA TWINS 1962-1969 (SECOND BOOK OF)
CATALOG OF BRITISH MOTORCYCLES (1951 MODELS)
DOUGLAS PRE-WAR ALL MODELS 1929-1939 (BOOK OF)
DOUGLAS POST-WAR ALL MODELS 1948-1957 FACTORY WSM
DUCATI 160cc, 250cc & 350cc OHC MODELS FACTORY WSM
HONDA 50 ALL MODELS UP TO 1970 INC MONKEY & TRAIL (BOOK OF)
HONDA 90 ALL MODELS UP TO 1966 (BOOK OF)
HONDA MOTORCYCLES 125-150 TWINS C/CS/CB/CA WSM
HONDA MOTORCYCLES 250-305 TWINS C/CS/CB WSM
HONDA MOTORCYCLES C100 SUPER CUB WSM
HONDA MOTORCYCLES C110 SPORT CUB 1962-1969 WSM
HONDA TWINS & SINGLES 50cc THRU 305cc 1960-1966 (BOOK OF)
HONDA TWINS ALL MODELS 125cc THRU 450cc UP TO 1968 (BOOK OF)
INDIAN PONYBIKE, BOY RACER & PAPOOSE ILL PARTS LIST & SALES LIT
LAMBRETTA ALL 125 & 150cc MODELS 1947-1957 (BOOK OF)
LAMBRETTA LI & TV MODELS 1957-1970 (SECOND BOOK OF)
MATCHLESS 350 & 500cc SINGLES 1945-1956 (BOOK OF)
MATCHLESS 350 & 500cc SINGLES 1955-1966 (BOOK OF)
NORTON 1932-1947 (BOOK OF)
NORTON 1938-1956 (BOOK OF)
NORTON DOMINATOR TWINS 1955-1965 (BOOK OF)
NORTON MODELS 19, 50 & ES2 1955-1963 (BOOK OF)
NORTON MOTORCYCLES 1957-1970 FACTORY WSM
NORTON PREWAR MODELS 1932-1939 (BOOK OF)
NSU QUICKLY ALL MODELS 1953-1963 (BOOK OF)
ROYAL ENFIELD SINGLES & V TWINS 1937-1953 (BOOK OF)
ROYAL ENFIELD SINGLES 1946-1962 (BOOK OF)
ROYAL ENFIELD 736cc INTERCEPTOR FACTORY WSM
ROYAL ENFIELD 250cc & 350cc SINGLES 1958-1966 (SECOND BOOK OF)
SUZUKI 50cc & 80cc UP TO 1966 (BOOK OF)
SUZUKI T10 1963-1967 FACTORY WSM
SUZUKI T20 & T200 1965-1969 FACTORY WSM
TRIUMPH PRE-WAR MOTORCYCLE 1935-1939 (BOOK OF)
TRIUMPH MOTORCYCLES 1937-1951 WSM
TRIUMPH MOTORCYCLES 1945-1955 FACTORY WSM
TRIUMPH TWINS 1956-1969 (BOOK OF)
VELOCETTE ALL SINGLES & TWINS 1925-1970 (BOOK OF)
VESPA 1951-1961 (BOOK OF)
VESPA 125 & 150cc & GS MODELS 1955-1963 (SECOND BOOK OF)
VESPA 90, 125 & 150cc 1963-1972 (THIRD BOOK OF)
VESPA GS & SS 1955-1968 (BOOK OF)
VINCENT MOTORCYCLES 1935-1955 WSM

**PLEASE VISIT OUR WEBSITE**
www.VelocePress.com
**FOR A DETAILED DESCRIPTION
OF ANY OF THESE TITLES**

# www.VelocePress.com

Ingram Content Group UK Ltd.
Milton Keynes UK
UKHW020715200423
420491UK00014B/463